T0270888

Thanks to European works council representatives social Europe is taking ground at the heart of societies. They are showing daily why collective organisation of interests is a core element of the well functioning of societies. From different national environments we are getting deep insights into how European identity can evolve. Trade unions can benefit from these insights by taking up the challenge to renew themselves in a European perspective.

(Norbert Kluge, ETUI)

Towards a European Labour Identity

Since 1996 a growing number of European employees have had access to a European Works Council (EWC), a transnational employee body designed to complement national forms of labour representation. This volume brings together a bee hive of contributors who present valuable new insights into how employee representatives from different European countries perform their jobs as members of European Works Councils and thus contribute to an emerging European identity for labour.

The transnational character of the EWC makes it an ideal microscopic structure through which the wider discourse on international labour representation and solidarity can occur. *Towards a European Labour Identity* examines not only the workings of EWCs, utilising individual case studies, but also analyses the link with the broader discussions on European identity as well as European trade union co-ordination and solidarity.

Michael Whittall is an associate professor at the Technical University in Munich and a European Union-level correspondent for the European Foundation for the Improvement of Living and Working Conditions.

Herman Knudsen is an associate professor in labour relations at Aalborg University, Denmark.

Fred Huijgen is a professor in business administration at the Nijmegen Business School, University of Nijmegen, the Netherlands.

Routledge Research in Employment Relations

Series editors:
Rick Delbridge and Edmund Heery
Cardiff Business School, UK

Aspects of the employment relationship are central to numerous courses at both undergraduate and postgraduate level.

Drawing from insights from industrial relations, human resource management and industrial sociology, this series provides an alternative source of research-based materials and texts, reviewing key developments in employment research.

Books published in this series are works of high academic merit, drawn from a wide range of academic studies in the social sciences.

Also available from Routledge:

Rethinking Industrial Relations
Mobilisation, collectivism and
long waves
John Kelly

**Employee Relations in the Public
Services**
Themes and issues
*Edited by Susan Corby and
Geoff White*

The Insecure Workforce
*Edited by Edmund Heery and
John Salmon*

**Public Service Employment
Relations in Europe**
Transformation, modernisation
or inertia?
*Edited by Stephen Bach,
Lorenzo Bordogna,
Giuseppe Della Rocca and
David Winchester*

Reward Management
A critical text
*Edited by Geoff White and
Janet Druker*

Working for McDonald's in Europe
The unequal struggle?
Tony Royle

**Job Insecurity and Work
Intensification**
*Edited by Brendan Burchell,
David Ladipo and
Frank Wilkinson*

Union Organizing
Campaigning for trade union
recognition
Edited by Gregor Gall

**Employment Relations in the
Hospitality and Tourism Industries**
Rosemary Lucas

Towards a European Labour Identity

The case of the European Works Council

Edited by
**Michael Whittall, Herman Knudsen
and Fred Huijgen**

Routledge
Taylor & Francis Group

LONDON AND NEW YORK

First published 2007
by Routledge
4 Park Square, Milton Park, Abingdon, Oxon OX14 4RN
605 Third Avenue, New York, NY 10017

Routledge is an imprint of the Taylor & Francis Group, an informa business

Typeset in Times New Roman by
Taylor & Francis Books

British Library Cataloguing in Publication Data
A catalogue record for this book is available from the British Library

Library of Congress Cataloging in Publication Data
Towards a European labour identity : the case of the European Work
  Council / edited by Michael Whittall, Herman Knudsen and Fred
  Huijgen.
    p. cm.
  Includes bibliographical references and index.
  1. Works councils–European Union countries. 2. International labor
  activities–European Union countries. I. Whittall, Michael. II.
  Knudsen, Herman, 1947- III. Huijgen, F.
HD5660.E85T68 2007
331.88094–dc22   2006031739

ISBN 13: 978-0-415-40396-2 (hbk)

Contents

Illustrations

Tables

Figures

Contributors

Monica Andersson is a former HRM practitioner at Volvo and SCA. She is currently completing her PhD at Göteborg University, Sweden. Her research interests include power relations, human resource management and communications between different professions and organisations. Although these interests are mainly related to MNCs and the Swedish public sector, they are also highly relevant to comprehending how European Works Councils function. The focus of her thesis is on call centres in Sweden, specifically telephone nursing advice in Swedish health care.

Sergio González Begega is a research fellow at the University of Oviedo, Spain. He is also an associate research fellow at the IRESCO-CNRS in Paris and has recently worked for the ETUI-REHS in Brussels. He is currently researching into industrial relations developments at firm and sector level from a southern European perspective, with a specific interest in European Works Councils. Other research interests concern diversity in Europe, articulation problems of European social partners, human resource policy and corporate governance in the automobile industry.

Helen Bicknell completed her PhD early in 2006 with the thesis 'How "German" are European Works Councils?' at the Institute for German Studies, Birmingham University in England. She is a Business English lecturer at the University of Applied Sciences in Mainz. She also works as a European Works Council consultant, specialising in comparative industrial relations and intercultural communications. Other areas of academic interest include European economic integration, labour economics and human resource management.

Michael Gold is senior lecturer in European business and employee relations at Royal Holloway, University of London. He is an acclaimed expert on European Works Councils, being one of the very first academics in Europe to address the importance of this European institution. A former editor of the *European Industrial Relations Review* and consultant editor of the *European Industrial Relations Observatory*, he has written widely on European employment relations and social policy. He is co-author of

Social Partnership and Economic Performance: The Case of Europe (2000), and recently edited *New Frontiers of Democratic Participation at Work* (2003).

Fred Huijgen is a professor in business administration at the Nijmegen Business School, University of Nijmegen, the Netherlands. He is especially interested in organisation theory and organisational design, HRM, quality of working life, labour market and European industrial relations. His main research activities concern international comparative empirical research on labour market flexibility and organisational renewal and participation of employees. He is also a key labour market policy advisor to the European Union.

Herman Knudsen is an associate professor in labour relations at Aalborg University, Denmark. He is renowned for his work on employment participation in Europe. His research includes studies of national systems of employee participation, European Works Councils, the Danish system of labour regulation, and European social policy. In addition, he has written and taught on such diverse areas as strikes, technology and work as well as labour market socialisation processes.

Holm-Detlev Köhler is professor at the University of Oviedo, Spain. He has worked in industrial relations and business strategies of transnational corporations in a wide range of countries and institutions. His research areas include the impact of HRM on workers and unions as well as the globalisation of industrial relations. He is the author of a leading manual on industrial relations in Spain, and has published detailed studies on the automotive, steel, coal and low-tech sectors in several languages.

Hermann Kotthoff is a professor at the Institute of Social Research (Landesinstitut Socialforschungsstelle) in Dortmund. He is the most prominent researcher of German works councils, with *Betriebsräte und Bürgerstatus* from 1994 as a central work. He is currently attached to a research programme on work politics in Europe and has recently investigated European Works Councils, the learning processes involved, and the significance for EWCs of the EU eastern enlargement.

Miguel Martínez Lucio is a professor at the University of Bradford in England. He has worked on industrial relations and change in a range of organisations and countries. His areas include the impact of new forms of management and workplace organisation on workers and unions, the emergence of new frameworks of firm-based regulation such as social partnership, the impact of organisational practices such as quality management, and the globalisation of industrial relations and HRM. He has also worked on the political dimension of employment relations including state–labour relations and the changing character and regulatory form of the state.

Torsten Müller is a member of the European and Global Industrial Relations Research Group at the University of Applied Sciences in Fulda, Germany. His main research interests are: the development of industrial relations at global level with a special focus on the structure and strategies of European and global union federations; the development of employee representation structures at global company level; and the implementation of international framework agreements. Prior to his work in Fulda, he was a research fellow at the University of Warwick in the UK, where he researched European Works Councils.

Valeria Pulignano is a professor in sociology of labour and industrial relations at the Katholieke Universiteit of Leuven, Belgium. She is also an associate fellow at the Industrial Relations Research Unit and the Industrial Relations and Organisational Behaviour Group at the University of Warwick, England. Her main research field is comparative industrial relations in European and non-European countries. A central aspect of her work concerns change in work organisation and company restructuring in the metalworking and chemical sectors. Currently she is involved in the project 'Trade unions anticipating change in Europe' for the European Trade Union Institute.

Stefan Rüb is a member of the European and Global Industrial Relations Research Group at the University of Applied Sciences in Fulda, Germany. His research focuses on the development of employee representation structures at European and global company level and trade union internationalism. He is currently writing his PhD on the transnationalisation of the German metalworkers' union IG Metall at Kassel University. Prior to this he was involved in several research projects on European Works Councils. He also works as an EWC consultant for trade unions and works councillors.

Volker Telljohann is a senior researcher at the Institute for Labour Foundation in Bologna and secretary general of the international network 'Regional and Local Development of Work and Labour'. Volker Telljohann has vast experience in European employment relations. His areas of interest include developments in regional, national and European industrial relations as well as the role of social dialogue for local development policies.

Christer Thörnqvist is an associate professor at the Department of Work and Society, Göteborg University, Sweden. His main research interests include industrial conflict, collective bargaining and employee influence within MNCs and SMEs. More recently he has focused on the connections between collective bargaining, family-friendly policies and gendered patterns and negotiations and conflict within the changing context of Swedish industrial relations. In addition, he is involved in various international networks concerned with European Works Councils and trade union influence in small and medium-sized companies.

Andrew R. Timming is a PhD student at Cambridge University. He is currently researching into the relationship between identity and trust in the context of European Works Councils. The project aims to formulate policy suggestions for the purpose of building long-term trust among European works councillors. His research interests also concern the impact within the UK of the recent European Union Directive on information and consultation.

Ulke Veersma spent many years teaching in the Netherlands, his home country, prior to becoming a senior lecturer in international human resource management at Greenwich Business School. For many years his research has focused on European industrial relations and the social dimension of the European Union. He has a special interest in European works councils and worker participation. He is currently involved in a European Union-funded project on board-level representation of employees in various European Union member states.

Syd Weston is a reader in European industrial relations at the University of Sunderland in England. He has worked on matters of deregulation, HRM and trade unionism in a variety of sectors. He has published in leading journals in economics and industrial relations, and has wide experience on matters related to trade union politics and strategy. He has also worked on the subject of change in the area of transportation, with the port transportation sector and the road haulage industry the focus of detailed and significant study.

Michael Whittall is an associate professor at the Technical University in Munich and a European Union-level correspondent for the European Foundation for the Improvement of Living and Working Conditions. A former Economic and Social Research Council Fellow, he is also senior lecturer in employee relations at Nottingham Trent University. Although in recent years he has focused specifically on European Works Councils, his work addresses a wide range of industrial relations subjects. These include: German industrial relations and corporate governance; managing insecurity within new workplace regimes; trade union organisation within the British car industry; and trade union recognition within the UK.

Acknowledgements

This book is the result of a two-year co-operation between the three editors and the additional fifteen authors who have contributed with their research findings and special knowledge. As editors we would like to express our thanks to a number of persons and institutions who have also played important roles in the process of creating the book:

- Peter Lesink and his associates at the School of Governance at the University of Utrecht for organising the IREC conference in August 2004, where the idea for the book was born;
- Jens Lind and his associates at Aalborg University for allowing the editors to organise a special workshop at the IERA conference in Aalborg in June 2005; this was where many of the authors had the opportunity to present drafts of their chapters and discuss them with each other;
- Sophie Vestergaard and Line Jensen at Aalborg University for their work on harmonising the manuscript and bringing it into line with Routledge standards;
- the Nederlands Participation Institute (NPI – www.snpi.ne), The Hague, for financial support, which made it possible for the editors to meet and helped to cover expenses for text processing;
- the Department of Development and Planning at Aalborg University for additional financial support for text processing;
- the Technical University of Munich and the University of Nijmegen for hosting editorial meetings;
- Sage Publications for giving permission to reproduce parts of an article that appeared in *European Journal of Industrial Relations*, vol. 6, no. 2, pp. 203–16, 2000: Miguel Martínez Lucio and Syd Weston, 'European Works Councils and "flexible regulation": the politics of intervention'.

The Editors

Abbreviations

BDI	Bundesverband der Deutschen Industrie; German Industrial Employers' Association
CCOO	Comisiones Obreras; Worker Commissions, Spain
CEEP	Centre Européen de l'Entreprise Publique; European Centre of Public Enterprises
CEO	Chief Executive Officer
CEOE	Confederacion Española de Organizaciones Empresariales; Spanish Confederation of Employers' Organisations
CGIL	Confederazione Generale Italiana del Lavoro, General Confederation of Italian Labour
CISL	Confederazione Italiana Sindacati dei Lavoratori, Conferation of Italian Trade Unions
DG	Directorate-General (of the European Commission)
DG5	European Commission's Directorate-General for Employment, Social Affairs and Equal Opportunities
DGB	Deutsche Gewerkschaftsbund; German Trades Union Confederation
DTI	Department of Trade and Industry (UK)
ECS	European Company Statute
EEA	European Economic Area
EEC	European Economic Community
EEF	European Employee Forum
EIF	European Industry Federation
EIRO	European Industrial Relations Observatory
EIRR	European Industrial Relations Review
ELA-STV	Euskal Langileen Alkartasuna, Solidarity of Basque Workers
EMCEF	European Mining Chemical and Energy Workers' Federation
EMF	European Metalworkers' Federation
EMU	European Monetary Union
ETUC	European Trade Union Confederation
ETUI	European Trade Union Institute

EU	European Union
EWC	European Works Council
EWCB	European Works Councils Bulletin
EWCD	European Works Councils Directive
FIET	Fédération Internationale des Employés, Techniciens et Cadres; International Federation of Commercial, Clerical, Professional and Technical Employees
FIOM-CGIL	Federazione Italiana Operai Lavoratori; Federation of Italian Metalworkers
FNV	Federatie Nederlandse Vakbeweging; Federation of Dutch Trade Unions
GM	General Motors
GME	General Motors Europe
HR	Human Resources
HRM	Human Resource Management
IG BAU	Industriegewerkschaft Bauen, Agrar und Umwelt; German Union for Construction, Agriculture and Environment
IG BCE	Industriegewerkschaft, Bergbau, Chemie, Energie; German Union for Mining, Chemical and Energy
IG Metall	Industriegewerkschaft Metall; German Metalworkers' Union
IR	Industrial Relations
ISS	International Service Systems (Danish company)
JNC	Joint Negotiating Committee
KAD	Kvindeligt Arbejderforbund; Female Workers' Union, Denmark
MNC	Multinational Company
NGG	Gewerkschaft Nahrung, Genuss und Gaststätten; German Union for Nutrition, Catering and Restaurants
PEPPER	Promotion of Employee Participation in Profits and Enterprise Results
PWA	Papierwerke Waldhof-Aschaffenburg (German company)
QMV	Qualified Majority Voting
SCA	Svenska Cellulosaaktiebolaget (Swedish company)
SE	Societas Europea (European company)
SME	Small and Medium-sized Enterprise
SNB	Special Negotiating Body
TNC	Transnational Company
TNE	Transnational Enterprise
UEAPME	Union Européenne des Artisans et des Petites et Moyennes Entreprises; European Union of Craft, Small and Medium-sized Enterprises
UGT	Union General de Trabajadores; General Union of Workers, Spain
UK	United Kingdom

UNI	Union Network International
UNICE	Union des Industries de la Communauté Europeénne; Union of Industrial and Employers' Confederations of Europe
Verdi	Vereinigte Dienstleistungsgewerkschaft; German United Services Union
WCA	Works Constitution Act
WEEC	Whirlpool Europe Employee Committee

Introduction
Process and structure of the book

The idea of producing this book was born at the Industrial Relations in Europe Conference (IREC) in Utrecht in 2004. The three editors all took part in the workshop on European Works Councils at the conference – Michael Whittall presenting a paper and Herman Knudsen and Fred Huijgen as co-ordinators of the workshop. At the workshop the development of a common, European identity within European Works Councils (EWCs) emerged as a central theme in the discussions. The formation of a collective identity was viewed by the participants as the decisive stage in ensuring that this structure becomes a key player in representing employee interests at a transnational level. This collective insight was not simply informed by chance. On the contrary, it was the result of a new empirical focus, the fact that a quantitative concern, especially prevalent in most of the 1990s, had given way to a qualitative and many-faceted interest in how this European institution functions – or perhaps does not function.

As prospective editors we approached presenters at the Utrecht workshop as well as other prominent researchers of EWCs and asked them to contribute to the book. By asking them to focus closely on the main theme, the development of a common European identity in EWCs and conditions promoting or preventing such a development, we hoped to be able to publish not just the latest research findings on EWCs, but also a coherent work on how processes within EWCs may be understood as a social laboratory for the development of a common identity for European labour. We believe we have achieved this goal, thanks to the collaborative efforts of eighteen researchers from eight different European countries – in itself a mini-project of European identity-building!

The book is not only of interest to students of EWCs. The transnational character of the EWC makes it an ideal microscopic structure through which the wider discourse surrounding identity, especially when associated with globalisation and mobility, can occur. Therefore, the book is able to link and contribute to the broader discussions on European identity and European trade union co-ordination and solidarity. Though the editors have had a long-standing interest in EWCs, the key theme – identity – represented an opportunity to address an issue that they increasingly found themselves unable to ignore when teaching organisational theory (Huijgen), employee participation (Knudsen) and human resource management (Whittall). By focusing on identities and identification processes, the editors have been forced to challenge traditional perspectives underpinning their earlier work and develop new ones. Evidence would suggest that all contributors have had similar experiences. In discussing EWCs, most have used this as an opportunity to grapple with theoretical issues that go way beyond our understanding of how EWCs function. As Hermann Kotthoff notes in Chapter 10, this involves returning to sociological theory. In fact, there have been very few employment-related books in the last twenty years in which the works of Durkheim, Goffman, Parsons, Sartre and other renowned sociologists have been used to develop the main arguments. Hence this is not a traditional labour relations book.

The common thematic basis for the work was a brief concept paper developed by the editors in late 2004. This paper was later developed into Chapter 1 of this book. An early version was presented at the IERA conference in Aalborg in June 2005, where six other chapter drafts were also presented and discussed.

The structure of the book is based on the following principles. Chapters 1 and 2 are broad, introductory chapters outlining the main theme of the book (the development of European identity in EWCs) and the regulatory framework (the European Works Councils Directive). Chapters 3–10 all present findings from empirical research on EWCs and relate these findings to the question of identity and, in some cases, also to the theoretical discussions on identity. Of these chapters, 3–6 are relatively narrow in the sense that they each build on just one or a few case studies. These studies make it possible to really follow the micro-processes and 'inner life' of EWCs at close hand. Chapters 7–10 are each based on a large number of case studies and/or a range of other empirical sources; correspondingly they tend to draw more generalised conclusions. Finally, the last chapters, 11–13, are even broader and more generalising. They do not present new empirical research; instead, while taking the vast material from prior research into account, they attempt to theorise and generalise on the question of identity-building in EWCs in particular and in the European labour movement in general. We will now briefly present the individual chapters of the book:

As already mentioned, Chapter 1, 'European Works Councils and the problem of identity' by Herman Knudsen, Michael Whittall and Fred Huijgen, contains the conceptual basis and framework for the book. It treats the debate on European identity in general as well as the more specific question of identity in EWCs and in the labour movement; discusses the concepts of identity and identification; and briefly reviews how prior research has contributed to our knowledge of identity-building processes in EWCs.

Chapter 2, 'The European Works Councils Directive: changing rationales for EU regulation of employee participation' by Michael Gold, presents the regulatory context of EWCs: the 1994 European Works Councils Directive, which provides EWCs with their formal identity. The chapter also examines the wider political processes and other initiatives on employee participation at the European Union level.

Chapters 3 and 4 are both case studies of restructuring processes, which put cross-national solidarity under strong pressure. In Chapter 3, 'Living apart together? A Chorus of multiple identities' by Andrew R. Timming and Ulke Veersma, restructuring in the Anglo-Dutch Corus company leads to mutual suspicion and sharply divided attitudes between the EWC representatives from the two countries. National identities triumph!

A more co-operative, yet also at times competitive, spirit is identified by Michael Whittall in Chapter 4, 'Beyond European Works Council networks: the break-up of the Rover group' in his study of relations between German and British representatives on the EWC of BMW. Whittall highlights the strong influence of national institutions and traditions, but also points at cross-border networking and mutual support as a tendency.

Chapter 5, 'Co-ordinating across borders: the role of European industry federations within European Works Councils' by Valeria Pulignano, deals with the crucial role of trade unions, and in particular European industry federations, in promoting a collective identity in EWCs. Pulignano studies the EWCs in an American multinational with activities in both the metal and the chemical sector, and she compares how the policies and support offered by the two corresponding industry federations affect the EWCs.

In Chapter 6, 'Regional clusters of communication: between national and European identities', Monica Andersson and Christer Thörnqvist report on motivations, expectations, communications and relations to trade unions among the representatives on the EWCs of two Scandinavian multi-nationals. By studying the patterns of communication they find on the one hand that interactions go beyond national borders, and on the other that they are not genuinely European by including everybody. In between, they identify 'regional clusters' based on language and cultural proximity.

As in Chapters 3 and 4, the theme of national identity versus European identity is at the core in Chapters 7–9. In Chapter 7, 'Ethno-, poly- and Eurocentric European Works Councils: how does German involvement influence their identity?', Helen Bicknell examines the specific influence of German representatives on EWCs and whether this influence is conducive to the development of a European identity. Her study deals with such factors as the numerical strength of German representatives, the German industrial relations and works council culture, and the EWC-related activities of German trade unions.

In Chapter 8, 'Still learning from Europe: Spanish participation in European Works Councils' by Holm-Detlev Köhler and Sergio González Begega, the somewhat ambivalent experiences of Spanish EWC representatives are presented. Spanish representatives have welcomed this new and European level of representation; yet they typically represent employees in subsidiaries owned by foreign multinationals and therefore find themselves in a peripheral position.

Chapter 9, 'Interest representation and European identity: a twofold challenge for European Works Councils' by Volker Telljohann, is based on a large amount of case material as well as other evidence dealing with the effects of restructuring on EWCs. From his Italian perspective he examines a number of cases in which restructuring has resulted in important learning within EWCs and led to a strengthening of a common identity, and he also sums up more generally the conditions which are critical for identity-building in EWCs.

Chapter 10, 'The European Works Council and the feeling of interdependence' by Hermann Kotthoff, analyses the interactions within EWCs and defines different types of EWCs based on the quality and quantity of interactions. Kotthoff also presents the different notions of identity developed by classical sociologists such as Durkheim, Weber, Parsons and Popitz, and links the evidence of identity development in EWCs to these notions.

Chapter 11, 'Preparing the ground for a social Europe? European Works Councils and European regulatory identity' by Miguel Martínez Lucio and Syd Weston, contains a theoretical discussion on the EWC as a form of regulation and its possible 'fit' with the challenges posed by economic and political integration in Europe as well as the transnationalisation of companies more generally. In this way the chapter offers a macro-perspective on the question of transnational identity-building in the labour movement.

In Chapter 12, 'Coming of age: the development of a collective identity in European Works Councils', Torsten Müller and Stefan Rüb apply their thorough knowledge of research on EWCs in constructing a model of the development of identity within EWCs. They identify the main factors which influence EWCs, and propose an understanding of EWC identity as composed of 'European identity', 'works council identity' and 'trade union identity'. They also point at critical dynamics over time, which may either foster or destroy a common sense of belonging among EWC representatives.

Finally, in Chapter 13, 'Tackling the identity dilemma' by Fred Huijgen, Michael Whittall and Herman Knudsen, the editors attempt to concentrate and integrate the main insights of the book. Factors hindering and promoting the development of a common identity in EWCs are identified, and it is discussed to what extent a common and collective identity can also be characterised as a specifically European one.

1 European Works Councils and the problem of identity

Herman Knudsen, Michael Whittall and Fred Huijgen

At the Conference for European Political Culture in Berlin in 2004, José Manuel Barroso, in one of his first speeches as European Union (EU) president, spoke of Europe's need to develop a soul. Terms such as 'soul', 'culture', 'social cohesion', 'citizenship' and 'identity' are buzzwords that increasingly penetrate the agenda of EU politicians. Although a common currency, the main symbol of economic integration, and the creation of supranational financial institutions have created a growing interdependence amongst the EU member states, such a fiscal convergence has not signalled the arrival of a common sense of belonging. On the contrary, Europe remains for many of its citizens an abstract idea, although as Wintle argues:

> Identity is usually multiple and potentially integrational, so there is no ostensible reason why European identity should not exist alongside a national one, in the same way that nations already exist alongside gender, race, age, and all the other aspects of identity which we have.
>
> (Wintle 1996: 2)

In a world where regionalisation often appears to represent nothing more than the forward march of shareholder value, the European project is associated with employment insecurity and sometimes decreasing labour standards (Grahl and Teague 2003; Dølvik 2002; Streeck 1991, 1995). With member states, excluding the UK, Denmark and Sweden,[1] abdicating responsibility over key economic variables with the introduction of the Euro (Buda 1998), not only have national systems of representation been undermined (Martin 1999; Hoffmann and Hoffmann 1997), but increased competition has led to a high degree of sectionalism (Hoffmann 2002). Many employees find themselves in a 'bidding war' over investment. Referred to at different times as social dumping, regime competition and negative integration within the context of the EU (Streeck and Vitols 1994; Streeck and Schmitter 1991; Streeck 1991), such a political and economic environment threatens to awaken latent nationalist tendencies and puts EU social cohesion at risk.

Since Jacques Delors' presidency, sections within the European Commission, particularly civil servants from the DG5, have been conscious of the lopsided character of the EU (Rhodes 1995). The emphases placed on social cohesion and the often praised European social model – i.e. rights to employment, protection and civilised labour practices (Visser and Hemerijck 1997) – represent subtle ways of acknowledging the harsh realities associated with neo-liberal economic integration. There prevails a risk that widespread resentment towards the EU will place in question the political legitimacy of Brussels. The Constitution Treaty, in which social and human rights are explicitly made pillars in the EU construction, represents one attempt to address this potentially damaging Achilles' heel. However, during 2005, now often termed the EU's *annus horribilis*, it became clear that the risk is real. The French and the Dutch electorates rejected the treaty, and at least in France it was evident that the lack of a 'social Europe' contributed to this major defeat for the EU elite. The sharpened competition on labour markets, propelled by EU enlargement and expected to be further increased by the much debated directive on cross-border services, became a prominent argument for saying no.

Another initiative is the Charter for Culture, which is planned as a bid to address regional anomie,[2] defined as a geographical area of governance in which there exists no sense of an attachment. Yet even more than the Constitution, this initiative will probably remain a non-tangible attempt to address the problem of a lack of social cohesion and common identity.

European social regulation

Although such legislative initiatives are commendable, there is an argument to suggest that historically the EU project has been reserved for elites and for this very reason has not acquired significance strong enough to change outlooks and identities among ordinary citizens. Governance from above ensures that an important ingredient is missing: 'negotiated interaction', the process of organicism in which the individual and groups of citizens, rather than the legislator, define the shape and form of European norms and value systems. What alternative path is available, though? What structures and opportunities exist that are able to convey a common sense of belonging? To answer this question we suggest that there is a need to comprehend developments within European social regulation in recent years, and in particular what is referred to as the transition from 'hard to soft' law (Dølvik 2000; Keller 2000; Wendon 2000).

In the 1970s and early 1980s the main regulatory approach was to harmonise existing national rules on the basis of the most advanced national standards (Keller and Platzer 2003). As an example, proposals for Community-wide provisions on workers' participation were heavily influenced by the German institutional set-up. With the growth in the number of member states and greater political diversity among them, the harmonisation approach proved increasingly futile. Then followed a period, from the late 1980s to the late 1990s/early 2000s, where the ambition was to set relatively loosely defined minimum standards in a number of areas, this constituting the so-called social dimension to the Single European Market. It included among other things directives on part-time work, fixed-term contracts, working time, and employee representation in multinational companies (European Works Councils). These initiatives leave considerable scope to nation-states and the social partners at national and local level. Finally, in recent years even softer approaches have become predominant. One approach is the 'open method of co-ordination' where the emphasis is put on benchmarking, the exchange of information and mutual learning processes. Another approach, which has been upgraded, is the social dialogue between employer organisations and trade unions at European level, at the general as well as at sector level. Both these approaches rest very much on voluntarism, and are problematic for labour because the right to negotiate is not accompanied by a right to strike, as is the case at the national level.

References to hard and soft law are used to denote a clear difference in Brussels' policy agenda. While hard law represents a commitment to European harmonisation in the field of social policy, the very basis for a supranational, vertically integrated industrial relations system, Streeck and Vitols note that recent developments represent

> An emerging commitment to a decentralized regulatory regime with preference for soft over hard law, private over public order, operating under a variable geometry of participants that are protected from central intervention by ample opportunities for opting out, as well as by a general presumption of precedence of both market forces and local traditions over unrealistic normative regulation.
>
> (Streeck and Vitols 1994: 18–19)

The crux of Streeck and Vitols' argument, one generally supported by other sources (Blank 1998; Keller 1998; Streeck 1997; Oechsler 1996; Altvater and Mahnkopf 1993), hinges on a view that the Commission's interpretation of 'civil society' is primarily directed by market rather than social commitments. In particular, they claim that first the Single European Act (1987) and then the Maastricht Treaty (1993) signalled a devotion to individualism over collectivism and subsidiarity over European-wide solidarity. Referred to by Marginson and Sisson (2004) as representing the 'Americanisation' of EMU, the main line of argument here suggests economic integration will lead to more rather than less labour market disaggregation.

Although we accept that first and foremost the EU project is concerned with economic power, at its centre guided by neo-liberal policies, we reserve our judgement with regard to the perceived negative consequences this has had on European social policy. Though agreeing that a homogenous social sphere is not on the agenda of EU economic integrationists, it would be wrong to forget that the character of Europe is a contested terrain. Certainly, since the foundation of the European Trade Union Confederation

(ETUC) in 1973 and the arrival of influential industrial confederations such as the European Metalworkers' Federation (EMF), European politicians have been unable to totally ignore the interests of labour. Returning to the issue of EU legitimacy, negotiations are not only a prerequisite of legitimacy, but determine some level of compromise. Because of this fact 'windows of opportunity' will intermittently appear.

With regard to the development of a European identity, we argue that Marginson and Sisson (2004) in their analysis of the EU policy shift from 'hard to soft' have located an important opening. Representing a tendency for EU regulation to emphasise rules of procedure and frameworks rather than specific rights and obligations, often discussed as the dilemma of subsidiarity, the current emphasis on a 'soft' legislative approach has the benefit of delegating 'responsibility to representatives at lower levels for implementation' (Marginson and Sisson 2004: 87). Of course, it would be wrong to deny that the ascendancy of procedure over compulsory obligations is not an expression of a rolling back of state rule, namely deregulation. However, the delegation of responsibility, to bring European law closer to the people it affects, we argue, is also an important 'window of opportunity' that cannot be ignored.

A role for organised labour

At the same time as regulatory approaches have become softer, organised labour has been granted a much more prominent role in EU social regulation. One decisive change was the Social Protocol connected to the 1993 Maastricht Treaty and later integrated into the 1997 Amsterdam Treaty. Here, the European peak organisations, UNICE and CEEP on the employer side and ETUC on the trade union side, were authorised to negotiate agreements that may function as alternatives to directives adopted by the political apparatus of the EU. The agreements can take the form either of directives, thus being implemented in the member states in the same way as any other directive, or of social partner agreements, in which case implementation is up to trade unions and employer organisations at national level. Through this opening, but also thanks to the fact that the EU political institutions lack the ability to agree on social regulation 'the hard way', the social dialogue has increased considerably in importance in recent years (European Commission 2004).

Although collective bargaining is still very much confined to national and local levels, this is another area where trade unions are beginning to orient themselves towards the European level. Following an initiative in 1997 from German IG Metall, the European Metalworkers' Federation decided to start a certain co-ordination of collective bargaining across borders, basically by agreeing to the principle that unions everywhere shall pursue wage increases that correspond to inflation plus increases in productivity (Schulten 2003).

A third playing field for European labour became a reality when the Directive on European Works Councils was adopted in 1994. It is the institutions created on the basis of this directive that constitute the case material for this book.

Given that organised labour has been granted, or has taken, roles to play at the European level, it becomes a question of the utmost importance how well suited labour is to play these roles. Is labour able to act as a collective actor at the European level? Labour *has* developed European organisations; labour *is* involved in a multitude of negotiations, consultations and projects at the European level. But how far has labour, trade unions and employee representatives, come in developing a collective, European identity? This is the central question for this book. The answer will be sought by studying the behaviour and attitudes of employee representatives acting at the European level in European Works Councils.

European Works Councils

In our view, one of the most interesting institutions as far as the development of a European identity for labour is concerned is the European Works Council (EWC). While globalisation generally and European economic integration in particular have brought about a wave of cross-national mergers and acquisitions, in turn leading to an increase in the number of workers dependent on employers/employees situated outside their own country, labour representation remains essentially a national concern. The 1994 European Works Council Directive (EWCD) acknowledges this fact. To redress the imbalance the EWCD grants employee representatives the right to meet across borders as well as to be informed and consulted by top management at least once a year. (See Chapter 2 for a more detailed review of the EWCD.)

A number of factors lend support to seeing the EWC as an important experiment in the development of a common identity for European labour. First and foremost, the EWC potentially oversees the regulation of what is central to most people's lives: employment. Not only is there a common reference point, work, virtually an inescapable part of the human condition (Thomas 1999), but there is a chance to observe the wider, transnational processes structuring and restructuring employment and work and to learn how these processes are not restricted to local environments, be they the immediate place of labour or the nation-state. Next, the EWC is a symbol of the contradictory forces that inhabit the EU's geographical realm. While the EWC represents a supranational attempt to consolidate the position of employees, its divergent nature cannot be ignored. It is generally acknowledged, for example, that management may try to use this European body to promote deregulation (Tuckman and Whittall 2002; Wills 2000) or to create an in-house company micro-corporatism detached from the influence of trade unionism (Schulten 1996). Yet at the same time the EWC represents an opportunity from below, our designated 'window of opportunity', for employees to cross-nationally address the tensions and injustices inherent within the neo-liberal regime of economic monetary integration, i.e. to interact and draw up alternative agendas to the many forms of insecurity inherent under modern-day capitalism (Standing 1999). In short, we believe that EWCs have a potential role to play in and against the new model of production and management characterised by Manuel Castells (1996: 238) as 'the simultaneous integration of the work process and disintegration of the workforce'.

Since the early 1970s various groups sympathetic to labour have campaigned to alleviate the negative consequences associated with the internationalisation of the economy and closer economic integration in the EU or, to put it differently: to close the employee representation gap. Although early attempts were unsuccessful, most notably the 1972 Fifth Directive, the 1975 European Company Statute and the 1980 'Vredeling' Directive (see Chapter 2), the adoption of the EWCD in 1994 represented a notable breakthrough in this area (Lecher 1998; Gold and Hall 1994). Initially the EWC was a somewhat exotic body, reserved for academic writings and contentious political wrangling. However, recent events have shown that EWCs may be able to play a role in developing supranational industrial relations (Müller and Hoffmann 2001; Weiler 2004). For instance, General Motors' restructuring of its European operations, involving several cutbacks in recent years, has been modified through interventions of the EWC (in close co-operation with the trade unions) (Knudsen 2003b). In addition, an increasing number of employees have discovered that their future fate can be influenced by this European institution.

Quantitatively, by 2004 the number of multinationals covered by the EWC Directive totalled 2,169, a 14 per cent increase on the 2002 figures (ETUI 2004). It was estimated that 737 EWCs had been established, this representing about two-thirds of all workers in multinationals coming under the jurisdiction of the directive (ETUI 2004). In his study of EWC agreements Paul Marginson (1999) found there were on average eighteen employee representatives on each EWC. This means that now more than 12,000 employee representatives have access to this new – European – level of representation. So, although the EWCD is another fine example of a topdown initiative (Miller 1999), as a soft piece of legislation it has the advantage that it empowers a large group of new actors to enter the European scene. Furthermore this is a group of actors who are deeply involved in solving problems in ordinary people's everyday lives.

The interesting question remains, though, whether EWC representatives can make sense of their new European role. Can they see the need of filling the representation gap pointed out to them by trade union leaders, academics and European Union legislators? Can they establish solidarity links with colleagues from other European countries in a fashion similar to the ones they are used to within local and national settings? Moreover, will EWC delegates be able to develop common perspectives, mutual understandings and a common identity in addition to their already local- and national-anchored identities?

Existing evidence indicates that actors find it extremely difficult to cultivate common positions. Resistance abounds on the part of EWC delegates to step outside their national environments, even after having acknowledged the necessity of developing supranational relations (Whittall 2003). Case studies have even demonstrated how the EWC can develop into a factional instrument (Tuckman and Whittall 2002; Wills 2000; Hancké 2000), the promoter of parochial as against supranational interests. Preliminary research on the interaction between EWC delegates has uncovered numerous factors as inhibiting actors' ability to identify with this still relatively new European institution. These include:

- EWC objectives (the role to be played by the EWC) (Weiler 2004; Huzzard and Docherty 2005);
- differences in national industrial relations background (Knudsen 2004; Whittall 2004);
- language and cultural obstacles (Stirling and Tully 2004);
- low intensity of communication (Weiler 2004);
- degree and type of trade union support and consciousness (Lecher *et al.* 2001);
- competing interests (visible notably during company restructuring processes) (Weiler 2004; Hancké 2000).

Although most representatives have in common a background as experienced employee representatives with an often well-developed sense of how to act in a solidaristic way, the result possibly of basic trade union principles (Miller 1999), they nevertheless arrive at the European scene with different experiences, perceptions and expectations. For example, in a recent comprehensive study of forty-one companies from six EU member states, Weiler (2004: 57) discovered that the functioning of the EWC is seen very differently by representatives in parent companies and foreign subsidiaries: 'In some cases, there seems to be more agreement between the management and the employee representatives in the headquarters than between the employees in the parent company and the subsidiaries.'

Differences among representatives could further be traced back to divergent national industrial relations practices and prior experiences with company employee representation. Tensions could be observed in particular between co-operative, social partnership approaches and adversarial, 'independent' employee representation traditions (Weiler 2004: 58). In addition, the research found great variance to the extent to which EWCs had developed a joint European perspective and strategy of employee representation. Only a few of the studied EWCs, among them those at Volkswagen and Whirlpool, were reported to have reached this advanced stage, corresponding to what Lecher (1998) refers to as a 'collective identity'.

It is by now evident from the research on EWCs that the issue of a collective identity within EWCs is a crucial step in these new bodies attaining a role that is more than merely symbolic or embryonic. This makes it important for us to approach a conceptual understanding of 'identity' and associate the concept to the knowledge we have on the functioning of EWCs.

Identity, labour and EWCs

Identity denotes sameness and congruence. Yet in these so-called post-modern times we are constantly reminded that identities are changing. Identity is no longer based on tradition, but on the roles and positions we are given or take on. For Stuart Hall (1996: 3–4) identity cannot be understood as 'that stable core of the self'; identities are 'increasingly fragmented and fractured' and 'multiply constructed across different ... discourses, practices and positions'. Identities are not stable, and in spite of the notion of sameness they are not self-sustaining; on the contrary, they are the product of differences: 'This entails the radically disturbing recognition that it is only through the relation to the Other, the relation to what it is not, precisely what it lacks ... that the positive meaning ... can be constructed' (Hall 1996: 4–5).

While a person's identity is constructed through intrapersonal processes interiorising experiences of the outside world, group or collective identity is created through interpersonal encounters, communications and experiences with other persons. Perhaps here it becomes clearer if we say that identity is the construct of differences. The group creates its norms and values *in contrast to* other actors and their different values. The notion of a group is for this reason a symbol of differentiation.

The important thing to note about the EWC as a group, however, is that it is not constructed in an organic, voluntaristic manner. Because the EU adopted this directive, and because trade unions urge employee representatives to take advantage of this window of opportunity, employee representatives find themselves situated in a body which initially hardly can be defined as a group. At the outset EWC delegates find themselves alongside other delegates from other plants and other countries, and each of them is already a member of other distinct groups. Jean-Paul Sartre (1976) called such a grouping 'a series' and used the example of a group of people queuing up for the bus. They have a common interest in travelling on the bus, but apart from that nothing binds them together. Similarly, EWCs start from a point of departure where the only thing the representatives have in common is that once a year they can participate in a meeting with the top management. What Lecher and associates (1999) term 'symbolic' EWCs are essentially EWCs that have not developed any further than the 'series'; there may be action, but no collective action. To move from a series to a genuine group, conscious efforts on the part of the EWC delegates are needed; only they can help transform the EWC into an entity with a more or less developed common sense of identity. Not only do the delegates have to communicate with each other so as to become conscious of common conditions and so develop what Goffman (1956: 26) refers to as 'interdependent activities of an on-going social system', but moreover this is an essential act in becoming a group subjectively.

Identity is constructed through identification processes. Identification implies recognising that conditions, characteristics and aspirations are shared with another person or group, either real or imagined, out of which a sense of belonging, allegiance and solidarity can emerge (Breakwell and Lyons 1996). It needs to be recognised, however, that although the processes of identification take place within determinate material and symbolic conditions, they are not only open-ended but also always ongoing and never completed (Hall 1996).

In considering identity within the context of EWCs there are a number of questions that need to be addressed. Who do employee representatives identify with in their role as employee representatives (disregarding that they probably also identify with their family, nationality, perhaps the local football club, etc.)? Is it the constituency that elected them or the trade union they belong to, or does identification stretch out to also encompass colleagues on the EWC or the whole workforce of the multinational company? Any representative will have his/her own answer – and the answer today might very well be different from that of yesterday or tomorrow. This is because environments, discourses and choices are in a constant flux of change, and because a position on an EWC inevitably involves learning processes. Identification and identity are complex issues; they combine elements from different worlds which not only have to grapple with their own internal (lack of) consistence but can end up being reoriented in the light of new events and experiences. In addition, we have to accept that employee representatives may be narrow-minded and identify almost exclusively with their immediate constituency. Alternatively, however, they may be broad-minded, identifying with the global cause of labour, or move from one identity to another influenced by changes occurring in their life and the discourses dominating it.

A crucial point seems to be how the collective 'we' is constructed *vis-à-vis* the Other. According to Marxist theory the Other will of course be the employer, the local management as well as the central management in the headquarters of the company. Against the employer the employees will construct a common identity based on a common condition of exploitation, and relations between them will be based on solidarity. Such a position assumes that in dealing with the harsh realities of increased international competition and what Hoffmann (1997) refers to as the threat of 'exit', the export of jobs abroad, labour representatives will seek to form alliances outside their immediate national environment to influence such processes (Whittall 2003; Knudsen, 2003a). In this perspective, the foundation of an EWC is symbolic of such a conscious decision. However, typically, a smaller or larger part of the representatives later elected to the EWC did not participate in the founding act.

Theoretically, at least, there exists a connection between employees divided by national boundaries. This involves awareness that globalisation and regionalisation are increasingly a general experience and not simply one restricted to a particular place or time. However, we contend that there are a number of problems associated with this position. Marxist theory was wrong in expecting the development of an interest-based class-consciousness to confront employers everywhere, eventually leading to the overthrow of the capitalist system. This is not to deny that the material interests underpinning capitalism are a strong vehicle for social orientations and change. We are not denying the universal subjugation of the working class within industrialised nations, nor Burawoy's (1985: 18) assertion that 'every particularity contains a generality; each particular factory regime is the product of general forces operating at a societal or global level'. Nevertheless, there is a need to guard against 'conflating' what Marx (1985: 51) referred to as the 'necessity of association', i.e. unbounded class solidarity. It needs to be recognised that, in constructing a 'we', employee representatives usually first and foremost interpret what is in the best interests of their immediate constituency, followed perhaps by an awareness of the interests of employees and trade unionism on a wider scale. This is because, as Offe and Wiesenthal (1980) observed, geographically labour is predestined to a degree of parochialism by the very fact that capital comes to labour and not vice versa. With capital being increasingly mobile and able to easily change the localisation of economic activities, the national scene, which the labour movement is so familiar with and where it has struck its compromises with capital in the past, is declining in importance. We need to recognise that capital can increasingly play nation-states and national labour movements off against each other (Knudsen 2003a). As witnessed by recent rounds of concession bargaining in Siemens, Scandinavian Airlines System and other big European companies, this opportunity is used to increase working time and/or reduce pay. Global labour solidarity is the obvious answer to capital mobility, but that answer is probably less developed today than it was a century ago (Hyman 1999, 2004). As both Flanders (1975) and Weber (1964) noted, as an interest group labour is marked by a high degree of sectionalism. Weber even demonstrated that the evolution of trade unions across Europe was closely associated with the process of 'exclusivity', labour organisations' primarily being concerned with restricting membership to their ranks as a means of improving the market power of their existing members. What this denotes is a historical predominance to focus on the immediate, which has led to the construction of company specific and national patterns of collective regulation, the very forbear of parochial sympathies (Lecher and Nauman 1994; Mittelman 1997). As Hyman argues in his critical discussion of the notion of universal labour solidarity:

> Reality is different. We are shaped by our direct experiences, immediate milieu, and specific patterns of social relations. Broader identities and

affiliations are founded on the direct, immediate and specific, through intersubjectivities which link these to the external and encompassing.

(Hyman 1999: 96)

The logic of this argument assumes, therefore, that if a plant forming part of a multinational company faces the threat of closure, the obvious response may be to mobilise resources in the local community, in local government bodies and in local management, while in a political and economic climate dominated by international factionalism it would perhaps seem much more unrealistic to contact employee representatives in other countries and seek their support for a united effort to change the decision of the parent company. At any event, the employee representative has to make choices regarding what is the most viable strategy to defend the interests of his/her constituency: to rely on known, tried-and-tested resources nearby, or to try to get help from the not-so-well-known resources of colleagues at the European or global level. Certainly, with the arrival of the EWC a European approach has become a more realistic option. However, given the obstacles mentioned above, is it worth while? Solidarity, according to Richard Hyman (2004: 42) 'involves the perception of commonalities, which extend, but do not abolish, consciousness of distinct and particularistic interests'. For EWCs to become transmitters of international solidarity, EWC representatives need to become aware of the commonalities that exist across all the differences and obstacles.

Thus, as a premise and point of departure for this book, we believe it to be an open question whether EWCs will remain 'series' in character or will develop into strongly integrated groups or even institutions with common identities. It is our proposition that common identities will only evolve in EWCs where communication between representatives is sufficiently intense and frequent; where methods have been developed to overcome language barriers and cultural suspicion; and where one or more events have demonstrated that a common effort on the part of the EWC can make a positive difference. So far, this seems to have been the case in, for instance, the EWCs of General Motors, Volkswagen and Whirlpool, but hardly in the majority of EWCs (Weiler 2004; Knudsen 2003b).

We will now let other researchers of EWCs take over from here, and enriched by their contributions we will return in the last chapter and attempt to conclude on the question of European identity-building in EWCs.

Notes

1 This is not to say that any of these countries are less committed to the neo-liberal course.
2 The 2004 Conference for European Political Culture in Berlin, committed Europe to passing a charter on culture.

References

Altvater, E. and Mahnkopf, B. (1993) *Gewerkschaften vor der europäischen Herausforderung*, Münster: Westfälisches Dampfboot.

Blank, M. (1998) 'Collective bargaining in the European Union: the standpoint of the IG Metall', in W. Lecher and H.-W. Platzer (eds) *European Union – European Industrial Relations?* London: Routledge, 157–68.

Breakwell, G. and Lyons, E. (eds) (1996) *Changing European Identities. Social Psychological Analysis of Social Change*, Oxford: Butterworth-Heinemann.

Buda, D. (1998) 'On course for European labour relations? The prospects for the social dialogue in the European Union', in W. Lecher and H.-W. Platzer (eds) *European Union – European Industrial Relations?* London: Routledge, 21–46.

Burawoy, M. (1985) *The Politics of Production: Factory Regimes under Capitalism and Socialism*, London: Verso.

Castells, M. (1996) *The Rise of the Network Society. The Information Age, Economy, Society and Culture*, vol. 1, Oxford: Blackwell.

Dølvik, J.-E. (2002) 'European trade unions: coping with globalisation', in J. Hoffmann (ed.) *The Solidarity Dilemma: Globalisation, Europeanisation, and Trade Unions*, Brussels: ETUI, 83–118.

—— (2000) 'Economic and Monetary Union: implications for industrial relations and collective bargaining in Europe', ETUI Discussion and Working Paper DWP, Brussels: ETUI.

ETUI (2004) *European Works Council Data Bank*, Brussels: European Trade Union Institute.

European Commission (2004) *Industrial Relations in Europe 2004*, Luxembourg: Office for Official Publications of the European Communities. Online. Available HTTP: http://europa.eu.int/comm/employment_social/publications/2004-3_en.html (accessed 15 March 2006).

Flanders, A. (1975) *Management and Trade Unions: The Theory and Reform of Industrial Relations*, London: Faber and Faber.

Goffman, E. (1956) *The Presentation of Self in Everyday Life*, New York: Doubleday.

Gold, M. and Hall, M. (1994) 'Statutory European Works Councils: the final countdown?', *Industrial Relations Journal*, 25 (3): 177–86.

Grahl, J. and Teague, P. (2003) 'The Eurozone and financial integration: the industrial relations issues', *Industrial Relations Journal*, 34 (5): 396–410.

Hall, S. (1996) 'Introduction: who needs "identity"?', in S. Hall and P. du Gay (eds) *Questions of Cultural Identity*, London: Sage, 1–17.

Hancké, B. (2000) 'European Works Councils and industrial restructuring in the European motor industry', *European Journal of Industrial Relations*, 6 (1): 35–60.

Hoffman, J. (1997) 'Geht das "Modell Deutschland" an seinem Erfolg zugrunde?', *Gewerkschaftliche Monatshefte*, 4: 217–23.

—— (2002) 'Introduction: the solidarity dilemma: globalisation, Europeanisation, and trade unions policy', in J. Hoffmann (ed.) *The Solidarity Dilemma: Globalisation, Europeanisation, and Trade Unions*, Brussels: ETUI, 1–6.

Hoffmann, J. and Hoffmann, R. (1997) *Globalization – Risks and Opportunities for Labour Policy in Europe*. Online. Available HTTP: http://www.etui-reks.org/europe_in_the_-context_of_globalisation/reports_and_discussion_papers.html (accessed 15 March 2006).

Huzzard, T. and Docherty, P. (2005) 'Between global and local: eight European Works Councils in retrospect and prospect', *Economic and Industrial Democracy*, 26 (4): 541–68.

Hyman, R. (1999) 'Imagined solidarities: can trade unions resist globalisation?', in P. Leisink (ed.) *Globalisation and Labour Relations*, Cheltenham: Edward Elgar, 94–115.

—— (2004) 'Solidarity for Ever', in J. Lind, H. Knudsen and H. Jørgensen (eds) *European Labour and Employment Regulation,* Brussels: PIE Peter Lang, 35–47.

Keller, B. (1998) 'National industrial relations and the prospects for European collective bargaining: the view from a German standpoint', in W. Lecher and H.-W. Platzer (eds) *European Union – European Industrial Relations?* London: Routledge, 21–46.

—— (2000) 'The emergence of regional systems of employment regulation: the case of the European Union', paper to 12th IIRA World Congress, Tokyo, May/June 2000.

Keller, B. and Platzer, H.-W. (2003) 'Conclusions and perspectives: European integration and trans- and supranational industrial relations', in B. Keller and H.-W. Platzer (eds) *Industrial Relations and European Integration*, Aldershot: Ashgate, 181–78.

Knudsen, H. (2003a) 'Between the local and the global – representing employee interests in European Works Councils of multinational companies', in D. Fleming and C. Thörnqvist (eds) *Nordic Management–Labour Relations and Internationalization*, Copenhagen: Nordic Council of Ministers, 47–77.

—— (2003b) 'Towards more influence. European Works Councils', report from the Conference in Aarhus, Copenhagen: LO/FTF/AC/ETUC, November 2002.

—— (2004) 'European Works Councils: potentials and obstacles on the road to employee influence in multinational companies', *Industrielle Beziehungen*, 11 (3): 203–21.

Lecher, W. (1998) 'Auf dem Weg zu europäischen Arbeitsbeziehungen? Das Beispiel der Euro-Betriebsräte', *WSI Mitteilungen* 50 (4): 258–63.

Lecher, W. and Nauman, R. (1994) 'The current state of trade unions in the EU member states', in W. Lecher (ed.) *Trade Unions in the European Union – a Handbook*, London: Lawrence and Wishart, 3–126.

Lecher, W., Nagel, B. and Platzer, H.-W. (1999) *The Establishment of European Works Councils: from Information Committee to Social Actor*, Aldershot: Ashgate.

Lecher, W., Platzer, H.-W., Rüb, S. and Weiner, K.-P. (2001) *Verhandelte Euro-päisierung: Die Einrichtung europäischer Betriebsräte – Zwischen gesetzlichem Rahmen und sozialer Dynamik*, Baden-Baden: Nomos Verlagsgesellschaft.

Marginson, P. (1999) 'EWC agreements under review: arrangements in companies based in four countries compared', *Transfer*, 5 (3): 256–77.

Marginson, P. and Sisson, K. (2004) *European Integration and Industrial Relations: Multi-Level Governance in the Making*, Basingstoke: Palgrave Macmillan.

Martin, A. (1999) 'Wage bargaining under EMU: Europeanisation, re-nationalisation or Americanisation?', ETUI Discussion and Working Paper, DWP, Brussels: ETUI.

Marx, K. (1985) *The German Ideology,* London: Lawrence and Wishart.

Miller, D. (1999) 'Towards a "European" Works Council', *Transfer,* 5 (3): 344–65.

Mittelman, J. (1997) 'Restructuring the global division of labour: old theories and new realities', in S. Gill (ed.) *Globalization, Democratization and Multilateralism*, London: Macmillan, 77–103.

Müller, T. and Hoffmann, A. (2001) 'EWC research: A Review of the Literature', Warwick Papers of Industrial Relations no. 65: Coventry: University of Warwick.

Oechsler, W. (1996) 'Europäische Betriebsräte', *DWB*, 5: 697–708.

Offe, C. and Wiesenthal, H. (1980) 'The two logics of collective action: theoretical notes on social class and organizational form', *Political Power and Social Theory*, 1: 67–115.

Rhodes, M. (1995) 'A regulatory conundrum: industrial relations and the social dimension', in S. Leibfried and P. Pierson (eds) *European Social Policy: Between Fragmentation and Integration*, Washington, DC: Brookings, 78–122.

Sartre, J.-P. (1976) *Critique of Dialectical Reason*, London: New Left Books.

Schulten, T. (1996) 'Der europäische Betriebsrat bei Nestlé', *Informationen über multinationale Konzerne*, 6: 42–52.

—— (2003) 'Europeanisation of collective bargaining: trade union initiatives for the transnational coordination of collective bargaining', in B. Keller and H.-W. Platzer (eds) *Industrial Relations and European Integration*, Aldershot: Ashgate, 112–36.

Standing, G. (1999) *Global Labour Flexibility*, London: Macmillan.

Stirling, J. and Tully, B. (2004) 'Power, process and practice: communications in European Works Councils', *European Journal of Industrial Relations*, 10 (1): 73–89.

Streeck, W. (1991) 'More uncertainties: German unions facing 1992', *Industrial Relations*, 30 (3): 317–49.

—— (1995) 'From market making to state building? Reflections on the political economy of European social policy', in S. Leibfried and P. Pierson (eds) *European Social Policy: Between Fragmentation and Integration*, Washington, DC: Brookings, 389–431.

—— (1997) 'Neither European nor works councils: a reply to Paul Knutsen', *Economic and Industrial Democracy*, 18 (2): 325–37.

Streeck, W. and Schmitter, P.C. (1991) 'From national corporatism to transnational pluralism – organised interests in the Single European Market', in W. Streeck (ed.) *Social Institutions and Economic Performance*, London: Sage, 197–228.

Streeck, W. and Vitols, S. (1994) 'European Works Councils: between statutory enactment and voluntary adoption', discussion paper, *Wissenschaftszentrum Berlin Für Sozialforschung, FSI*, 93–112.

Thomas, K. (1999) *The Oxford Book of Work*, Oxford: Oxford University Press.

Tuckman, A. and Whittall, M. (2002) 'Affirmation, games and increasing insecurity: cultivating consent within a new workplace regime', *Capital and Class*, 76: 64–94.

Visser, J. and Hemerijck, A. (1997) *A Dutch Miracle: Job Growth, Welfare Reform, and Corporatism in the Netherlands*, Amsterdam: Amsterdam University Press.

Weber, M. (1964) *The Theory of Social and Economic Organisation*, New York: The Free Press.

Weiler, A. (2004) *European Works Councils in Practice,* Dublin: European Foundation for the Improvement of Living and Working Conditions.

Wendon, B. (2000) 'The Commission as the venue entrepreneur in the EU social policy', *Journal of European Public Policy*, 5 (2): 339–53.

Whittall, M. (2003) 'European Works Councils – a path to European industrial relations? The case of BMW and Rover', unpublished PhD thesis, Nottingham Trent University.

—— (2004) 'European labour market regulation: the case of European Works Councils', in L. Vosko and J. Stanford (eds) *Challenging the Market: The Struggle to Regulate Work and Income*, McGill-Queens University Press, 152–72.

Wills, J. (2000) 'Great expectations: three years in the life of a European Works Council', *European Journal of Industrial Relations*, 6 (1): 85–107.

Wintle, M. (1996) *Culture and Identity in Europe*, Aldershot: Avebury.

2　The European Works Councils Directive

Changing rationales for EU regulation of employee participation

Michael Gold

Of all the areas regulated by the social and employment policy of the European Union (EU), worker participation has proved over the years to be the most controversial. EU provisions on, for example, equal opportunities, working time and non-standard contracts have all, at one time or another, provoked fierce opposition among employers, but those on worker participation – by apparently imposing constraints on management prerogative – have been widely viewed as the most threatening and intrusive. The Union of Industrial and Employers' Confederations (UNICE), for example, bluntly rejected the draft Directive on European works councils on its publication in 1991 as a 'false start' and as 'over-institutional, over-rigid and bureaucratic in character' (UNICE 1991: 1).

Problems surrounding the introduction of worker participation at EU level have been compounded by a variety of factors. One is the sheer diversity of existing institutional and legal frameworks across the member states of the EU. Employee representation at board level, for example, is required in the private sector in Austria, Germany, Luxembourg and most Nordic countries. France and the Netherlands provide for 'hybrid forms' of representation, while several countries, such as Greece and Spain, allow for such representation only in the public or socialised sector. Belgium, Italy and the UK make no provision at all (EIRO 1998; Group of Experts 1997). Regulations governing works councils and union representation at workplace or sub-board levels are equally complex. In the Nordic countries, Ireland, Italy and the UK, there are 'single channels' of representation through the unions, though these are sometimes supplemented by joint representation bodies. In 'dual-channel systems', employees are represented by works councils, which operate alongside the unions. In Belgium and France, the employer chairs the works council, whereas in most other cases – such as Germany, the Netherlands and Portugal – it consists only of employee representatives. In Ireland and the UK, employee representation has traditionally been placed solely on a voluntary basis, though elsewhere it is governed by statute or collective agreement (Group of Experts 1997).

The role of the trade unions therefore also varies widely. The dual system of industrial relations in Germany has kept collective bargaining and the determination of pay and conditions apart from issues of participation, such as information disclosure, consultation and co-determination. In the UK, unions view the world through the prism of collective bargaining, which has lent industrial relations an adversarial orientation. The German system of industrial relations has been characterised as 'legalised, centralised and co-operative', contrasting with the 'voluntary, decentralised, conflict-based system' in the UK (Williams 1988: v). In the early days, the Commission of the European Communities did not always take these divergences into account when proposing models of participation. In the 1970s, the European Company Statute and the Fifth Directive were based broadly on the German and Dutch models, which had little appeal for the UK and Ireland, who joined in 1973.

Furthermore, attitudes towards worker participation among the key actors, notably governments, have undergone phases of interest and hostility. Taking successive UK governments as examples, both Conservative and Labour governments in the 1970s were generally favourable to the proposals contained in the European Company Statute and the Fifth Directive for employee representation at board level. However, Conservative governments in the 1980s and 1990s were implacably opposed to all forms of worker participation, though these positions were at least partially reviewed when the incoming Labour government signed the social chapter in 1997, and thereby introduced European Works Councils into the UK. Even so, the same Labour government subsequently opposed the adoption of the 'general framework' Directive on information and consultation of employees in the European Community.

Despite these complications, the EU did eventually adopt the European Works Councils Directive in 1994, a breakthrough followed later by the European Company Statute (2001) and the 'general framework' Directive (2002). This chapter will track the emergence of worker participation as an area for EU regulation, along with the changing rationales for its development. It will examine in particular the following measures and the relationships between them:

- European Company Statute;
- draft Fifth Directive;
- draft 'Vredeling' Directive;
- European Works Councils Directive;
- 'general framework' Directive for informing and consulting employees;
- miscellaneous provisions for participation (relating to redundancy, health and safety and other areas); and
- recommendation on financial participation.

Throughout this chapter, quotations from these texts are taken from the sources listed in Table 2.1.

Table 2.1 Sources of principal EU legislation regulating employee participation

Title	Date adopted	Official Journal reference	European Industrial Relations Review	European Works Councils Bulletin (first issue 1996)
(Draft) Fifth Directive* [withdrawn]	Revised text, 1983	OJ C240/83	117, p. 8 (October 1983) Text: 117, p. 25	N/A
(Draft) Vredeling Directive* [withdrawn]	Revised text, 1983	OJ C217/83	115, p. 7 (August 1983) Text: 115, p. 26	N/A
European Works Councils Directive	1994	OJ L254/94	250, p. 14 (November 1994) Text: 251, p. 27 (December 1994)	N/A
European Company Statute	2001	OJ L294/01 (regulation and directive)	336, p. 21 (January 2002) Text: 335, p. 32 (December 2001)	37, p. 7 (January/February 2002); 38, p. 10 (March/April 2002) Text: 37, p. 16 (January/February 2002)
General framework Directive	2002	OJ L80/02	340, p. 13 (May 2002) Text: 339, p. 30 (April 2002)	38, p. 4 (March/April 2002) Text: 39, p. 17 (May/June 2002)
Statute for a European Co-operative Society	2003	OJ L207/04 (regulation and directive)	358, p. 35 (November 2003)	48, p. 12 (November/December 2003)

(continued on next page)

Table 2.1 (continued)

Title	Date adopted	Official Journal reference	European Industrial Relations Review	European Works Councils Bulletin (first issue 1996)
Miscellaneous provisions				
Collective redundancies	1975	OJ L48/75	13, p. 4 (January 1975) Text: 13, p. 24	N/A
Collective redundancies	1992	OJ L245/92, OJ L311/92	225, p. 24 (October 1992) Text: 226, p. 29 (November 1992)	N/A
Transfer of undertakings ('acquired rights')	1977	OJ L61/77	38, p. 21 (February 1977)	N/A
Health and safety framework directive	1989	OJ L183/89	181, p. 21 (February 1989) Text: 181, p. 24 (February 1989)	N/A
Company takeover bids	2004	OJ L142/04	N/A	52, p. 14 (July/August 2004)
Recommendation on PEPPER	1992	OJ L245/93	224, p. 2 (September 1992) Text: 224, p. 31 (September 1992)	N/A
Cross-border company mergers	2005	Not published in OJ at time of writing	N/A	60, p. 12 (November/ December 2005)
(Draft) temporary agency work*	2002	COM (2002) 149	339, p. 15 (April 2002) Text: 339, p. 33 (April 2002)	39, p. 3 (May/June 2002)

Notes:
Instruments marked with an asterisk exist in draft form and have not yet been adopted by Council. The Social Charter was adopted by the European Council in 1989: EIRR (1989), no. 190, November, p. 17; text, p. 26.

Rationales

The terms 'industrial democracy', 'employee participation' and 'employee involvement' have long been contested. The extent to which organisations, private or public, are prepared to allow their employees to participate in decisions concerning their lives at work is 'one of the most complex, dynamic and controversial aspects' of employment relations as they have evolved in industrialised countries (Hyman and Mason 1995: 1). All parties involved have widely varying interests and perspectives. Employers generally believe that employees need to be integrated into organisational structures to ensure that they understand the organisation's aims and objectives and can contribute to its success. Unions, by contrast, may be eager to extend their influence over organisational decision-making to ensure that their own priorities – such as control over work practices or stable employment patterns – are properly met. Governments too vary by political persuasion, with some adopting ostensibly free-market or non-interventionist policies in employment relations, while others are much more 'hands on' and proactive with respect to issues like participation. However, employee participation schemes can all be analysed with respect to the following elements:

- *forms*: direct forms involving all employees, and representational forms involving employee representatives;
- *levels*: such as workplace, company or group;
- *methods*: such as negotiation, consultation and information disclosure;
- *stages*: involvement at different phases of decision-making, such as planning, implementation and monitoring;
- *subject areas*: from 'tea, towels and toilets' at workplace level up to investment decisions at board level.

Using this typology, we can identify a 'continuum of participation' (Blyton and Turnbull 2004: 255). At one end of the spectrum there lie 'weak' arrangements, such as team briefings at workplace level that rely on one-way communication and limited subject areas. These may be termed 'integrationist', as they attempt to integrate the interests of workers and unions into company structures by improving their understanding of the business. They are generally voluntary and based on management initiative. By contrast, at the other end of the spectrum there are 'strong' arrangements, such as works councils or employee representation on company boards with certain rights to co-determination over areas of company strategy. These may be termed 'redistributive', as they attempt to redistribute power towards workers and their unions. At the far end of this spectrum can be found workers' self-management in co-operatives.

The EU has rarely focused on direct forms of participation, except in its recommendation on financial participation. It has, rather, focused on representational forms, at workplace, company and group level, and on information and consultation, rather than negotiation. Its measures have generally been designed to give workers influence at ever earlier stages of decision-making, and in relation to subject areas likely to have substantial effects on their lives.

This angle, generally referred to as 'employee participation', can be located towards the redistributive end of the 'continuum', which is why neo-liberal governments – notably, but not exclusively, governments in the UK – and employers' organisations have viewed EU activities in this arena with suspicion, if not hostility. For this reason – and particularly because the EU has enjoyed some remarkable success over recent years in advancing its agenda – we need to review some of the rationales for employee participation. What might be the underlying reasons for introducing employee participation, and how might changing economic and social circumstances support its introduction?

Along with social factors widely noted in the 1960s and 1970s – such as higher levels of education and training among the working population, a decline in deference and rising expectations – there are, broadly construed, four sets of rationales that underpin the Commission's interest in employee participation:

1   company law harmonisation;
2   participation seen as a productive factor;
3   prevention of social dumping; and
4   political factors, such as union and political pressures for workers' rights.

The Commission has long been committed to creating a unified framework of legislation designed to harmonise the regulation of company activity across the member states (the first company law Directive, dating from 1968, covered disclosure requirements). It believes that harmonisation is required to 'close the gap' between the economic realities facing European companies (the prospect of widening and deepening economic integration) and the legal obstacles that hinder them from taking full advantage of these realities (such as complex and fragmented regulation of taxation, reporting standards and decision-making systems across the member states). Its series of company law directives has covered non-contentious areas like accounting standards, company prospectuses and auditors' qualifications, as well as the seriously contentious area of employee participation.

Alongside these concerns, participation may also be viewed as a 'productive factor' in the success of enterprises. The introduction of works councils has been regarded as a means of securing co-operation between management and workers, explaining company policies and facilitating the process of restructuring (Streeck 1992). The Commission, as we see below, has often mobilised such arguments in justifying its proposals.

EU-level measures are also a means of preventing 'social dumping'. Some countries, with advanced worker rights, have expressed concerns that sharpening competition between member states would exert downward pressure on these rights – as a way of reducing labour costs – without appropriate safeguards. The European Company Statute, for example, states that 'special provisions' have to be established to ensure that the formation of a European Company does not entail 'the disappearance or reduction' of existing practices of employee involvement in the companies affected (Article 3 of the preamble). Finally, political factors have also played their part in creating groundswell for employee participation. Unions and progressive parties have supported the extension of workers' rights to information and consultation in exchange for support for trade liberalisation and the creation of 'business Europe'.

These rationales have not always been evenly weighted. For example, the draft Fifth Directive was explicitly based on rationales for company law harmonisation (rationale 1), and the European Company Statute, as a voluntary scheme, implicitly so, though Vredeling and the EWC Directive reflected to a greater extent rationales based on productive factors (rationale 2) and social dumping (rationale 3). However, the European trade unions have seen all proposals in terms of workers' rights (rationale 4), which is why the issue – the introduction of worker participation – has frequently become heavily confrontational. UNICE, for example, claimed that the EWC Directive was 'unfair and conflictual' and that it undermined 'the authority of management' (UNICE 1993: 1). Indeed, one of the principal tensions in debates on employee participation – at all levels, not just the EU – focuses on where it may be located along the 'continuum' – that is, the extent to which a particular arrangement is primarily integrationist (rationale 2) or redistributive (rationale 4). EU proposals, as we have noted, tend to be representational and seen as redistributive. Progress in securing the adoption of proposals has generally depended on the willingness of the parties involved to negotiate and compromise and to use productive-factor rationales to convince employers of the need for participation to help strengthen the Single European Market. Progress has also, crucially, depended on political factors, and the confluence of interests among the Commission and Council, and employers and unions.

The evolution of worker participation provides an object lesson in the operation of multi-level forms of EU governance, particularly social dialogue, and the result of the proposals noted above has been diverse. The European Company Statute has been adopted, though in diluted form; the Fifth Directive and Vredeling have both been withdrawn; and the EWC Directive and the 'general framework' Directive have been adopted by qualified majority vote on the Council, following failed attempts by the Commission to secure EU-level agreements between employers and unions.

The European Company Statute and the Fifth Directive

Worker participation became an issue for the Commission in 1970, when it published the first draft of its European Company Statute (ECS), and in

1972, when it published the first draft of its Fifth Directive on company structure and employee representation, in a series of instruments on company law harmonisation. At that time, the German model of industrial consensus was widely regarded as a major factor in Germany's remarkable economic performance, and the provision of 'worker directors' on the supervisory boards of large companies as the 'jewel in the crown'. Policy-makers in the Commission, in attempting to formulate a pan-European system of corporate governance, integrated the introduction of worker directors into their framework. Among the six then member states of the European Economic Community (EEC), France and the Netherlands, along with Germany, already had their own provisions for worker directors in the private sector – Belgium and Italy did not (Luxembourg was to introduce them in 1974). Furthermore, all six had provisions for works councils within companies (Daniel 1978), so it would not have seemed strange that the early drafts of the ECS contained provisions for a European works council.

The rationale for both proposals was based principally on company law harmonisation. The Commission argued in its original proposal for the European Company Statute that undertakings 'should be able to plan and carry out the reorganization of their activities at Community level'. Since the establishment of European undertakings was the 'obvious and normal means of achieving that result', it regarded the ECS as a 'necessary instrument for the attainment of one of the objectives of the Community' (Bulletin 1970: 5). Though the idea itself went back to 1959 (Sanders 1973), the ECS had a long and troubled history. It was amended in 1975 – particularly to allow for the co-option of independents on to the supervisory board – but it then entered a state of suspended animation until its revival as part of the Single European Market programme in 1987. Following protracted negotiations, the Council finally adopted both the Regulation and Directive on the ECS in October 2001. They took full effect three years later, from October 2004.

The key feature of the ECS is that it is voluntary, an option that companies registered in the European Economic Area (EEA) may wish to consider but are not required to adopt. The incentive is that European Companies are regulated by a unified legal framework designed to harmonise their management and reporting systems. Restructuring is also simplified, as registered offices may be relocated across member state boundaries without incurring the intervention of the national authorities involved. The Regulation allows the formation of a European Company in four ways: through a merger, the creation of a holding company, the creation of a subsidiary or the transformation of companies already registered in a member state. The directive provides for employee representation at two levels within the new company: through a 'representative body' (such as a works council) and through board-level representation. The provisions are designed both to prevent the dilution or abolition of existing arrangements and to prevent the imposition of board-level representation in member states where it is not

presently required. A Special Negotiating Body plays a major role in negotiating appropriate forms of employee representation throughout the European
Company, but 'standard rules' contained in the Annex apply either by mutual
consent or if there is failure to agree after due process (Goulding 2004).

So far, fewer than a dozen companies have either set up as a European
Company or expressed an interest in doing so (EWCB 2005b). However, in
September 2005 Allianz – one of the world's largest financial services companies, with 162,000 employees across some seventy countries – announced
plans to become one, following a merger with an Italian subsidiary (EWCB
2005c).

The rationale for the draft Fifth Directive was similar to that of the ECS,
though the approach was quite different. While the ECS was designed to
transcend national legislation by promoting the formation of an entirely
new legal entity – the European Company – with the same status throughout the EEA, the Fifth Directive aimed at harmonising systems of corporate governance across the EEC. That is, the draft Fifth Directive, which
was first published in 1972, would have *imposed* a certain model of company structure and employee representation on all companies with over
1,000 workers within the EEC. The original proposals were based firmly on
either the 'German model', under which employees elect a proportion of the
members of their company's supervisory board, or the 'Dutch model',
under which employee representatives are co-opted on to the supervisory
board. In the UK, which joined the EEC in 1973, the government set up the
Bullock Committee to examine the issue of board-level employee representation, but employers and sections of the labour movement proved hostile, and Conservative governments elected throughout the 1980s and 1990s
precluded any chance of legislation on the issue, as it required a unanimous
vote on the Council. Nevertheless, the Commission published a Green
Paper in 1975 to examine the main controversies aroused, and the Economic and Social Committee and the European Parliament both debated
the topic in depth. The Commission finally adopted an amended text on the
draft Fifth Directive in 1983.

The amended text, like the previous versions, covers two separate but
linked issues: the structure of company boards and the nature of employee
representation on them. Member states would have been required either to
introduce a two-tier board structure (management and supervisory boards)
or else to allow companies to select for themselves a single or two-tier
structure. On single boards, a distinction would have been drawn between
executive directors with a management role and non-executive directors,
who would have been in the majority but in a purely supervisory capacity.
Shareholders would have retained final control over the company through
its annual general meeting.

The amended text adopted a more flexible approach towards the nature
of employee representation on boards, reflecting the diverse systems operating across the EEC (by 1983, Denmark, Greece, Ireland and the UK had

also joined, and Portugal and Spain were preparing to do so). Member states would have been required to apply one of four systems to all companies with over 1,000 workers, with employee representation: either on a supervisory board or among the non-executive members of the management board (essentially the 'German model'); or on a supervisory board appointed through co-option (the 'Dutch model'); or on a special 'company council' comprising only employee representatives, with rights to information and consultation like those of a supervisory board, but no veto over management decisions; or through other company-level schemes negotiated through collective bargaining, provided that they reflected the basic principles of the other three systems.

While the third system would have required legislation to ensure the introduction of a standard 'company council', the fourth merely placed a statutory obligation on companies and employee representatives to negotiate over the introduction of company-level participation schemes. In this way, the directive reflected a more negotiable and less legalistic approach towards participation, in line with the traditions of certain member states such as the UK. However, in the case of failure to agree, statutory fall-back provisions would have applied and one of the other three systems would have been introduced. After years of deadlock, the Commission formally withdrew the draft in January 2004.

'Vredeling' Directive

At the same time as debates on the draft Fifth Directive were continuing, an entirely separate directive was proposed in 1980. While the draft Fifth originated in DG III of the Commission, the Directorate-General dealing with the internal market and industrial affairs, the 'Vredeling' Directive was proposed by DGV, the Directorate-General dealing with employment, social affairs and education. This directive – named after Henk Vredeling, the Dutch Commissioner then responsible for social affairs – governed employees' rights to information and consultation in companies with complex structures, primarily multinationals. It adopted a more pragmatic approach than the ECS and Fifth Directive by adapting itself to existing information and consultation procedures rather than imposing certain models. The preamble to the directive stated that procedures for informing and consulting employees were 'often inconsistent' across the member states, which consequently led to unequal treatment of employees affected by decisions taken by the same undertaking.

Following the usual round of consultations, the Commission issued an amended text in 1983. It proposed new rights for workers employed in those subsidiaries across the EEC which formed part of a group of companies employing at least 1,000 workers. Such workers would have acquired three major rights. First, they would have received annually from the parent undertaking, through the management of the subsidiary, 'general information giving a clear picture of the activities of the parent undertaking and its subsidiaries as a whole', as well as any specific information relating to the sector or geographical area in which the subsidiary was operating. Second, if the management of the parent undertaking intended to take a decision 'liable to have serious consequences for the interests of the employees of its sub-sidiaries in the Community', it would have been required to give the man-agement of each subsidiary precise details 'in good time' about its proposals for submission to the employee representatives. Third, following disclosure of this information, the management of each subsidiary would have been required to request the opinion of the employee representatives about the proposed measures within thirty days and to have held consultations with them in an attempt to reach agreement. The decision could not have been implemented until at least thirty days following the opening of consultations.

The text also dealt with issues regarding confidentiality, appeals and sanctions in cases of failure to comply with the directive's provisions, among others. Though the Irish Presidency of the Council proposed further amendments to the text in 1984 in an attempt to unblock objections to it, work on it was suspended in 1986 for three years, but then never revived.

Changing circumstances

Renewed impetus for worker participation developed against the back-ground of industrial restructuring across the EU that characterised the 1980s. Cross-border mergers and acquisitions activity had been increasing, along with the impact of competitive pressures on company operations, such as the introduction of new technologies, innovatory forms of work organisation and team-working (Cressey 1985). In 1985, the Commission published its White Paper *Completing the Single Market*, and embarked on the Single European Market programme, designed to eliminate or reduce a wide range of remaining non-tariff barriers to trade, including customs posts, differing tax rates and technical barriers by the end of 1992. A key objective of this programme was to promote the competitiveness of Eur-opean companies by facilitating their restructuring and supporting pro-cesses that were taking place in any case as a result of more integrated trade relations among member states (Cecchini 1988).

The implications for workers of EU-wide industrial restructuring, and the need to expedite measures to help safeguard their interests, were well understood within the EU. The Single European Act, which established the SEM project in 1987, introduced qualified majority voting (QMV) on the Council for measures regulating health and safety at work, the first time that QMV had been extended to an employment issue. It also enshrined the social dialogue – arrangements at EU level for discussions and consultation between employers and unions – as Article 118B in the Treaty (now incor-porated as Article 139 of the consolidated Treaty), which formed the foun-dation for further advance at Maastricht, four years later. In addition, the

European Council adopted the Social Charter in 1989 (though without UK support), which was designed to protect the rights of workers across the EU in relation to the freedom of movement, employment and remuneration, social protection and equal opportunities, among many others. Article 20 covered the right of workers to information, consultation and participation, which 'must be developed along appropriate lines' and should 'apply especially in companies or groups of companies having establishments or companies in several member states of the European Community'. Article 21 developed this point by requiring the implementation of such provisions 'in due time' in a number of situations, including technological change, restructuring and collective redundancies.

The Social Charter was accompanied by a social action programme containing forty-seven proposals, of which seventeen were draft directives (EIRR 1990). Three of these proposals concerned worker participation:

- revision of the 1975 Directive on collective redundancies, principally to ensure its application to multinational companies;
- an instrument on equity sharing and financial participation (later to become the recommendation on the promotion of employee participation in profits and enterprise results, or PEPPER); and
- an instrument on the procedures for the information, consultation and participation of the workers of European-scale undertakings.

The rationale for the third proposal was that cross-border company restructuring had led to the subjection of increasing numbers of workers to decisions taken at headquarters in other countries. National systems of employee representation were simply no longer appropriate under such circumstances. In order to ensure the acceptability of the restructuring required by the completion of the SEM, some form of employee representation at European group level was needed.

It might have seemed logical for the Commission, in preparing its directive, to have returned to the Vredeling proposal that was then still in abeyance. This proposal, as we have noted, had already been extensively debated, and its time appeared to have come. However, instead, the Commission adopted a different tack: it began work on a new directive on European works councils. There are three main reasons for this. First, the European Trade Union Confederation (ETUC) was eager to promote collective bargaining across multinational companies located in the EU. The formation of EWCs would help to establish a firm foundation for EU-level industrial relations within multinationals. They were supported in this by the Economic and Social Committee, which also advocated an EU-wide framework for information and consultation arrangements (Hall 1992).

Second, during the 1980s and since the suspension of work on Vredeling, a number of multinational companies had set up their own information and consultation committees on a voluntary basis. They began in several French multinationals – notably BSN, Bull and Thomson Grand Public – but by the early 1990s had spread to nine companies, including Allianz and Volkswagen in Germany (Gold and Hall 1992). It was possible to identify a number of core characteristics of these arrangements including their competence, method of employee representation, size and procedures. They had developed as they allowed group-level management the opportunity to explain corporate strategy, facilitate company restructuring and create the sense of belonging to an international company. Such examples proved very influential with the Commission, which used this emerging practice as the model for the draft of its EWC Directive in 1991. However, as we shall see below, the directive differed from practice in two significant ways: it gave EWCs an explicit role in consultation (whereas practice had till then generally favoured information disclosure only) and it granted no explicit role to trade unions. This was left to national legislation to determine, even though both national unions and European industry federations had played a major part in the operation of existing voluntary arrangements.

Third, although the EWC Directive was drafted by DGV and has been dubbed 'son of Vredeling' (Cressey 1993: 99), the Commission drew heavily on the existing proposals for the European Company Statute, dating from 1970 and 1975. As well as board-level representation, the ECS had also required the introduction of a European works council. This proved a helpful precedent, and the Commission successfully adapted the concept for the purposes of its new directive.

The European Works Councils Directive

The first draft of the EWC Directive was published in the *Official Journal* in February 1991. Employers' reactions were generally hostile, though certain employers' organisations, such as the European Round Table, recognised the need for information disclosure at EU level. The Commission, the European Parliament and the ETUC supported the directive and its amended version in September 1991, but because it had been proposed under Article 100 of the EEC Treaty it required a unanimous vote on the Council of Ministers. Given that the UK government was opposed to the directive (Hall 1992), it seemed as though it would become deadlocked, just as Vredeling had done beforehand.

However, the Maastricht summit in December 1991 provided the escape route. The summit debated the 'social chapter' for integration into the EU's Treaty base. The social chapter contained two principal provisions: it extended QMV to a yet wider range of subjects, including working conditions, equal opportunities and, in particular, 'the information and consultation of workers'; and it introduced a new 'negotiation track' for the proposal of directives. This enabled the Commission to convert an agreement concluded between employers and unions at EU level into the text of a directive, for implementation through the normal EU procedures. In this way, responsibility for the content of directives could be devolved to the social partners, the parties most likely to be affected. However, the UK government was unable to stomach the social chapter. The result was that it became an agreement – the 'social protocol' – between the other eleven member states and excluded the UK, a state of affairs that lasted until 1997, when the incoming Labour government signed the social chapter for the UK (now Articles 136–45 of the consolidated Treaty).

When the Maastricht Treaty came into effect in November 1993, the way was cleared for the eleven signatories to adopt the EWC Directive under the terms of the social protocol. Given the controversial nature of the proposal, the Commission itself appealed to the social partners to open negotiations on the text, using the negotiation track of the social dialogue. UNICE agreed, on the grounds that it was then more able to control the contents of an agreement, and talks opened between UNICE, CEEP (the EU-level public sector employers' organisation) and ETUC in November 1993. They lasted until the end of March 1994, when the Confederation of British Industry withdrew, claiming that the latest proposals had conceded too much towards the establishment of transnational structures. The deadline for agreement then expired and the way was open for the Commission to legislate (Gold and Hall 1994).

The EWC Directive – fairly described as the 'most controversial and far-reaching industrial relations measure ever to reach the statute book of the European Union' (Hall *et al.* 1995: 1) – was eventually adopted by the Council of Ministers on 22 September 1994, under the terms of the social protocol of the Maastricht Treaty. It applied to the eleven signatories of the social protocol, as well as to the other countries in the EEA (Iceland, Liechtenstein and Norway), and to Austria, Finland and Sweden, the three new member states that acceded to the EU in 1995. These countries had until 22 September 1996 to implement the directive. In June 1997, on signing the social chapter, the UK also became party to the EWC Directive. Finally, on the accession of ten new member states to the EU in May 2004, coverage rose to twenty-eight countries, with a substantial rise consequentially in the number of multinational companies affected.

The principal requirement of the EWC Directive is the establishment, on request or by management initiative, of an EWC or an information and consultation procedure in every multinational company that has at least 1,000 workers in the countries covered by the directive, with at least 150 in a second country. However, Article 13 exempted those companies that already had agreements providing for transnational information and consultation prior to 22 September 1996. Indeed, the directive lays great emphasis on the negotiation of 'tailor-made' information and consultation arrangements through a Special Negotiating Body (SNB) established for the purpose.

Members of the SNB are elected or appointed in line with the domestic regulations governing works councils or other representative structures in each member state. It must include one employee representative from each country in which the company operates, with supplementary members in proportion to the number of workers employed in each country up to a maximum. It may also call on experts to assist in the performance of its functions. Once the SNB has convened, there may be four results to its deliberations. First, by a two-thirds majority, it may decide not to initiate negotiations with central management for an EWC, or to abort those already in progress. Second, it may conclude a written agreement with central management establishing an EWC. Article 6 of the directive outlines the scope required in such an agreement, including the composition of an EWC, its functions and operations, the frequency of its meetings, relevant resourcing, and the duration of the agreement. Third, the SNB may establish an information and consultation procedure instead of an EWC, and the means by which employee representatives are to convene to discuss the information disclosed to them. Or fourth, the SNB may register a failure to agree with central management either by mutual consent, or if central management refuses to open negotiations within six months of a request or if agreement is not concluded within three years of such a request. In that case, certain 'subsidiary requirements' (or fall-back provisions) become binding:

- An EWC must be set up with a maximum thirty members drawn from existing employee representatives.
- The competence of the EWC is limited to transnational issues.
- There must be an information and consultation meeting with central management at least once a year.
- Further meetings between central management and an 'executive committee' of the EWC may be possible in cases where restructuring has a significant impact on employees.
- The company must defray operating costs.

Since the adoption of the directive, the number of EWCs has burgeoned. By the end of 1999, there were 507 attested EWCs, 386 of which had been set up under Article 13 of the directive and a further 121 under Article 6 (Carley and Marginson 2000). As noted above, Article 13 had granted exemptions from the directive to those multinationals that had negotiated voluntary agreements establishing EWCs by September 1996, or two years after adoption, while Article 6 required such negotiations between central management and the SNB thereafter. There is only one recorded example of an Article 7 EWC, set up in accordance with the subsidiary requirements of the directive (Lecher *et al.* 2002: 51). By November 2004, the total number of EWCs had reached 737 of the 2,169 companies covered by the terms of the directive following enlargement of the EU the previous May, a density of 34 per cent (ETUI 2004). By April 2005 this estimate had risen to around 750 (EWCB 2005a: 9).

The EWC Directive required the Commission to review its operation within five years of adoption: that is, by September 1999. The Commission's report was published in 2000, but restricted itself to examining the transposition of the directive into national systems of regulation. It argued that a more general assessment should await adoption of the ECS and the directive establishing a general framework for informing and consulting employees (both of which have now been adopted). However, the Commission did note certain problems, such as the low level of transnational information and consultation in some agreements, the absence of measures focusing on restructuring and the requirement to ensure the provision of timely information. The new Commission, which took office in November 2004 for five years, has now published its *Social Agenda 2005–2010* (February 2005). This was followed by a Communication, *Restructuring and Employment*, in which the Commission called on the social partners to strengthen the role of EWCs in restructuring and change, prior to a review of progress on updating the directive at a tripartite social summit scheduled for 2006.

It has been observed that the European Company Statute and the Statute for the European Co-operative Society may lead to a 'ratcheting up' effect on EWC rights, as they have stipulated stronger entitlements for 'representative bodies' than in the EWC Directive itself (EWCB 2003: 14). In the Annex on 'standard rules' appended to the final version of the ECS (2001), the 'representative body' may be elected directly by all company employees (Part 1a); it enjoys competence over issues 'that exceed the powers' of decision-making organs in a single member state (Part 2a); and, if the company does not act in accordance with its views on major issues, it has the right to a further meeting 'with a view to seeking agreement' (Part 2b). All three of these provisions exceed those granted to EWCs in the 1994 directive. The Statute for the European Co-operative Society has gone even further, as it lays down requirements for gender balance among employee representatives and inclusion of corporate social responsibility as an area for information and consultation. These developments may act as precedents when the EWC Directive comes up for revision.

Meanwhile, it is significant that the social partners – ETUC for the unions and UNICE, UEAPME (small businesses) and CEEP for the employers – released a joint statement in April 2005 reviewing the operation overall of EWCs. The first 'lesson learned' stated:

> Practice shows that EWCs can help management and workers to build a corporate culture and adapt to change in fast-evolving transnational companies or groups ... The existence of a good social dialogue climate of confidence and a constructive attitude to change are key factors which may contribute to ease the management of change in companies.
> (EWCB 2005a: 9)

This is as clear a statement of the 'productive' or business rationale for EWCs as any likely to be found.

Directive establishing a general framework for informing and consulting employees

The adoption of the EWC Directive highlighted an anomaly in the practice of worker participation in a minority of EU member states, notably Ireland and the UK. These two countries lacked what every other member state had established – namely, some system or other providing for the rights of worker representatives to information, consultation and even co-determination at national level. The European Court of Justice had ruled in 1994 that every member state is responsible for designating the worker representatives to be informed and consulted over collective redundancies and transfers of under-takings. However, in the UK and Ireland, where representation takes place only through the unions, this left large gaps in provision in those enterprises where union membership was either weak or non-existent.

These considerations, along with 'productive' rationales, led to the adoption in February 2002 of the 'Directive establishing a general framework for informing and consulting employees in the European Community'. Anna Diamantopoulou, the EU Commissioner for employment and social affairs at the time, commented that 'used intelligently [the directive] can be a modern business tool. Enlightened self-interest is already driving companies to anticipate and manage change. Many businesses already involve employees in this. All businesses should provide a baseline level of involvement' (EWCB 2002a: 2).

The development of this directive had been as fraught as that of the EWC Directive. The idea for a directive covering national-level rights to information and consultation had first been mooted in the Commission's medium-term social action plan published in April 1995. However, it did not publish its draft until November 1998. During the intervening period, the Commission had tried to induce UNICE, CEEP and the ETUC to negotiate an EU-level agreement on the topic, but UNICE had eventually rejected this course of action. The UK government firmly opposed the directive, and reportedly reached an understanding with the German government: the Germans would oppose the directive in exchange for UK support for the inclusion of provisions in the European Company Statute protecting board-level employee representation in German companies choosing to adopt European Company status (EWCB 2002b). As a result, discussions on the directive stalled until the French Presidency of the Council in 2000. Even then, when the UK blocked debate at a Council meeting in December 2000, the *Financial Times* informed its readers that a French and British minister had 'traded insults' over the matter (21 December 2000). Denmark, Germany, Ireland and the UK, all of which expressed reservations about the proposal and could block it under qualified majority voting rules, accordingly prevented the adoption of the 'common position' required to take matters forward.

However, once political agreement had been reached on the European Company Statute, it became clear that the German government would not continue its opposition after the UK general election in June 2001. Amendments to the text reassured Denmark and Ireland, and the UK's blocking minority collapsed. The Council of employment and social affairs formally adopted a common position in July 2001. Under the co-decision procedure, a joint Parliament–Council conciliation committee was convened to hammer out the text, which was agreed in December and finally adopted the following February. The main points of the directive are as follows:

- The directive applies to all undertakings with at least fifty employees or to establishments with twenty.
- Information must be provided to employee representatives on the 'recent and probable development' of the undertaking/establishment's activities and economic situation.
- Information and consultation is required on a range of employment matters, particularly when employment is under threat.
- Information and consultation is also required, with a view to reaching agreement, on decisions likely to lead to major changes in work organisation or contractual relations.
- Various provisions cover confidentiality and sanctions for non-compliance.
- Member states must have implemented the directive by March 2005, though extensions are permitted mainly for Ireland and the UK. In those countries, there are sliding deadlines reducing the size thresholds, until the directive is fully implemented by March 2008.

Miscellaneous provisions

Historically, the Commission has been most successful in gaining acceptance for worker participation when it is associated with specific areas of industrial relations. The Directive on collective redundancies (1975, amended 1992) requires employers, when considering collective redundancies, to inform worker representatives about the details and to consult them with a view to seeking an agreement. Similar provisions are contained in the Directive on transfers of undertakings (1977), sometimes known as the Acquired Rights Directive. The Health and Safety Framework Directive (1989) granted workers the right of access to information on risk assessments and protection measures, along with the right to consultation on a range of issues, including the planning and implementation of health and safety training. More recently, the Statute for the European Co-operative Society was adopted in July 2003, while the Directive on company takeover bids, adopted in April 2004, grants employee representatives in the companies involved certain rights to information and consultation, without prejudice to those they may already exercise at national level. The Directive on cross-border mergers, adopted in September 2005, governs the rights of employees to participation in the companies affected. The draft Directive on temporary agency work would also enhance worker participation in the areas within its remit.

The exercise of these rights has frequently proved problematic in the UK, because the directives leave the definition of 'worker representatives' up to national legislation. In the context of generally declining union membership, and before the advent of statutory provisions for union recognition, let alone employee representation, this has meant that employers often do not have representatives to inform or consult. Two judgments of the European Court of Justice in 1994, in cases brought against the UK for failure properly to implement the directives on collective redundancies and transfer of undertakings, ruled that member states are required to establish procedures for designating appropriate employee representatives. This issue has now been systematically dealt with through the adoption of the 'general framework' Directive on informing and consulting employees.

PEPPER

The social action programme accompanying the Social Charter in 1989 contained a recommendation on the promotion of employee participation in profits and enterprise results (PEPPER). Sporadic interest had been expressed before in the promotion of financial participation, with the adoption of memoranda and resolutions in 1979 and 1983, though little interest was kindled at the time. The Commission published a draft Recommendation in 1991 designed to encourage all forms of financial participation, including profit-sharing, employee share-ownership schemes, share-option schemes and employee buy-outs. The Council adopted the Recommendation in July 1992, which – though not binding – invites member states to introduce appropriate legal and tax regimes.

Conclusions

In recent years, the EU has – at last – begun to create a genuine 'space' at EU level for worker participation: besides a variety of miscellaneous measures, the European Works Councils Directive, the European Company Statute and the 'general framework' Directive on information and consultation have now been successfully adopted. The anomaly of the lack of national-level rights to participation in certain countries has been dealt with, and the measures implemented all reflect a generally flexible approach. The 'old' model of rigid participation structures, enshrined particularly in the Fifth Directive, has evolved through a greater stress on procedures (Vredeling) to an approach based on negotiation – the use of Special Negotiating Bodies and fall-back requirements – as found in the EWC Directive and the European Company Statute. This approach has led to greater flexibility, with EWCs more readily adaptable to the organisational requirements of individual companies.

The Commission used the procedures available under the social chapter to secure adoption of its proposals. It sought the agreement of the EU-level social partners on appropriate texts through the 'negotiation track', though in both cases where this was tried (the EWC Directive and the 'general framework' Directive) the employers either pulled out at a late stage or else refused to begin. In both cases, it then used the legislative route, through QMV. The EWC Directive was adopted under the terms of the 'social protocol' – and then subsequently by the UK – while UK opposition to the 'general framework' Directive was eventually undermined when it found itself isolated in the Council, and unable to mobilise a blocking minority.

Recent advances have also owed their success to an evolution in the rationales supporting them. Reference to workers' rights has given way to the 'productive' or business case for participation. This shift is underlined by research that suggests that employers in the UK who have introduced EWCs now recognise their effectiveness in providing a forum for exchanging information and explaining the business case for change (Gold 2003). A similar shift can be found in the joint text on restructuring adopted by the social partners in October 2003, which states that it is essential for management to explain changes 'in good time' (EWCB 2004: 13). Such considerations may be consolidated at the review of progress on revising the EWC Directive scheduled in 2006.

A cynic might conclude that such moves give workers the chance to participate in their own exploitation, in that restructuring generally leads to uncertainty, work intensification and possible redundancy. However, employee representatives and unions can use changing rationales for their own purposes too. For example, they can extend the competence of EWCs into new areas, such as collective bargaining, and campaign for earlier and more effective degrees of information and consultation. Reports that EWCs at companies like General Motors, Ford and General Electric Advanced Materials have developed a bargaining role are encouraging. Such developments may feed into alternative strategies to deal with the employment effects of restructuring – such as new products, retraining and redeployment. The structures are there – but the issue now is: will EWCs rise to meet the challenges?

References

Blyton, P. and Turnbull, P. (2004) *The Dynamics of Employee Relations*, Basingstoke: Palgrave Macmillan.
Bulletin (1970) Supplement 8/70 to *Bulletin of the EC*, Luxembourg: Office for Official Publications of the European Communities.
Carley, M. and Marginson, P. (2000) *Negotiating EWCs under the Directive: a Comparative Analysis of Article 6 and Article 13 Agreements*, Dublin: European Foundation for the Improvement of Living and Working Conditions.
Cecchini, P. (1988) *The European Challenge, 1992. The Benefits of a Single Market*, Aldershot: Wildwood House.

Cressey, P. (1985) *The Role of the Parties Concerned in the Introduction of New Technology*, Dublin: European Foundation for the Improvement of Living and Working Conditions.

—— (1993) 'Employee participation', in M. Gold (ed.) *The Social Dimension. Employment Policy in the European Community*, Basingstoke: Macmillan, 85–104.

Daniel, W.W. (1978) 'Industrial democracy', in D. Torrington (ed.) *Comparative Industrial Relations in Europe*, London: Associated Business Programmes, 49–63.

EIRO (1998) 'Board-level representation in Europe', *Observer Supplement* 5/98, Dublin: European Industrial Relations Observatory, i–iv.

EIRR (1990) 'Social Charter: Action Programme released', *European Industrial Relations Review*, 192 (January): 11–15.

ETUI (2004) *European Works Councils Database 2004* (CD Rom), edited by P. Kerckhofs and I. Pas, Brussels: European Trade Union Institute.

EWCB (2002a) 'Final text of EU employee consultation directive agreed', *European Works Councils Bulletin*, 37 (January/February): 1–2.

—— (2002b) 'Final approval given to EU consultation directive', *European Works Councils Bulletin*, 38 (March/April) 38: 4–6.

—— (2003) 'Employee involvement in the European co-operative society', *European Works Councils Bulletin*, 48 (November/December): 12–14.

—— (2004) 'EU social partners issue joint text on restructuring', *European Works Councils Bulletin*, 49 (January/February): 13–15.

—— (2005a) 'Joint statement on EWCs published by EU social partners', *European Works Councils Bulletin*, 57 (May/June): 8–10.

—— (2005b) 'European company statute update', *European Works Councils Bulletin*, 59 (September/October): 10–14.

—— (2005c) 'Allianz to become an SE', *European Works Councils Bulletin*, 60 (November/December): 1.

Gold, M. (2003) 'European works councils: who benefits?', in M. Gold (ed.) *New Frontiers of Democratic Participation at Work*, Aldershot: Ashgate, 51–72.

Gold, M. and Hall, M. (1992) *Report on European-level Information and Consultation in Multinational Companies – An Evaluation of Practice*, Dublin: European Foundation for the Improvement of Living and Working Conditions.

—— (1994) 'Statutory European works councils: the final countdown?', *Industrial Relations Journal*, 25 (3): 177–86.

Goulding, P. (2004) *European Employment Law and the UK*, London: Sweet and Maxwell, 8.87–88.138.

Group of Experts (1997) *European Systems of Worker Involvement*, Final Report, Brussels: European Commission.

Hall, M. (1992) 'Behind the European works councils directive: the European Commission's legislative strategy', *British Journal of Industrial Relations*, 30 (4): 547–66.

Hall, M., Carley, M., Gold, M., Marginson, P. and Sisson, K. (1995) *European Works Councils: Planning for the Directive*, London: Eclipse Group; Coventry: Industrial Relations Research Unit, University of Warwick.

Hyman, J. and Mason, B. (1995) *Managing Employee Involvement and Participation*, London: Sage.

Lecher, W., Platzer, H.-W., Rüb, S. and Weiner, K.-P. (2002), *European Works Councils: Negotiated Europeanization*, Aldershot: Ashgate.

Sanders, P. (1973) 'Structure and progress of the European company', in C.M. Schmitthoff (ed.) *The Harmonization of European Company Law*, London: UK National Committee of Comparative Law, 83–100.

Streeck, W. (1992) *Social Institutions and Economic Performance*, London: Sage.

UNICE (1991) 'UNICE's approach to Community-action with regard to information and consultation', 7 October, Brussels: Union of Industrial and Employers', Brussels: Confederations of Europe.

—— (1993) 'Proposal for a directive on the establishment of a European works councils. UNICE comments', 10 May, Brussels: Union of Industrial and Employers', Brussels: Confederations of Europe.

Williams, K. (1988) *Industrial Relations and the German Model*, Aldershot: Avebury.

3 Living apart together?

A Chorus of multiple identities

Andrew R. Timming and Ulke Veersma

In his study of the European works council (EWC) at BMW, Whittall (2000) highlights a convincing example in which a cross-national act of solidarity among workers' representatives from the UK and Germany helped to establish trust and co-operation within and beyond the forum. He exemplifies a case in which, when faced with the possibility of a plant closure in the UK, the German delegates mobilised in order to prevent the occurrence. With some optimism, he concludes that 'European regulation is a real possibility' (ibid.: 80). We agree. However, we also realise that the outcome of cross-national EWC interaction is not always as positive as in the case of BMW. In this chapter, we provide an alternative case study of Corus, an Anglo-Dutch metals firm, and its EWC. The chapter looks at the failure of workers' representatives to resolve in a mutually satisfactory way the company's proposed sale of its profitable aluminium assets in 2002.

In the section that follows, we provide some historical background to Corus and its EWC. It will be argued that the crisis-laden history of the company does not facilitate the procurement of cross-national solidarity and co-operation. We will then lay out a theoretical framework through which we analyse what we will hereafter call the 'aluminium debacle'. The theoretical framework will attempt to contextualise the central concept in this collection: the problem of identity in EWCs. We will argue that social identities on the labour side of the Corus EWC are stratified along the lines of national cultures and divergent industrial relations and corporate governance systems. On the basis of ethnographic fieldwork conducted by the lead author, we will then set out an empirical foundation to the theoretical discussion. Hence, we outline the events and circumstances leading up to and following the aluminium debacle, and then go on to demonstrate how it relates to the concept of identity in EWCs. Finally, we close the chapter with a discussion of its findings and conclusions.

Historical background

Corus is an Anglo-Dutch metals firm headquartered in London. It was created in 1999 from a merger between what was then known as the British

Steel Corporation and Koninklijke Hoogovens in the Netherlands. The aim of this section is to recount a brief history of the two companies leading up to the merger and also to provide some background information on what the Corus EWC has had to cope with in more recent years.

Steel production within the UK dates back to the early stages of the Industrial Revolution, but for our purposes we will focus on recounting the post-war evolution of the industry only. Following the Second World War, the great demands placed on rebuilding the UK infrastructure were such that by 1967, the year in which the British Steel Corporation took form, the industry enjoyed a period of relative prosperity and job security. However, the epoch of 'good times' came to an end in the mid-1970s, at which time the world plunged into an era of economic crisis. The steel industry in the UK was hit particularly hard, especially in light of the fact that in '1974, the [Iron and Steel Trades Confederation, Britain's main steel union] had 120,000 members in 854 branches administered by 31 full-time officers. In 1994, it had 34,000 members with 480 branches and only 20 full-time officers' (Bacon and Blyton 1996: 772). As these numbers indicate, the massive scale of the job cuts was sufficient to install an almost perpetual sense of vulnerability among the British steelworkers who survived the restructuring.

In an attempt to decentralise collective bargaining in the UK steel industry, British Steel central management implemented in 1979 a government-backed plan, aptly called 'Slimline'. The ensuing localisation of wage negotiations led in January of 1980 to a thirteen-week national strike involving up to 100,000 workers (Hartley 1989). It is widely agreed that the strike was unsuccessful on the basis of the fact that collective bargaining was further decentralised to plant level. The result of the ordeal was a much weakened workforce in terms of both power and numbers.

As in the UK, post-war steel production in the Netherlands was prosperous in the first instance. As Stewart (1974: 160) points out, the steel industry in Holland was 'virtually strike-free for 15 years after the end of the Second World War'. Ironically, it was not until 1973, at the zenith of the steel industry's prosperity, that Hoogovens experienced its first major strike in which an estimated 2,300 employees participated (Nieuwenhuys 1993: 154) at the dominant IJmuiden plant. Oddly, from the beginning of the steel crisis in 1975, through the tumultuous 1980s and into the early 1990s, the Dutch steel industry escaped industrial action. This lack of strike activity indicates a successful bout of restructuring, especially inasmuch as employment at the IJmuiden plant fell from 22,500 in 1974 to 11,500 in 1993 (ibid.: 8).

Production at British Steel and Hoogovens stabilised for the most part in the 1990s. This period of relative stability led in 1999 to the creation of Corus. The so-called 'merger' between British Steel and Hoogovens is said to have been more of a 'takeover' on the part of the UK operations than anything else (Looise and Drucker 2002: 44). Almost immediately, performance began to slip on the British side of the firm. From February 2001, Corus central management announced the projected loss of some 6,000 UK jobs, in addition to the 4,500 redundancies that were realised from the time of the merger (Parker 2001). While the steel and aluminium operations in the Netherlands remained profitable, the UK operations haemorrhaged money. As a result, net operating losses totalled £458 million by 2002. In order to repay its debts, company headquarters in London sought in that year to sell off its Dutch aluminium assets for some €750 million to Pechiney, a French metals firm. This attempted sale is what set into motion what we have called the aluminium debacle. This was to be the first major test of the Corus EWC in reference to its capacity to withstand the class-based tensions between the workers' and employers' representatives, and also the nation-based tensions between the dominant British and Dutch delegations.

For the purposes of our analyses, at least two important lessons can be drawn from this truncated history of Corus. The first is that steelworkers, particularly British ones, are cognisant of the human costs of crisis. It is an inevitability that when 'times become tough', so to speak, concomitantly jobs become scarce. Though parochialism among workers is commonplace during the 'good times' of, for example, investment, protectionism is particularly strong during the 'bad times' of crisis. Second, the Dutch employees learnt that in order to protect the integrity of their industry, they sometimes had to mobilise the national workforce, even if such action appeared to contradict the co-operative nature of their so-called Polder model. Thus, when push comes to shove, the Dutch workers are willing to fight for their jobs.

Theoretical framework

In order to capture the essential problem of the aluminium debacle from an industrial relations point of view, it is useful to apply a sociological approach to the question of identity. The resultant union of sociology with industrial relations serves as the cornerstone of the theoretical framework laid out in this section. Although the two disciplines are closely aligned, the former is perhaps more often concerned with issues of identity and social psychology. We wish to accentuate the importance of two closely related social psychological theories, both of which fit in the context of what most sociologists will refer to as the symbolic interactionist tradition. Thus, we draw from the 'dramaturgical framework' as it is outlined in Goffman (1959) and from the 'ethnomethodological framework' as it is articulated by Garfinkel (1963, 2002). Both of these frameworks are foundations of contemporary sociological theory, but neither is used commonly in the study of industrial relations.

An important premise of our study is that, insofar as social identities in EWCs are mutually exclusive (for example, I identify myself with group X and you identify yourself with group Y, but not with group X), social interaction will probably be oriented towards competition as opposed to co-operation. In other words, provided that groups of non-compatriotic EWC delegates identify themselves first as national citizens and second as Europeans, the labour side of the forum will be unable to advance a unified and collective front to employers' representatives. As such, it is clear that the question of national identity is intimately tied to the question of class identity in multinational companies like Corus. After all, effective cross-national action among employees and their representatives depends in large part on a class-based nexus through which their collective interests as workers come to overshadow their political affiliations.

We focus on two manifestations of multiple identities in order to understand the aluminium debacle: (1) nation-based identity constructs and (2) what we will call industrial relations system and corporate governance identity constructs. First, nation-based identity constructs are politico-cultural divisions that effectively set the stage in EWCs for a perceived conflict of collective interests among employee representatives and along the lines of national cultures. As such, it is hypothesised that, on the whole, 'European' works councillors will tend to prioritise their identities first at national and then at European level. Second, what we call industrial relations system and corporate governance identity constructs refer to the qualitatively different forms of industrial relations and management practices that are characteristic of the diversity of European Union (EU) member countries and, in this case, of the UK and the Netherlands.[1]

Ifversen (2002: 14) rightly argues that the 'construction of identity takes place in a multi-layered context where "multiple identities" confront each other. Europe is thus one level of identity formulation that intersects with the national level or other levels'. In this light, all workers' representatives who sit on EWCs are compelled to 'juggle' multiple senses of self. At the same time, they are at once European, but also, for example, Dutch, British and – to further complicate matters in the case study EWC – English, Welsh and Scottish. But these six social categories (Europe, the Netherlands, Great Britain, England, Wales and Scotland) are ordered according to a certain logic. Europe is the least culturally homogeneous construct while the British regions are the most culturally homogeneous constructs. On this basis, we argue that the nation-state in Europe is a more tangible and culturally coherent entity than is Europe. It follows that the representatives can be expected, on the whole, to prioritise their nation-based identities over and above the 'imagined community' (Anderson 1983) that is Europe.

One caveat to the argument thus far deserves mention. In spite of the fact that we are only concerned to cast light on the identity-based tensions between the nation-state and Europe, this dynamic is not the only one worth examination. One could, for example, look at regional differences within the UK in much the same way that one examines national differences within the EWC, as is the case in this chapter. Further, one could also quite rightly examine parochialism along the lines of religious identity in the Netherlands. Such dynamics are, we concede, all very important and worthy of consideration in future research, but for the purposes of circumscribing the problem our focus in this chapter will be on the tensions between nation-based and European identification in the case study EWC.

The prioritisation of nation-based identity constructs in EWCs translates into what we consider to be fertile ground for the emergence of dramaturgical interaction. By dramaturgy, we are referring to the general framework outlined in Goffman (1959) in which actors (performers) seek to control the outcome of social interaction via the creation of 'impressions' of reality. The aluminium debacle can be explained in part via dramaturgical lines of inquiry. First, we want to argue that nation-based identity constructs are prioritised over and above the idea of Europe. In this light, 'European' works councils are thought to be something of a misnomer, as Streeck (1997) argues. Second, the resultant national 'teams' (Goffman 1959) confront one another on the basis of what are perceived by the workers to be different sets of collective interests. Workers' representatives of each 'team' subsequently implement strategies by which to achieve their parochial aims. Third, following Goffman, these strategies usually involve surreptitious and manipulative action whose purpose is to 'dupe' or 'contain' members of the rival team. The mutually recognisable absence of fiduciary obligations (Barber 1983) that follows from this scenario, we argue, creates a low-trust atmosphere in which perceived conflicts of collective interests are brought to the fore. The dramaturgical framework thus provides a unique set of lenses through which the aluminium debacle can be viewed as an episode of conflicting interests.

In addition to these interest-based divisions whereby the representatives often must compete cross-nationally for jobs and investment, we also want to point out that normative obstacles can be equally factious in the context of the Corus EWC. On this note, we now turn our attention to the idea of what we have called industrial relations system and corporate governance identity constructs. In order to explain this concept in contextual reference to the EWC at Corus, we need to outline clearly the tenets of what Garfinkel (2002) has called 'ethnomethodology'.

The ethnomethodological branch of the symbolic interactionist tradition seeks to understand social interaction in terms of actors' intersubjectively shared normative values. In other words, the framework posits that the rules of social interaction can be grasped by coming to terms with the common methods of cognition that are practised by a set of actors. Within a given cultural space, group members will share a 'world in common' with each other that can serve as a basis for trust (see Lane 2002). Their commonly held background assumptions will thus tend to overlap. However, beyond the confines of an integrated cultural space, and in a cross-national context such as an EWC, the methods of cognition and background assumptions are often qualitatively different. For the purposes of our analysis, the problem is that when members of two or more different cultural spaces merge into one common space, at least some degree of cognitive dissonance (Festinger 1957) is likely to stem from the divergence in cultural practices.

We argue that industrial relations and corporate governance practices within a given nation-state set the normative basis for common cognitions, or a common way of 'thinking' about the employment relation. We want to emphasise that the dominant actors in the Corus EWC define that which is 'normal' according to a divergent set of criteria with respect to the processes for 'conventional' engagement with employers' representatives. Workers from the United Kingdom will refer to a form of 'voluntarist adversarialism' as their so-called 'world in common', for example. Thus, their frame of reference will spontaneously generate a set of culturally unique assumptions which are associated with typical industrial relations practices in the UK: the differences between employees and employers are class differences; employers cannot be trusted; the state is unlikely to side with employees in the event of a dispute; the employment relation is based upon sentiments of mutual antagonism; and trade unions are the main channel of representation. These attitudes are expressed in the Corus EWC by a lack of trust in employers' representatives on the part of the British delegates. For a more in-depth discussion of typical UK industrial relations, see Edwards *et al.* (1998).

Worker representatives in the Netherlands broadly assume a co-operative set of attitudes towards the employment relation (Visser 1998). The Dutch background assumptions thus markedly contrast with those of their British counterparts. The legally regulated system of co-determination that characterises Dutch industrial relations establishes a qualitatively different order of things to which workers' representatives from the Netherlands refer in order to define normal conventions for employer–employee engagement. According to the cultural mores of industrial relations practices in their country, the Dutch works councillors tend to formulate a set of nationally specific assumptions: for example, we live in a comparatively 'classless' society; on the whole, workers can trust employers, and vice versa; the state enforces statutory regulations and some are advantageous to the representation of the interests of workers; though we do not always get along with one another, generally speaking, employees and employers in the Netherlands will continue to treat each other with respect. These attitudes are expressed in the EWC by a greater level of trust in management and an expectation of partnership that is similar to what they find in their own national works councils.

In sum, we have theorised in this section the concept of multiple identities in EWCs. Two manifestations of identity are outstanding in this respect. Drawing from the dramaturgical framework of Goffman (1959), we argued that interaction in EWCs is stratified along the lines of national cultures. As such, cross-national engagement is thought to be corrupted by the parochialism of national interests. Drawing also from the ethnomethodological framework set out in Garfinkel (1963, 2002), we argued that, in addition to interest-based conflicts, different methods of cognition can also hamper co-operation and trust among non-compatriotic workers. As a result of the different conventions associated with the British and Dutch industrial relations models, a form of cognitive dissonance is thought to emerge in the Corus EWC. We will now apply the aforementioned theoretical framework in an empirical context.

A case in point: the aluminium debacle

As part of a broader research project, the lead author was able to interview twenty-five workers' representatives and trade union delegates from the Corus EWC, nineteen of whom were British and six of whom were Dutch. (In the text below, the acronyms 'BWR' and 'DWR' and a number will be used as identification of the quoted British and Dutch workers' representatives, respectively.) The interviews were geared in large part towards gaining a better understanding of the representatives' identity constructs in the context of the EWC. This section will report some of the findings in respect of the representatives' views on the proposed sale of the aluminium operations.

We argue that the aluminium debacle is a direct consequence of: (1) competing nation-based identities among the Corus European works councillors, and (2) a lack of common cognitions in regard to industrial relations systems and corporate governance practices between the UK and the Netherlands. The trouble started in October 2002, at which time Corus management announced publicly that it had agreed 'in principle' to sell off its profitable aluminium assets to Pechiney, a French metals firm. The revenue that was to be made from the proposed sale, some £543 million, was probably sought out by the Corus Board of Directors in order to counterbalance the massive losses that were being incurred by the British steel operations.

The prospects for a cash injection into some of the Corus operations created an atmosphere of competition for investment. On the one hand, the British delegation of works councillors supported the Board's decision to sell the aluminium assets on the basis of the potential for that sale to provide a badly needed lifeline to the UK side of the industry. This unity of interests between workers' and employers' representatives exemplifies the extent to which national cultures can override feelings of transnational class identity. On the other hand, the Dutch delegation generally opposed the selling of the aluminium assets inasmuch as the UK-dominated Board of Directors offered no assurance that the proceeds of the sale would be redirected into Corus Netherlands.

Although we were unable to observe the proceedings within the EWC itself, the lead author was able to discuss the delegates' attitudes on the aluminium debacle 'after the fact', so to speak. During one of these interviews, the Dutch position was made extremely clear:

> Well, it's quite simple … Corus Aluminium is making money. It's profitable. Why would you sell a profitable company? Why would you? … In fact, if you sell it, and it makes seven hundred, eight hundred

million, do we put it in England before they restructure? ... That's where it would go. And we have the feeling that it will end in a bottomless pit ... We think that if we throw in ... six, seven hundred million dollars, if we throw it in England, we throw it in a bottomless pit and that bottomless pit is so deep that we don't even hear it splash. That's the true feeling.

(DWR3)

This explanation is a good example of how 'logic' can be culturally specific and also dependent on nation-based identities. There was a real sense in talking with the Dutch EWC delegates, many of whom represent the workforce in national and plant works councils, that the merger was not universally in the best interests of the Dutch metals industry. It was widely thought: (1) that the impressive profits that were being posted in Corus Netherlands were being 'cancelled out' by the massive losses in the UK, and (2) that the UK-dominated Board of Directors was not properly looking out for the interests of the Dutch workforce. One employee representative from the Netherlands pointed out that times had changed more recently for the better: 'At the moment, the Board is good. We have a Dutchman on the Board [laughing]' (DWR4). This sort of national parochialism is illustrative of the argument that transnational class interests often do come second to what are perceived to be national interests.

The Dutch workers' opposition to the selling of the aluminium assets reached its culmination when the Corus Netherlands Supervisory Board – a body that consists of both workers' and employers' representatives – exercised its mandate to block the proposed sale. Much to the disdain of the British elements of Corus, the Dutch Court of Appeals upheld the blockage. The resultant debacle, according to one of the British works councillors, almost brought the company 'to its knees' (BWR7).

Many of the British delegates were quick to point out how they thought they were viewed by the Dutch side. For example, BWR1 admits:

When we merged, I don't think they thought a lot of us because I think we were, some people described us as parasites, living off their good fortune. Because when, you know, the time of the merger, the Dutch plant started making money and the UK side of it was losing. So they thought they were 'carrying' us, so to speak ... That's the feeling you got because of when they blocked the merger with the Aluminium. They didn't want that money to go into a UK loss-making business.

(BWR1)

Another delegate took a more aggressive tone:

So far as this Aluminium business was concerned, selling it off, you know, if it comes to a decision as to whether we should or whether we shouldn't and it was down to the European works council to decide, I mean, of course I would. It's in our interests in the UK to sell that off because we need that money to survive and reinvest over here to make more money and become more efficient ... I mean, you look at what's going to benefit you as a site, and I'm afraid in [the UK], as in Europe, it's dog eat dog, because if it means another plant shuts for us to survive, so be it.

(BWR10)

Accusations of national parochialism were commonplace. In what follows, a British representative accuses the Dutch delegation of seeking to protect its national interests, but then goes on to admit reluctantly that similar protectionism is often sought in the UK as well:

The last couple of years, we've had an argument of whether we should sell Aluminium or not. British interest suggests that you should sell Aluminium. Dutch interests said, 'Yes, we should sell Aluminium, but ... we should have some guarantees that some of that money should be invested in IJmuiden, where I work.' We thought that the money should be invested Europe-wide. They were singular. We were more plural.
Interviewer: Why do you say that?
Because I think that this is all that the Dutch are concerned about. The Dutch are concerned about the Dutch, and I think there is, we're more ... concerned about UK, which is Britain, it's England, Scotland and Wales.

(BWR8)

Delegates from both sides of the channel assigned blame in this manner. There was a real feeling that the aluminium debacle had severely impaired the prospects for cross-national co-operation on the EWC. We now want to illustrate why this was found to be the case.

Recall that we explained the difficulties of cross-national industrial relations by drawing from the dramaturgical and ethnomethodological frameworks developed by Goffman (1959) and Garfinkel (2002), respectively. Using these two approaches, we argued that conflicting national interests and a lack of common cognitions both contributed to the aborted attempt to sell Corus' aluminium assets. In order to make this connection, we need to corroborate empirically the existence of both nation-based and industrial relations system and corporate governance identity constructs.

The tendency towards national protectionism in the Corus EWC can be well documented. On a number of occasions, workers' representatives were honest and open about the perceived conflict of interests between the UK and the Netherlands. For example, one British representative noted that 'It's not really a spirit of total co-operation because all countries have their own agendas ... They all have their very strong agendas and they want to make sure that the best was going to come forward for *their* area of representation' (BWR15). Another British representative confirms, 'There was always going to be an interest there with the Dutch people looking after the Dutch and the British looking after the British side' (BWR1). Even the Dutch workers' representatives agreed that national parochialism was at times a problem:

> I would be giving a wrong answer if, when I say it doesn't matter, because it matters. The Netherlands said, 'The Netherlands is the Netherlands and the UK is the UK' ... Of course, we look what's good for, from the Netherlands, of course. We look what are good at IJmuiden, what is good for Aluminium.
>
> (DWR1)

Perhaps BWR6 summarises in the clearest of terms what we mean by the nation-based parochialism:

> If there was going to be an axe that fell, I believe that all of us would think, 'Well, I'm glad it's over there and not over here for a change,' you know, and I suppose that's natural. I take no pleasure out of a plant [in the UK] closing. I take no pleasure from that at all. I hate to see people lose their livelihood and everything that comes with that, but I'd feel a bit better about it if it happened in Germany or if it happened in Holland ... So there's always a little bit of self-preservation in there, and you are a little territorial.
>
> (BWR6)

On the basis of these comments, we want to argue that cross-national relations in the Corus EWC, at least at the time of the aluminium debacle, were biased towards nation-based parochialism, with each delegation striving to 'define the situation' (Goffman, 1959) in accordance with what it perceived to be in its own interests.

Another element that we highlighted as a contributing factor to the aluminium debacle was cognitive dissonance. We argued that, as a result of the varying methods by which British and Dutch workers' representatives 'think' about industrial relations and corporate governance, it was difficult to find a common basis for communication and trust. For example, BWR17 links this point directly to the aluminium debacle:

> British Steel, the old British Steel management, had a sort of arrogance, they used to treat us with disdain, and it was, 'We know best. There's no discussion on this.' That was why they got a bloody nose from the Dutch over the Aluminium business. Because it was, they said, 'We know best. We're selling it off.' 'Well, no you're not. You might be able to do that in the UK, but you can't do it over here.'
>
> (BWR17)

Another British workers' representative, BWR8, describes the differences as such:

> In their system, they've got union members, non-union members and management. Most of the senior officials, other than a couple of them, are from management, which would concern me, because then I think that they would lean more towards the management's ideas of what is needed than what the workforce probably really need. I may be totally wrong because I don't understand. I've not worked in their system, their system of co-determination.
>
> (BWR8)

The Dutch representatives tended to emphasise the legalistic differences between the two systems:

> When you look to the Dutch and to the people in the UK, we have more, a totally different relationship between our employers and the workforce also in the UK. Why? There is a long history in the Netherlands. There's the works council law, and, yeah, we have stronger regulation ... and when you look to the UK, it's more the unions represent the workforce, and, yeah, it's more of a battle than information and consultation. The British law is totally different than law in the Netherlands.
>
> (DWR2)

There are two important consequences of the existence of different industrial relations system and corporate governance identity constructs. First, the different methods of 'thinking' about the employment relation can and often do generate a lack of mutual understanding. For example:

> The way we have agreements and the way the Dutch have agreements is completely different, you know what I mean? Even the payments and bonuses that we have in England are completely different than the Dutch, know what I mean? ... You'll say something at the council and they'll look at you as if 'What do you mean?'
>
> (BWR4)

Second, at least from the perspective of the British representatives, there was a strong sense of what we will call 'system jealousy'. As one British employee representative stated, 'We're envious of their system and we would very much like to have the same sort of privileges which they enjoy. And I think we should all enjoy them together on the European works council' (BWR9). We want to argue that: (1) the inability of the workers' representatives to find themselves on an even playing field, (2) the fact that their background assumptions in relation to cultural mores and industrial relations and management practices diverged, and (3) the absence of an overarching and European 'world in common', *sui generis*, played an active role in the aluminium debacle.

Discussion and conclusions

In sum, perceptions of conflicting interests and a lack of common cognitions are serious obstacles to effective transnational co-operation and trust in the context of an EWC. The aluminium debacle, as it unfolded in the Corus EWC, demonstrates the practical consequences of parochialism, protectionism and the absence of a commonly shared cultural space. First, it was shown that nation-based identity constructs in the EWC served to reinforce the boundaries that generally divide workers' representatives along the lines of their national cultures. Thus, that which they share in common, i.e. that they are all workers, is marginalised *vis-à-vis* that which separates them, i.e. that they are concomitantly British and Dutch workers. On the basis of their nation-based identities, it was argued that interaction in the EWC was dramaturgical and low-trust. Second, in consequence of the qualitatively different mores associated with national industrial relations and business practices, we have furthermore argued that cognitive dissonance stemming from the merger of cultures hampered the workers' ability to communicate, co-operate and trust one another on the basis of an overarching 'world in common'.

What does all of this suggest in relation to the concept of class identity? It is obvious from the case of the aluminium debacle that class consciousness seems to be a national construction; stated alternatively, recognition of the points of conflict that characterise worker–employer relations would appear to be strongest within national boundaries and weakest across national boundaries. In a transnational context, it could be argued that nation-based alliances and antagonisms cut across the material fact that steelworkers, irrespective of nationality, are all agents of production from more or less similar class locations. In effect, what we have spelt out in this chapter is nothing less than the quintessential problem of labour internationalism, i.e. that wage-labourers do not easily recognise what is in their collective interests (Offe and Wiesenthal 1985).

But we do not mean to conclude on a pessimistic note. Having identified the mechanisms underlying the aluminium debacle, it would now make sense to address what, if anything, can be done to prevent it from occurring again. Paradoxically, the solution lies within the problem. What is needed, above all else, is a 'transcendental shift' from the nation-state to Europe as the primary category of identification. The primacy of Europeanism would not only tear down the boundaries that demarcate 'us' against 'them' in the EWC, but it would also establish a necessary 'world in common' to which the representatives could refer in order to gain a sense of common direction. Under such circumstances, one can reasonably speculate that co-operative employee relations would have enabled Corus workers' representatives to address the proposed sale of the aluminium operations with one voice.

How, precisely, does one go about promoting the elusive European identity? To be sure, there is room for Europeanism to emerge from the 'bottom up', as was demonstrated to an extent by Whittall (2000). Simultaneously, there is much that can be done at the level of public policy for both the European Union and member states in order to persuade their constituencies of the advantages of 'thinking' and 'acting' European. Furthermore, implementation of the EU Directives is most definitively a step in the right direction. Beyond this, the most useful suggestion that we can make for both the Corus European works councillors specifically, as well as for all EWC delegates more broadly, is that they learn to accept their common class interests as a reality. It is on this note that we conclude by pointing out the dialectical nature of the aluminium debacle. Despite the internal strife – which incidentally has been the main subject-matter of this chapter – the debacle itself did give occasion to the opportunity for transnational collective action. In the aftermath of the aborted sale, Corus workers across the UK and the Netherlands drew from a common grievance against the former Chief Executive in order to push collectively and successfully for his resignation. It is in this light that we conclude optimistically by suggesting that, as indicated, perhaps the solution is intrinsic to the problem.

Note

1 Industrial relations are historically embedded in the development of the nation-state and therefore have a strong national identity and meaning (Crouch 1992). Dunlop (1993), one of the founders of the field of industrial relations, for this reason distinguishes national systems of industrial relations.

References

Anderson, B. (1983) *Imagined Communities: Reflections on the Origin and Spread of Nationalism*, London: Verso.
Bacon, N. and Blyton, P. (1996) 'Re-casting the politics of steel in Europe: the impact on trade unions', *West European Politics*, 19 (4): 770–86.
Barber, B. (1983) *The Logic and Limits of Trust*, New Brunswick: Rutgers University Press.
Crouch, C. (1992) *Industrial Relations and European State Traditions*, Oxford: Clarendon Press.
Dunlop, J. T. (1993) *Industrial Relations Systems*, Boston: Harvard Business School Press.
Edwards, P., Hall, M., Hyman, R., Marginson, P., Sisson, K., Waddington, J. and Winchester, C. (1998) 'Great Britain: from partial collectivism to neo-liberalism to where?', in A. Ferner and R. Hyman (eds) *Changing Industrial Relations in Europe*, 2nd edn, Oxford: Blackwell.
Festinger, L. (1957) *A Theory of Cognitive Dissonance*, Evanston: Row.

Garfinkel, H. (1963) 'A conception of, and experiments with, "trust" as a condition of stable concerted actions', in O.J. Harvey (ed.) *Motivation and Social Interaction: Cognitive Determinants*, New York: Roland Press.
——(2002) *Studies in Ethnomethodology*, Cambridge: Polity Press.
Goffman, E. (1959) *The Presentation of Self in Everyday Life*, New York: Doubleday.
Hartley, J. 1989 'Leadership and decision making in strike organization', in B. Klandermans (ed.) *Organizing for Change: Social Movement Organization in Europe and the United States*, Greenwich: JAI Press.
Ifversen, J. (2002) 'Europe and European culture – a conceptual analysis', *European Societies*, 4 (1): 1–26.
Lane, C. (2002) 'Introduction: theories and issues in the study of trust', in C. Lane and R. Bachmann (eds) *Trust Within and Between Organizations: Conceptual Issues and Empirical Applications*, Oxford: Oxford University Press.
Looise, J.K. and Drucker, M. (2002) 'Employee participation in multinational enterprises: the effects of globalisation on Dutch works councils', *Employee Relations*, 24 (1): 29–52.
Nieuwenhuys, W. (1993) *Company on the Move: Seventy Five Years of Hoogovens*, Wormer: Hoogovens Groep BV.
Offe, C. and Wiesenthal, H. (1985) 'Two logics of collective action', in C. Offe (ed.) *Disorganized Capitalism*, Oxford: Polity Press.
Parker, J. (2001) 'Government supports steel workers hit by Corus restructuring', *European Industrial Relations Observatory*, European Foundation for the Improvement of Living and Working Conditions. On-line. Available HTTP: http//www.eiro. eurofound.eu.int/2001/07/feature/uk0107140f.html (accessed 9 April 2004).
Stewart, M. (1974) *Trade Unions in Europe*, Epping: Gower Economic Publications.
Streeck, W. (1997) 'Rejoinder: neither European nor works councils: a reply to Paul Knutsen', *Economic and Industrial Democracy*, 18 (2): 325–37.
Visser, J. (1998) 'The Netherlands: the return of responsive corporatism', in A. Ferner and R. Hyman (eds) *Changing Industrial Relations in Europe*, Oxford: Blackwell.
Whittall, M. (2000) 'The BMW European Works Council: a cause for European industrial relations optimism?', *European Journal of Industrial Relations*, 6 (1): 61–83.

4 Beyond European Works Council networks

The break-up of the Rover group

Michael Whittall

The break-up of Rover in 2000 helped bring together and galvanise an amalgamation of different interests. The very public campaign to stop BMW's proposed sale of the Longbridge and Solihull plants involved Rover and component factory employees, senior Rover managers, the local community, Rover dealers, politicians of all persuasions, the British government and labour activists up and down the country. On 1 April 2000 this unusual alliance converged on the city of Birmingham to voice its discontent with BMW's new strategy.

A group of people most conspicuous by their absence in Birmingham on April Fool's Day were Austrian and German delegates to the BMW EWC. At the time Rover employees could have been forgiven for critically noting the EWC's non-appearance. As one Rover member of the BMW EWC noted: 'Well, it is a sad thing to say but I've been hearing about international solidarity since I first went to work in 1955 and I have to confess that I have never seen any of it.'

For a European institution designed among other things to facilitate cross-border employee cohesion, the break-up of Rover represented an ideal opportunity for the EWC to demonstrate its transnational value. Its absence in Birmingham – and, moreover, BMW employee representatives' support of management's strategy, the very same people who attended EWC meetings – poses serious questions for EWC research. The event certainly seems to validate the sceptical view of the European Works Council Directive (EWCD) held by a prominent group of writers referred to widely as the pessimists. According to Wills (2000), Keller (1998), Streeck (1997) and Streeck and Vitols (1994), deprived of co-determination rights and a unified form of employee representative procedures, the EWCD hinders the development of a transnational collective identity. If anything it represents an instrument for promoting regime competition, delegations using this forum to lobby management on behalf of national interests, a process Wills (2000) ironically refers to as 'international nationalism'.

However, as argued on previous occasions, I believe the 'pessimistic' stance offers a too 'narrow' understanding of EWCs' potential (Whittall 2000, 2004), failing as it does to acknowledge the windows of opportunity offered by this European institution. The BMW EWC, for example, played a very active role in halting the closure of Longbridge in 1998 and 1999. Having already studied these two events (Whittall 2000, 2003, 2004), in this chapter I will outline the role, even if unsatisfactory at times, played by the BMW EWC after the German car manufacturer's decision to break up Rover in 2000.

In throwing light on the role played by German EWC delegates in the break-up of Rover, the chapter addresses a number of factors. It aims: first, to rectify any misconceptions – and there are many – relating to the role played by the BMW EWC in this critical period; second, to use this event to study an issue which has become central to EWC research, EWC collective identity (Stirling and Tully 2004; Whittall 2003; Lecher *et al.* 2001). The interest here relates not only to common experiences, although this is ultimately an impotent prerequisite of a collective identity, but equally to an awareness that an association with other groups and individuals can be mutually beneficial. The fact remains, however, that the histories of most EWCs to date demonstrate the existence of obstacles, not yet properly substantiated by research, that impede the development of such an EWC collective identity. Concerned with making a contribution to this research void, the chapter is structured as follows: after outlining the way information was gathered, a brief review of key events in the history of the BMW EWC leading up until March 2000 is presented. Concentrating on the character of the BMW structure, this section also serves a double purpose in that it addresses key aspects of the EWC Directive. I then consider the crisis that engulfed Rover in 2000 and the part played by the EWC. This is followed by a consideration of the lessons to be gleaned from the Rover experience in 2000.

Research design

A four-year case study of BMW's EWC between 1998 and 2002 and a total of seventy-six interviews were conducted with EWC delegates, management representatives, European Commission officials and relevant trade union officers. The chapter benefits from having important access to key individuals at the height of the Rover group's break-up.

The 2000 crisis proved most beneficial for the research. Not only did it help to improve trust relations with individuals already part of the research programme, it also brokered new relations with individuals who had been less forthcoming in the past. On top of this, it became most noticeable that BMW and Rover respondents were far more candid in their responses to questions after March 2000. At times it appeared the interview situation represented a cathartic experience for respondents, individuals eager to communicate their side of the story.

The BMW EWC prior to 2000

Founded in 1996, the BMW EWC utilised Article 13 of the EWCD. The eventual agreement, however, followed very closely the overall character of the EWCD in that it agreed to:

- yearly meetings (rotation);
- respecting national employee representative practices;
- management communication and consultation on
  - financial situation;
  - production;
  - sales;
  - employee development;
  - capital expenditure;
  - relocation of production;
- extraordinary meetings.

Part of what Lecher *et al.* (2001) refer to as a negotiated process, i.e. not dominated by one particular nation (usually representatives from the country where the holding is based), the BMW agreement tried to accommodate the interests of employees in Austria, Britain and Germany, all countries where it had plants. The number of employee delegates, nine BMW and six Rover seats, was based on the respective number of plants in each country: one in Austria, five in Germany and four in the UK.

Though Austrian, British and German employee representatives were very keen to set up an EWC structure, relations were initially marked by low trust and factionalism (Whittall 2000, 2003, 2004), a common experience (Knudsen 2004; Wills 2000; Lecher *et al.* 1998). Wide-ranging differences arose over the nature of employee representation, which in turn had consequences for the character and role of the EWC. The quite different industrial relations practices, British voluntarism versus Austro-German state regulation, strongly influenced perspectives on EWC seat allocation, accountability, confidentiality, trade unionism and negotiation procedures (Whittall 2000). This represents what Levinson (1972) terms the 'polycentric' problem of transnational employee relations. Consequently these differences became obstacles in the development of a collective identity, the emergence of a transnational consciousness, of which an active EWC is the ultimate expression and mediator of such a state. The lack of a collective identity among EWC delegates within the BMW group became most evident in 1996, when BMW globally restructured its engine production, the EWC playing no significant role (Whittall 2000).

The years 1998 to 1999, however, represented a major improvement in EWC relations. Following a number of exchange visits and an inter-cultural workshop in 1997, relations between BMW EWC delegates markedly improved. The culmination of this improvement saw German employee representatives lobby to stop the closure of the Longbridge plant as well as the introduction of new working time practices at Rover acceptable to British employees (Whittall 2000). This period confirms Knudsen's (2004) observation that 'multi-nationality' (his term), the continuing hold that national identities have over EWC delegates, can be 'diminished considerably' through training and intensified communication. This period suggests that the BMW EWC was moving towards the formation of a transnational consciousness prior to 2000, the collective experience of joint activities helping to develop a greater sense of bonding – an acknowledgement that employment terms and conditions were no longer a national affair. The EWC was no longer an abstract idea, but a body which had begun to demonstrate its value in co-ordinating joint transnational strategies.

The break-up of Rover

After six years of trying to rectify decades of poor management, bad product design and low levels of investment (Whisler 1999), a process greatly hampered by the UK's non-affiliation to the Euro-zone, BMW decided on a radical new course in Britain (Brady and Lorenz 2001; Batchelor 2001). In March 2000 BMW announced it would be severing its ties with Longbridge, the manufacturing plant of the Rover 200 and 400 models, and Solihull, the producer of off-road vehicles.

By the end of 1999 BMW's strategy to halt Rover's losses, known as the Turnaround Programme, was not having the desired effect. Involving the removal of the Rover board, the transfer of 120 experts from BMW's Munich headquarters to Britain (Büschemann 1998) and the implementation of the 'sister plant' concept,[1] this strategy failed to have the intended impact. In fact, the financial results in the 'Turnaround Year' were slightly worse. Rover sales fell by 150,000 units (Büschemann 2000), representing a loss of £750 million, compared to £642 million in 1998 (Brady and Lorenz 2001: 140).

Significantly, Rover's losses had an adverse effect on BMW's share price. Between September 1999 and January 2000 their value fell from €32 to €23 (*Süddeutsche Zeitung* 2000a). This led to speculation that the Quandt family, BMW's leading shareholder, was considering selling its stake, a suggestion that sent shock waves through the company's factories, the workforce fearful that any potential takeover could lead to an export of jobs (Hasel and Bellauf 2000).

A number of factors conspired to undermine the Turnaround Programme. The thinly veiled threat at the 1998 British Motor Show by Bernd Pischetsrieder, BMW's CEO, to close Longbridge unwittingly sabotaged the launch of the Rover 75, the very vehicle designated to save Rover. Although BMW estimated it could sell between 70,000 and 80,000 units a year (*Süddeutsche Zeitung* 1999), by the end of 1999 these figures seemed to be over-inflated.

In addition, a buoyant pound hampered Rover's cause. As the value of sterling increased, so did the price of Rover cars, affecting even the company's most marketable product, Land Rover's Discovery (see Table 4.1).

Table 4.1 demonstrates that an increase in the value of the pound by virtually 1 DM over a five-year period, meant that a prospective German customer had to pay DM 23,400 more in 2000 than in 1995 for the same product.

Table 4.1 Exchange losses

	1995	2000
Cost of Land Rover Discovery in sterling	26,000	26,000
Rate of sterling	2.25 DM	3.15 DM
Price of Land Rover Discovery in Deutschmarks	58,500	81,900

Source: BMW (2000)

16 March 2000 *Aufsichtsrat* meeting: break-up of Rover

By the end of 1999 Joachim Milberg, newly elected BMW CEO, publicly at least still supported the original 1994 expansion strategy implemented by his predecessor, Bernd Pischetsrieder. Privately, however, he was under pressure, particularly from the Quandt family, to change BMW's six-year course in Britain (*Die Welt* 2000a). According to Brady and Lorenz (2001) BMW began exploring alternative avenues in October 1999, a fact subsequently confirmed by BMW respondents. In fact, from October 1999 to March 2000 various secret meetings took place between BMW and a potential buyer, Alchemy, a British venture capitalist. Initially these meetings represented nothing more than provisional discussions. BMW finally concluded that it would have to sell Longbridge and Solihull in December 2000.

Once the BMW board had decided on its course of action, namely to break up its British subsidiary, it was required by Article 111, paragraph 4, of the German *Aktiengesetz* (shareholder law), to seek the backing of its *Aufsichtsrat* (supervisory board). On 16 March BMW's CEO approached the *Aufsichtsrat* to ask permission to enter into negotiations with Alchemy and Ford over the sale of Longbridge and Solihull respectively. This meeting was a simple formality, a mere legal requirement. In the tradition of most *Aufsichtsrat* meetings, according to BMW respondents, the 16 March gathering was convened merely to rubber-stamp a decision that in principle had already been agreed within the *Aufsichtsrat* presidium.

A point that needs to be recognised is that BMW at this stage was very concerned with retaining a high level of secrecy. Conscious that it had intentionally reiterated its commitment to Rover, there was a concern that a sudden change in strategy would have a negative effect on the firm's share price. BMW was also concerned that any bad publicity, particularly the reaction of Rover's workforce and the British government, could both hinder ongoing negotiations and ultimately harm BMW sales in Britain. With Britain accounting for a massive 28 per cent of BMW's European market, representing 9.3 per cent of BMW's total sales,[2] Munich had due reason to be concerned.

This covert approach, however, was ruined by an article appearing in the *Süddeutsche Zeitung* on 15 March (2000a): '*BMW will sich von Rover trennen*' (BMW wants to dispense with Rover). The piece reported that an *Aufsichtsrat* meeting had been called for the next day to announce the sale of the Longbridge plant, with BMW retaining the Mini and Land Rover models. This news scoop was public knowledge on the evening of 14 March, tradition in Germany seeing the next day's newspaper appear on the street the night before. British news agencies were quickly alerted to BMW's intentions, the possible sale of Rover cars even reported on that evening's nine o'clock news.

However, not everybody was aware of the events unfolding just twenty-four hours before the planned *Aufsichtsrat* meeting on 16 March. Although their German colleagues on the EWC had been aware of these developments prior to 16 March, possibly as early as October 1999 (the same month that an EWC meeting was convened), they failed to forewarn their British counterparts.

Campaign to save Rover

Trade union delegation to Munich

In the months that followed, a protracted struggle took place, initially over the break-up of Rover but then later over the future ownership of Long-bridge. Between March and May 2000, British trade unionists, including Rover delegates on the BMW EWC, tested the resolve of transnational employee relations mediated through the EWC. At first the prospects did not appear good. A trade union delegation (including all Rover EWC representatives) to Munich a day before the all-important *Aufsichtsrat* meeting was convened, was not greeted by welcoming trade union banners or pledges of international support. On arriving at the Munich headquarters, BMW personnel shuttled their Rover guests into a basement conference room. Straight away it became obvious that relations were somewhat strained and that friendships built up through the EWC appeared to count for nothing. One British respondent present noted, 'The atmosphere was not convivial, let me put it that way. I got the feeling "this is not like it was".'

However, on the evening of 15 March, even given the tension that prevailed between EWC delegates, with the British delegation making it quite clear that it felt betrayed by their German colleagues, BMW and Rover trade unionists were still able to draw up a plan of action. It was agreed that Manfred Schoch, chair of the EWC and deputy chair of the *Aufsichtsrat*, would communicate to BMW management and the Quandt family the position of their British employees, i.e. that Rover should be retained within the BMW group.

It needs to be noted, though, that the German BMW EWC members at this stage in the developments at no time indicated they would support the retention of Rover. In fact, they were very careful not to be drawn on their position. Rover delegates suspected that their BMW counterparts were simply trying to pacify them, having already decided to support management's strategy, which as it turned out they eventually did. Nevertheless,

German employee representatives stated categorically that they would do everything in their power to alleviate the fallout associated with any decision, namely safeguard as many jobs as possible.

Although this first British delegation was unable to achieve its original goal, a reverse of BMW's strategy and the unconditional support of their German colleagues, it was able to clarify a number of important points. Apart from gaining an insight into BMW's proposed plan to sell Longbridge to Alchemy and Land Rover to Ford, along with a commitment on the part of BMW board to consider alternative bids, it allowed Rover trade unionists to touch base with the German BMW EWC members. There remained a belief (even if slight) that these individuals might still have a role to play in any eventual outcomes.

The Phoenix campaign

Conscious that any campaign to retain Longbridge and Solihull within the confines of the BMW group was a virtual impossibility, British trade union organisers and Rover EWC delegates turned their attention to opposing the proposed deal with Alchemy. With Land Rover seemingly well catered for (Ford committed to its long-term future), attention focused on Alchemy's plans for Longbridge. This new course was unwittingly helped by the bluntness and at times seemingly heartless statements of Alchemy's CEO, John Moulton. Talking of the potential redundancies that might occur, Moulton noted: 'Making people redundant is not a nice thing to do; but nor is removing haemorrhoids, and sometimes that needs to be done' (O'Grady 2000).

On successfully concluding an agreement with BMW, Alchemy announced it would turn Longbridge into a niche car producer. Although figures continually changed, it was estimated that Longbridge would produce around 100,000 units per year (*Die Welt* 2000b). Such yearly production figures, it was calculated, would cost around 8,000 jobs at Longbridge (Wompel 2000) and anything up to 50,000 at component suppliers and car dealers throughout Britain.

In the following weeks the Joint Negotiating Committee, Rover employees' main representative body, went to great lengths to depict Alchemy as an asset-stripper in the eyes of the general public, the British government, the BMW board and, most of all, influential German BMW employee representatives. One German EWC respondent noted that the message of the numerous trade union trips to Munich between March and April 2000, consisting of either JNC or simple shop steward delegations, was always the same: 'Tony Woodley and the English representatives said that Alchemy was a gravedigger in their opinion. That they would run the company down, pick out the cream and close the plant' (BMW EWC member).[3]

Nevertheless, a campaign based on opposition alone, a fact that BMW EWC members were keen to point out, had no future. Success ultimately depended on a rival bidder coming to the fore, one that would have not only the workforce's backing but that of the government, too. A key breakthrough occurred when the Department of Trade and Industry (DTI) changed its position, according to Brady and Lorenz (2001), at the beginning of April. Initially adhering to the BMW stance that 'some jobs were better than none', the DTI first backed the Alchemy bid. Steven Byres, the then trade and industry minister, even met John Moulton to discuss his firm's plans for Longbridge on 16 March (Graves *et al.* 2000). The government, however, soon became very conscious of the general anti-Alchemy feeling up and down the country. A rally in Birmingham on 1 April, involving an estimated 100,000 people, helped to demonstrate the political seriousness of the Rover crisis to Downing Street. Consequently, the government switched its alliance, Stephen Byres founding a task force consisting of the engineering group Mayflower (leading components supplier), Rover dealers and John Towers, the former CEO of Rover. Their task was to draw up an alternative bid.

By the beginning of April the trade unions' 'anti-Alchemy' campaign had become something quite substantial, a powerful alliance consisting of the government, industry and the Rover workforce. Moreover, trade union delegations to Munich now had the benefit that they could present a potential alternative of some substance. However, for the rival bid, named the Phoenix Consortium and headed by John Towers, to stand any chance of success, it required not only influential support but also time to draw up a viable business strategy (Brady and Lorenz 2001). As in 1998 and 1999, British trade unionists once again turned their attention to lobbying their German colleagues on the EWC:

> We were saying, 'we need your help', because at the time the Phoenix Consortium was having trouble getting off the ground, and we were asking for more time ... All our objective was to get time for serious, maybe not negotiations but exploratory talks about talks.
>
> (Rover EWC member)

This new twist in developments asked potentially compromising questions of BMW German employee representatives. After the 16 March *Aufsichtsrat* meeting, German trade unionists hid behind a management smokescreen, arguing that the break-up of Rover was a decision they could not reverse, with superior management numbers on the *Aufsichtsrat* predetermining a level of control beyond their power. This was a reference to the weakness often associated with the 1976 Co-determination Act, the fact that the legislation only achieved a notional sense of parity between management and employee representatives. With management guaranteed an employee seat, as well as the chair (delegated to management) having the casting vote in the case of a tie, employee influence becomes moderated. Once an alternative bid began to materialise, one committed to superior levels of employment than those offered by Alchemy, BMW trade unionists were faced with a dilemma. Having assured Rover employees that their main concern was to secure as many jobs as possible, this part and parcel of an attempt to demonstrate their trade union credentials, they were now presented with an ideal opportunity to fulfil such a pledge.

BMW EWC members, though, were conscious of certain dangers associated with alternative bids. First, another bid would lengthen Munich's association with Rover. Haemorrhaging an estimated €5 million a day (Rubython 2000), there was more than a level of urgency on the part of BMW to find a new owner. Joachim Milberg was certainly under pressure from shareholders to bring this chapter in BMW's history to an end by 16 May, the day of the company's annual general meeting (*Süddeutsche Zeitung* 2000b). Second, other potential offers might not prove as lucrative to that being drawn up together with Alchemy. With these concerns in mind the arrival of another interested party, the Phoenix Consortium, offering to buy Longbridge in the first week of April (Brady and Lorenz 2001) represented a scenario that neither BMW management nor employee representatives had calculated for.

Although Phoenix had tabled its offer, BMW was still involved in an exclusivity arrangement with Alchemy. This meant that BMW could not open up its books to a third party until after 28 April, by which time the German car producer was hopeful that an agreement would have been reached with Alchemy. This did not deter the Rover trade unionists. April signalled an intensive period of lobbying BMW EWC delegates on behalf of what had commonly become known as the Towers bid, a reference to the Phoenix Consortium's head, John Towers. On 26 April, two days before Longbridge was due to be sold to Alchemy, a trade union delegation travelled to Munich in one final attempt to convince the BMW board of the virtues of the Phoenix offer (Atkinson 2000). This appeared to have the desired effect.

The collapse of the Alchemy negotiations

On the afternoon before the period of due diligence was set to end and an agreement between BMW and Alchemy to be announced, the negotiations unexpectedly collapsed. Various reasons have been given as to why half a year of talks and six weeks of intense negotiations came to a sudden halt. According to Alchemy, the deal was jeopardised by last-minute demands that they cover the compensation costs for franchise dealers in the region of £500 million. Alchemy estimated that, together with potential claims by suppliers for terminated contracts and redundancy payments, these extra costs amounted to around £600 million not calculated for in their original business plan (Maguire *et al.* 2000). BMW on the other hand blamed Alchemy for the failure to reach a settlement, noting that John Moulton's original demand that BMW contribute £500 million for restructuring purposes was suddenly increased by £200 million at the last minute (Brady and Lorenz 2001: 157).

John Moulton has rejected these accusations. In fact, the Alchemy CEO even threatened to prosecute BMW after discovering that Joachim Milberg intended to make such a claim public at the forthcoming shareholders meeting. Interestingly, faced by the prospect of prosecution the BMW CEO left this section out of his address. The implication, supported by Brady and Lorenz (2001) and Schneider (2000), is that BMW raised the stakes as a pretext for sabotaging the deal.

But why sabotage the deal when, as noted above, each extra day that Rover remained within the BMW group not only cost Munich money, but also harmed the firm's much guarded image? According to Brady and Lorenz (2001) there were a number of aspects that combined to 'spook' BMW, for example the threat of legal action on the part of British dealers. However 'more importantly they [BMW] had been taken aback by the strength of union, government and public resistance to the Alchemy bid' (Brady and Lorenz 2001: 157–8).

The question that remains unanswered, then, is what bearing international trade union links, developed between 1994 and 2000 through the EWC, had on the course of events from March to May 2000. Did EWC meetings, the final one convened on 26 April in which Rover delegates pleaded with their German counterparts to steer the BMW board towards the Phoenix bid, influence what appears to be BMW's management's decision to intentionally jeopardise the negotiations with Alchemy?

The value of international links

When Phoenix finally purchased Rover for a symbolic £10 on 9 May 2000, Rover trade unionists could once again reflect on another remarkable outcome. Compared to 1998 and 1999, however, employee plaudits were reserved for John Towers and not for their BMW counterparts. At the press conference on 9 May to announce the success of the Phoenix bid, Tony Woodley did not praise Anglo-German trade union relations as he had done just over a year earlier.

What, then, does the break-up of the Rover group say about the value of EWC relations, in particular the notion of transnational employee solidarity? When this question was put to Tony Woodley directly after the 16 March *Aufsichtsrat* meeting, he suggested there were obvious limitations associated with this institution:

> Let us be clear here. EWCs are designed for consultation purposes more than anything else and it would be extremely naïve of any trade unionist to think that under these circumstances you would end up with the German workers on the streets for British workers. I only wish international trade union solidarity would stretch to those boundaries.

Unfortunately, that is not the case. At the end of the day each country will unfortunately look at its own prospects of survival and its own prospects for plants. Human nature and selfishness will always play a part in something like this.

(Tony Woodley)

In the weeks that followed, however, Tony Woodley and his colleagues never lost sight of the fact that important access and potential influence could be gleaned through the BMW EWC. Although there was an initial anger towards their German colleagues, there existed a general feeling 'that they [BMW EWC members] were our only hope' (Rover EWC member).

Not surprisingly, BMW respondents were very keen to play up their role, a concern with demonstrating their trade union credentials regarding how instrumental they had been in both steering management towards Phoenix and in brokering a payment of £500 million to help the launch of the new company. It was also pointed out that Manfred Schoch, chair of the EWC and vice-chair of the *Aufsichtsrat*, on more than one occasion symbolically sat next to Tony Woodley while the latter presented Longbridge's case to the BMW board. Rover respondents corroborated many of these claims. In fact, once the deal with Phoenix was completed, Rover informants generally indicated that their German colleagues had made an important contribution: 'They [BMW EWC delegates] did what they could to get the Brits the best deal, even though it would have been more costly, potentially more costly to BMW, as long as it did not threaten their survival' (Rover convenor).

Moreover, the break-up of Rover did not dampen respondents' commitment to the EWC idea; rejection of this new institution was not to be observed. Although it was suggested that relations would initially be strained, there was a realisation that the EWC would continue to serve a purpose in developing transnational employee relations. Various influential factors need to be considered here. First, Rover trade unionists acknowledged the precarious position of their German counterparts, recognition that BMW's independence was being threatened. Second, they acknowledged that BMW EWC delegates had 'saved their bacon' twice, as Tony Woodley vividly suggested. And finally there was a deep-rooted belief that trade union values stood for something. This last point was instrumental in making British trade unionists believe that there was still some benefit in appealing to German BMW EWC delegates, even though they had supported the management's strategy at the all-important March *Aufsichtsrat* meeting.

The challenge of EWCs: obstacles to developing collective identity

Networks and beyond

While contacts attained through the EWC were an important factor in helping steer BMW towards the Phoenix bid, we should not lose sight of the fact that German BMW EWC delegates did not forewarn their British colleagues of management's plans to break up Rover. The development of a collective identity, which appeared to be a real possibility after the intervention of the BMW EWC in the first two Rover crises in 1998 and 1999, did not materialise. Solidarity proved to be a very fragile affair, not sustainable under certain circumstances. One British trade union officer summarised the problem as follows:

> You get periods where the parameters of competition that exist between different groups of workers in a sector are actually quite sympathetic to solidarity and building common conditions and so on. You then get periods that open up where actually the gap is too big.

Hyman's (1999, 2004) work on solidarity is very informative here, describing as it does how solidarity is the construct of objective and subjective interests. While a general subjugation of labour produces the objective conditions for international solidarity, often the very reason why trade unionists support the foundation of EWCs in the first place, such mutual employee empathy is mitigated by immediate experiences and interests. Consequently, although British trade unionists could turn to this European institution for backing on three separate occasions, the interplay of objective and subjective interests at this particular stage in the development of the BMW EWC meant any assistance was never unbridled. Most notably, before German EWC members committed themselves to their British colleagues' cause in 2000, they first endorsed management measures perceived as ensuring their own long-term future. As for 1998 and 1999, two occasions when they played a decisive role in halting the closure of Longbridge, this was done at no real expense to German employees.

How, then, should one conceptualise the function of the BMW EWC in 2000, 1999 and 1998? Although objective solidarity and what Miller (1999) refers to as 'core' trade union values helped procure common points of reference that led to the foundation of the BMW EWC, a collective identity could not be observed. What emerged can be best described as a network of contacts. Although membership to such a structure might prove beneficial, the different nodes representing potential points of assistance, this is neither assured nor ultimately sustainable. Therefore, though the BMW EWC network allowed British trade unionists to call on the co-determination influence of their German BMW colleagues in 1998 and 1999, events surrounding the break-up of the Rover group in 2000 demonstrated the susceptibility of such a structure. This is because an EWC network represents the amalgamation of independent interests and identities, such a structure determining that any notion of solidarity is conditioned first and foremost by accommodating subjective interests, i.e. actors' immediate concerns. As a respondent noted above, BMW EWC delegates only supported the Phoenix bid once they felt German jobs were safe.

The EWC network does not represent a pure form of polycentrism. EWC delegates assume that there are areas of common interest, out of which windows of opportunity can emerge. In the negotiations to save Longbridge in 1998, both BMW and Rover employees benefited from the eventual introduction of the thirty-five-hour week (Whittall 2000, 2003). While for British workers it meant a shorter working week, for their German counterparts it removed a potential threat to jobs in Germany, with management now unable to point to the longer hours worked by Rover employees.

Although the usefulness of EWC networks should not be underestimated, it is necessary to acknowledge that support through EWCs at a stage where a common identity does not exist can prove sporadic, sensitive as it is to subjective interests. Surpassing the network juncture brings us on to the issue of discerning EWC obstacles, a key concern of current research (Stirling and Tully 2004; Whittall 2004; Knudsen 2004), that hinder the emergence of a collective identity. Stirling and Tully (2004), for example, locate four factors: EWC objectives, industrial relations backgrounds, cultural differences and language. In addition to these hindrances present within the BMW EWC, the study also came across two further issues that proved obstacles to effective communication, namely the dynamic of corporate identity and what is here referred to as the catch-22 syndrome of EWCs.

Corporate identity

In terms of corporate identity, EWC delegates continued to demonstrate a close association with their respective company prior to BMW acquiring Rover in 1994. A 'common' sense of belonging to the BMW group proved quite abstract. Once again the parochial aspect of solidarity proved decisive, with individuals' immediate vicinity of paramount importance. In some cases the issue of company association was quite profound. Employees at Solihull, for example, were very keen to point out that they were one of the world's most prestigious off-road automobile producers. They viewed Land Rover as something apart from Rover, never mind BMW. Such a stance noticeably changed in times of crisis: Rover employees, with the exception of Solihull, were keen to be associated with BMW once mass redundancies loomed. Ultimately, however, in addition to the existence of a close affinity with their plant, respondents also demonstrated that they were either BMW, Land Rover or Rover employees.

These clear divisions in corporate identity were facilitated by the managerial structure imposed by BMW after the acquisition of Rover. Initially Munich was very concerned that Rover should not be incorporated into the BMW group but should remain an independent entity. Such strategy was viewed as an important prerequisite for ensuring that Rover retained its very British sense of style and engineering. After all, Rover was bought to add to BMW's portfolio and not to be a German screwdriver plant in Britain.

Another key factor that influenced the persistence of a multiplicity of corporate identities related to German corporate governance. Unlike at Daimler-Chrysler, BMW did not make provisions for Rover employees to have a seat on the *Aufsichtsrat*. A key co-determination structure, not only did the absence of a Rover presence deprive British employees of an insight into and influence over restructuring and investment plans (a fact that became only too startling in March 2000), it also deprived them of membership to the BMW employee group, a body with a clearly defined collective identity. Within the confines of German industrial relations, in particular through the *Aufsichtsrat* and *Gesamtbetriebsrat*, BMW EWC delegates have been able to co-ordinate common positions as part of a strategy to counteract potential management whipsawing. Through this process of interaction, one from which Rover trade unionists were excluded, a mutual sense of responsibility developed, albeit one categorically marked by a concern with BMW production sites. Consequently, from the perspective of BMW employee representatives, challenges faced by the BMW group did not automatically include Rover. Thus, although BMW EWC respondents implied that 'core' trade union values brought about a concern that the break-up of Rover should involve the least number of redundancies, the question remains to be answered as to what course of action would have been followed had a BMW plant been threatened. The insight offered by the following BMW EWC respondent suggests another solution would have been sought:

> Because we, the employee representatives, have a good working relationship, we can control the competition to a certain extent, the ball has to be played backwards and forwards ... Then we have to talk, exchange information and see what everybody has to say, and then we need to attempt to find a common solution.

Evidence would suggest, therefore, that corporate identity, a term used to define employees' association with a particular company structure, can hinder the development of a cohesive EWC.

Catch-22 syndrome

Finally, decision-making processes within the BMW EWC are considered. In terms of agenda-setting and communication, both within and between EWC meetings, chairs of the BMW EWC played the role of conductor discussed in the work of Lecher *et al.* (1998). Even after relations between delegates improved towards the end of 1998, the BMW EWC continued to be marked by what can be termed an 'involvement deficit'. This mirrors Stirling and Tully's (2004: 75) argument 'that questions of communication are not simply related to issues of exchanging information, but are inextricably linked with questions of power and control'. In the case of the

BMW EWC, lay delegates played a superficial role, restricted as they were to offering short plant reports. This practice neither helped to develop a notion of ownership, nor facilitated a closer interaction between representatives. The claustrophobic character of EWC meetings is summed up by the following Rover respondent:

> I was always keen to mix socially with them, whether it was in Brussels or wherever it was, 'Let us get out of here (EWC meeting), let us get together and share information, and let us talk about the taboo things as well. Let us be open about these things.'

Two factors appear to have contributed to the 'involvement deficit' problem. Like Stirling and Tully (2004), the case study discerned that language proved a major barrier to improving communications. Consequently, although most Austrian and German respondents were actually quite competent in English, their British counterparts possessing virtually no knowledge of German, the BMW EWC chair's office remained the central juncture of communication. This was partly due to the fact that it was widely acknowledged that Manfred Schoch and his assistant possessed excellent language skills, representing a useful translation service in which miscommunication and embarrassing pauses could be avoided.

Although the language issue forced delegates to be practical in using Manfred Schoch's office to co-ordinate EWC activities, a more influential factor concerned the continuing pull and influence of delegates' respective industrial relations systems. It needs to be recognised that this represents something quite distinct from the oft-cited problem of 'polycentrism' discussed in much of the literature on EWCs. Although this problem was characteristic of the BMW EWC directly after its foundation in 1996, by 1998 a combination of training and the active role of German delegates in campaigning to stop the closure of Longbridge helped to militate against such industrial relations chauvinism. The concern here is with what we refer to as the catch-22 syndrome of EWCs, delegates trying to straddle the past and the present. Committed to moving forward, developing new appropriate modes of representation in a world of increased global competition, delegates are nevertheless forced to acknowledge the continued importance of their respective industrial relations systems. Even taking into consideration the depreciation that has occurred within such systems, they continue to be their main source of power.

The catch-22 syndrome was most notably, although not exclusively, a problem of Austrian and German respondents. Access to key co-determination institutions meant that the national pull was extreme. BMW respondents were forced to acknowledge, however, that *Modell Deutschland* found itself in a period of transition. Marked by decentralisation of sectoral collective bargaining (Bispinck 2003) and the advance of concession bargaining (Rehder 2003), *Modell Deutschland* is experiencing a change in power relations between capital and labour. With the EWC offering a potential outlet for company collective bargaining and management already using this institution to promote benchmarking (Tuckman and Whittall 2002; Wills 2000), delegates have to plot a course that will not hasten the decline of German corporatism. BMW EWC delegates find themselves having to weave a fine line between national and transnational interests, usually to the disadvantage of the latter.

Although this proved a less pervasive issue among Rover respondents, with the EWC in fact a source for compensating for the lack of rights enjoyed by employees under British legislation, the catch-22 syndrome was to be observed here as well. The main concern relates to the role and influence of trade union officers. Not only does the EWCD fail to provide full-time union officers with a position beyond that of external experts, but works councils are generally deemed an employee body only, independent of 'direct' trade union influence. Such an arrangement runs counter to the tradition of British industrial relations, in which trade unions have not been banned from the shop floor as they were in Germany with the passing of the Works Constitution Act in 1952. Thus a fear prevailed among Rover respondents that the absence of a union officer could precipitate the marginalisation of organised labour. Unlike in Germany, British trade unions do not play a significant role outside of plants, with involvement in drawing up government policy and industrial collective bargaining an anomaly in the UK.

Even though the circumstances of BMW and Rover delegates were quite different, the centralised structure that evolved within the BMW EWC served to reinforce national systems. It ensured that any delegate interaction had to be mediated through the recognised national channels. Such a communication process helped guarantee that the respective sources of power were not threatened. This structure, however, did not facilitate the development of a collective identity, but rather a network of interests in which the close association with traditional national customs and practices continued to be a defining characteristic.

Conclusion

During the break-up of Rover in 2000, the BMW EWC did not initially prove to be a durable institution. On the contrary, the German delegates to the BMW EWC supported management measures that potentially involved massive job losses. The predominance of subjective interests thus seems to concur with critics' assumption that the EWCD only helps to promote division among employees, with this institutional shortfall ultimately the result of an inability to develop a transnational collective identity. As noted in the first part of this chapter, however, such a narrow analysis surrounding the events in 2000 is incomplete. For example, though BMW EWC delegates did not attend the Birmingham Rally on 1 April, we have to be able to explain their assistance in steering management eventually towards the Phoenix Consortium.

Although evidence demonstrates the limitations associated with EWCs when a collective identity is absent, this does not undermine its value. The fact that employee representatives were conscious of the need to develop transnational relations as a potential answer to increased product market competition helped procure what I term an EWC network. This represents a loose amalgamation of distinct interests in which joint activity or assistance can potentially be attained.

Solidarity based on a network structure, though, is conditional. Because self-preservation is the first prerequisite of joint action, any support will be fragile – ultimately a hostage to changes in employment circumstances. In 1998 and 1999 BMW EWC delegates could come to the aid of their Rover colleagues, hoisting up their international banner knowing that any assistance in halting the closure of Longbridge would not have negative repercussions in Germany. When BMWs' share price later fell because of Rover's continued poor performance, potentially threatening the independence of BMW, the solidarity gap became too large; hence support was temporarily withheld.

The task facing EWC delegates, to which researchers are already trying to contribute (Stirling and Tully 2004; Whittall 2004; Knudsen 2004), consists of discerning ways in which the network stage, a developmental point which appears to characterise the situation of the most advanced EWCs to date, can be surpassed. Drawing on evidence gleaned from this case study of the BMW EWC, the chapter locates two further problems that need to be considered. In addition to the recognised obstacles of language, culture, industrial relations differences and the objectives of the EWC, corporate identity and the EWC catch-22 syndrome can hinder the transition to a transnational collective identity. Ultimately the ability to come up with solutions to these barriers will determine the long-term future of this still relatively new European institution.

Notes

1 The 'sister plan' concept saw BMW plants adopt their Rover equivalent in an attempt to school British employees in the new production and organisational practices.
2 These figures are calculations drawn up by the author based on market share and sales data taken from BMW's website (www.bmweducation.co.uk/facts).
3 Tony Woodley at the time was a national officer in the Transport and General Worker's Union and was responsible for the car industry. Later he became the union's general secretary.

References

Atkinson, M. (2000) 'Rover unions demand more time as Towers bid teeters', *Guardian*, 24 April 2000.

Batchelor, J. (2001) *Employment Security in the Aftermath of the Breakup of Rover Group*, Warwick Papers in Industrial Relations 342, Coventry: Industrial Relations Research Unit, University of Warwick.

Bispinck, R. (2003) 'Das deutsche Tarifsystem in Zeiten der Krise – Streit um Flächentarif, Differenzierung und Mindeststandards', *WSI Mitteilungen*, 7: 395–404.

BMW (2000) *Exchange Losses*, Munich: Internal Document.

Brady, C. and Lorenz. A. (2001) *End of the Road*, London: *Financial Times*/Prentice Hall.

Büschemann, K.-H. (1998) 'Pischetsrieder hofft auf das Ende der Pechsträhne', *Süddeutsche Zeitung*, 30 March 1998.

—— (2000) 'Ein Bild der Verzagtheit', *Süddeutsche Zeitung*, 22–23 January 2000.

Die Welt (2000a) 'Quandt-Familie hält zu BMW-Chef', *Die Welt*, 22 March 2000.

—— (2000b) 'Ford übernimmt Land Rover von BMW', *Die Welt*, 18 March 2000.

Graves, D., Jones, G. and Levi, J. (2000) 'Alchemy aims to turn Rover's ruin into gold', *The Daily Telegraph*, 17 March 2000. Online. Available HTTP: http://www.telegraph.com.html (accessed 17 March 2000).

Hasel, M. and Ballauf, H. (2000) 'The meeting that saved Rover', *Die Mitbestimmung*, 8: 12–15.

Hyman, R. (1999) 'Imagined solidarities: can trade unions resist globalization?', in P. Leisink (ed.) *Globalisation and Labour Relations*, Cheltenham: Edward Elgar, 94–115.

—— (2004) 'Solidarity for ever?', in J. Lind, H. Knudsen and H. Jørgensen (eds) *Labour and Employment Regulation in Europe*, Brussels: PIE-Peter Lang, 35–47.

Keller, B. (1998) 'National industrial relations and the prospects for European collective bargaining: the view from a German standpoint', in W. Lecher and H.-W. Platzer (eds) *European Union – European Industrial Relations?* London: Routledge, 21–46.

Knudsen, H. (2004) European Works Councils: potentials and obstacles on the road to employee influence in multinational companies, *Industrielle Beziehungen*, 11 (3): 203–21.

Lecher, W., Nagel, B. and Platzer, H.W. (1998) *Die Konstituierung Europäische Betriebsräte – Vom Informationsforum zum Akteur?* Baden-Baden: Nomos Verlagsgesellschaft.

Lecher, W., Platzer, H.-W., Rüb, S. and Weiner, K.-P. (2001) *Verhandelte Europäisierung: Die Einrichtung Europäischer Betriebsräte – zwischen gesetzlichem Rahmen und sozialer Dynamik*, Baden-Baden: Nomos Verlagsgesellschaft.

Levinson, C. (1972) *International Trade Unionism*, London: George Allen & Unwin.

Maguire, K., Bannister, N. and Milner, M. (2000) 'How the Alchemy deal fell apart', *Guardian*, 29 April 2000.

Miller, D. (1999) 'Towards a "European" Works Council', *Transfer* 5 (3): 344–65.

O'Grady, S. (2000) 'John Moulton: the man who walked away', *Independent*, 29 April 2000.

Rehder, B. (2003) *Betriebliche Bündnisse für Arbeit in Deutschland*, Frankfurt am Main: Campus Verlag.

Rubython, M. (2000) 'Bernd Pischetsrieder: the man with Volkswagen's future in his hands,' *Euro Business*, July: 52–8.

Schneider, M. (2000) 'Stoppte Blair Rover-Deal?', *Die Welt am Sonntag*, 30 April.

Stirling, J. and Tully, B. (2004) 'Power, process and practice: communications in European Works Councils', *European Journal of Industrial Relations*, 10 (1): 73–89.

Streeck, W. (1997) 'Neither European nor works council: a reply to Paul Knutsen', *Economic and Industrial Democracy*, 18 (2): 325–37.

Streeck, W. and Vitols, S. (1994) 'European Works Councils: between statutory enactment and voluntary adoption', Discussion Paper *Wissenschaftszentrum Berlin für Sozialforschung*, FS I: 93–312.

Süddeutsche Zeitung (1999) 'BMW muß für Rover noch stärker bluten', *Süddeutsche Zeitung*, 24 June 1999.

—— (2000a) 'BMW will sich von Rover trennen', *Süddeutsche Zeitung*, 15 March 2000.

—— (2000b) 'BMW sucht schnelle Rover-Entscheidung', *Süddeutsche Zeitung*, 6–7 May 2000.

Tuckman, A. and Whittall, M. (2002) 'Affirmation, games and increasing insecurity: cultivating consent within a new workplace regime', *Capital and Class*, 76: 64–94.

Whisler, T. (1999) *The British Motor Industry 1945–94*, Oxford: Oxford University Press.

Whittall, M. (2000) 'The BMW European Works Council: a cause for European industrial relations optimism?', *European Journal of Industrial Relations*, 6 (1): 61–84.

—— (2003) 'European Works Councils – a path to European industrial relations? The case of BMW and Rover', PhD thesis, Nottingham Trent University.

—— (2004) 'European labour market regulation: the case of European Works Councils', in L. Vosko and J. Stanford (eds) *Challenging the Market: The Struggle to Regulate Work and Income*, Montreal: McGill-Queens University Press, 152–72.

Wills, J. (2000) 'Great expectations: three years in the life of a European Works Council', *European Journal of Industrial Relations*, 6 (1): 85–108.

Wompel, M. (2000) 'Rover hätte BMW gefährdet', *Labour Net*, 21 March 2000. Online. Available HTTP: http://www.labournet.de

5 Co-ordinating across borders

The role of European industry federations within European Works Councils

Valeria Pulignano

The aim of this chapter is to critically analyse variables that may inhibit as well as promote employee representatives' independent networks and social cohesion within European Works Councils (EWCs). These variables include the intensity of communication and the exchange of information within (and around) the EWCs as well as the support of European trade union organisations for the procurement of a collective identification among the employees represented within the EWCs. The main object is to politicise the creation of union internationalism, one that acts along the horizontal and vertical lines of the trade union structure. Our aim is to explain how far European trade union organisations' support and engagement with EWCs can affect these institutions' social cohesion and capacity to be proactive. Thus, the chapter discusses the way this influence is exercised, its limits and how it is interfaced with the new dynamics of political and social regulations and employee representation within Europe. In short, we are concerned with discerning, first, the extent to which the European Union organisations are able to affect the functioning of EWCs while fostering actors' identification with them. Second, we critically examine the channels through which this influence is exercised, looking at its outcomes in terms of connecting the responses of employee representatives across borders. Third, we assess how far this influence ensures that national and local union policy is embedded in framework agreements: that is, in supranational trade union policy.

The vision of a European internationalism able to create a multi-tiered web of ties to overcome the national isolation and the diversity of conditions faced by employees within the global economy has been open to extensive analysis and discussion in the literature since the beginning of the 1990s (Hoffmann 2000; Dølvik 2000). It requires trade unions at the European level to devise new ways of organising which reinforce the vertical links to the national and the local union representatives on the one hand, while attempting to co-ordinate horizontally (across companies) within the EWCs on the other hand. What this chapter suggests is that in the light of these developments there is justification to locate EWCs within the complex political and social environments that envelop the creation of mechanisms for the promotion of 'solidarity'. More specifically, the chapter addresses these issues by considering the sector-based orientations of the trade unions and company structures. In particular, it is highlighted that sector-specific factors, specifically European industry federations' (EIFs') activities in co-ordinated policy-making, create the structural conditions for employee representatives to more easily network across borders and, thereby, to generate closer identification with the EWC.

As such, EWCs are seen as potentially able to develop into 'organic' or 'flexibly co-ordinated' networks of individuals (Hyman 1999: 107) rather than becoming 'factional' instruments (Hancké 2000) of differentiated employee interests. This may be of particular importance in accounting for the intriguing location of EWCs within the new multi-dimensional relations of transnational and, in particular, European identity. Thus, we emphasise the significance of co-ordination between employee representatives within EWCs as the result of the European sectoral federations' attempts to articulate within the trade union structure. Regarded in this way, the co-ordination of activities among employee representatives at the European level requires articulation between the diverse union levels. This implies the reinforcement of interdependence between central (European trade union federations) and national trade unions' collective interests (Pulignano 2005a). Crouch (1993) considers interdependence (or articulation) as crucial to guarantee consensus from local to central structures of collective representation. Hence, an important issue in the area of articulation is trade unions' efforts to reshape relations along the vertical levels of the union structure. This implies creating interdependence among the different union levels and widening the scope for union benchmarking across borders.

The chapter, therefore, looks at the ways and factors through which interdependence can be promoted and adopted while understanding labour representation and its complex environmental context at the European level. How far can interdependence (if any) promote a potential framework for developing co-ordination as an effective labour response to transnational capital? What are the prospects and limitations faced by supranational trade union structures in endorsing interdependence with the lower levels of trade union organisation? These questions are of great relevance since they emphasise cross-border co-operation versus competition between plants as the response to the strategies pursued by multinational companies (MNCs). Specifically, the aim is to promote co-operation rather than to break potential cross-border employee alliances, the latter being a method often used by multinationals to weaken workplace-based collective action. This is notably the case with American multinationals, which have acquired a special reputation for being more repressive towards trade unions (De Vos 1981).

In discerning the extent of articulation as a dynamic force for the creation of interdependence as a crucial element for the procurement of a European collective identity, this chapter will take a closer look at the experience of three EWCs in the metalworking and chemical sectors within the same

American MNC and their corresponding integrative dynamics with both national, local and European industrial relations levels and actors. Specifically, I explore prospects and limitations of EWCs to strategically co-ordinate among different employee representatives' responses and identities. I examine how far co-ordination is the result of articulation between the European and the national (and local) union levels and the extent to which it helps in promoting a European collective identity.

Implementing 'co-ordination' within the European Works Councils?

The discussion on EWCs has been laced with many critical interventions. A quite wide range of concerns have been raised with regards to the functioning of EWCs as a transnational forum fostering progress towards employee transnational interests at the European level. As Martínez Lucio and Weston (2000) observe, the 1994 Directive on EWCs responded to an ongoing concern within the international labour movement with regard to the regulation of new forms of international capital. An assumption appeared that the procurement of interaction, networking and collective identity (Lecher 1999) represent the main prerequisites of this European institution developing into a functional structure through which collaborative relations can be established. With regard to the constitution of EWCs, the creation of interaction is assessed as a process through which both horizontal and vertical co-ordination among and between diverse levels of employee and union representation needs to be guaranteed. This is necessary so as to prevent EWCs becoming 'isolated and marginalized and, hence, bereft of legitimacy' (Lecher and Rüb 1999: 11) and, conversely, to establish a link, in structural or communications terms, which may stimulate social cohesion among the delegates as the main manifestation of their identification with the EWC.

There is growing evidence, however, which suggests EWCs face difficulties co-ordinating specific issues and developments. Specifically, this is because delegates have found it problematic to step out of national environments. As Hyman (2001) remarks, this is due to the practices of MNCs, which on the one hand encourage territorial dispersal of the workforce and thereby tend to exacerbate sectional interests among different groups of employees within any workplace. This limits the scope for collective identity as the aggregation of interests, which is essential for any coherent action, involving the establishment of priorities among a variety of competing grievances and aspirations (Hyman 1999). On the other hand, institutional constraints which are present in the EWC Directive aim at supplementing, not substituting, existing national systems of workplace representation, with largely firm-specific representation arrangements for European workers at the headquarters of transnational companies taking precedence (Streeck 1998). As a result, EWCs may be seen as potential instruments for the establishment of 'parochial interests' (Tuckman and Whittall 1997). Crucial here is the belief that local trade union attitudes seem to limit opportunities to forge networks and co-ordination between employees across the EU. They mostly embrace national and company-level unions' willingness to preserve their domestic sphere and space of autonomy in regulating labour issues, and therefore they hinder the development of a European identity.

In particular, the study by Wills illustrates how the defence of autonomy by national institutions across borders has the potential to generate a lack of unity between employee representatives, arguing this 'can further undermine employee representatives' case and arguments at the EWC' (Wills 2000: 98). She suggests this lack of unity is shaped by the heterogeneous union culture and traditions within the EWC. The result is the development of a path of 'international nationalism' (Wills 2000), which leads to 'concession bargaining' where employee representatives become principally the defenders of local interests (Schulten 1996). Hence, some concerns have been raised about the EWC becoming a tool to consolidate management strategies of control over labour, rather than an effective instrument for trade unions to influence the employment relations for more positive outcomes (Keller 1995; Streeck 1997). This is also because of the prevalence of the national dimension within industrial relations arrangements concerning the implementation of the Directive on the rights and the obligations accorded to EWCs in the company's country of origin (Rehfeldt 1998).

Whereas there is the tendency to present EWCs as nationally based structures of employee consultation where co-ordination between representatives of diverse national backgrounds may be problematic, recent research has also pointed out the relevance of 'sector-effects' (Marginson 2000; Rivest 1996) for initiating and co-ordinating negotiations and activities within specific EWCs. In this chapter we draw attention to this bulk of literature by pointing out the importance of engaging in assessing the relevance of sector-based supranational trade union intervention in the operations of EWCs, and thereby highlighting the crucial role European trade union organisations should play in providing new mechanisms for facilitating reciprocal relations between employees across diverse European areas. In so doing, we stress the importance of sector-specific and actor-related factors (within the sector), rather than structures and institutions, in the process of constituting EWCs as independent networks of employee representation.

Overall, the evidence on the complex nature of co-ordinating systems of employee representation at the European level points to the crucial need to integrate central and local-level actors while at the same time including national and company level institutions. Hence, the co-ordination approach seeks to situate local labour within the transnational regime where synergies or interdependence between central and local-level organisations and institutions are generated. Along with a great sensitivity to the relevance of these intangible outcomes, such as the development of interdependence, information exchange and broader social actors and processes in and around labour, we argue that co-ordination within EWCs can become a potential catalyst for the creation of alliances among employee representatives, on which transnational solidarity may be systematically constructed. Specifically, what is required within the European context is that trade unions and employee representatives at different levels have to embark on new learning processes characterised, first and foremost, by the need to incorporate and develop political strategies and rules based on consensus and mutual exchanges of information that serve all parties. Therefore, we consider ramifications of articulation between the central (European) and local (national) union structures as particularly salient in establishing horizontal co-ordination and networks which can potentially foster actors' common identification with EWCs.

The EWCs in the case study companies

In the following a brief presentation is given of the three business units and the EWCs studied. The units are all owned by the same American multinational. The collection of data took place between 2003 and 2004. A total of forty semi-structured tape-recorded interviews with international, European and national-level union officers, local representatives at the EWC level and key management were conducted. In addition, an analysis of European trade union documents; participation in workshops and shadowing of EWC meetings, where possible, also took place.

USMetA

USMetA is the electrical and control subdivision of the American corporation. In April 2004, together with the lighting and the industrial subdivision, it was merged into a new larger business unit, this leading to the transfer of the EWC headquarters from Spain to Hungary. However, when our research commenced the EWC covered the European operations in eight western countries (Germany, Spain, Netherlands, Belgium, Italy, France, Portugal and Britain) with the European headquarters based in Spain. The European HR department has the function of co-ordinating and integrating the diverse European operations, aligning them to the HR corporate policies, which are centralised and follow an American orientation. Within the Spanish head office there are both American and European HR directors. However, the Chief Executive of the division is American. The setting up of an EWC occurred in 1999. Spanish law does not provide for any legal obligation on the part of management to adhere to the general rules outlined in the EWC Directive regarding the participation of an external expert on the employee side. This generated a situation where an internal expert from within the company could be used before any external expert was elected to assist the Special Negotiating Body (SNB) in the course of the negotiations to found an EWC. Pressure from the European Metalworkers' Federation (EMF) was decisive in ensuring a role and function for an external expert. Only since April 2004 has this expert been given authority to participate in the meetings with management, under the condition that the participation is agreed by the central management and the select committee.

USMetB

The EWC covers the European operations in eleven EEA countries (Italy, France, Britain, Norway, Germany, Spain, Sweden, Finland, Netherlands, Ireland and Austria). USMetB is one of the three business units producing power-generating systems equipment within the American MNC. Other businesses include aircraft engines and energy. A multi-business focus characterises the division. USMetB has a single central management structure at European level, where the global headquarters are located. The global direction is based in Italy. While the origin of HR managers is mixed, American and Italian, the head of HR and the Chief Executive are both American. The EWC expert, who attends meetings with management, is an Italian union official from the most representative union within the company (Federazione Impiegati Operai Metallurgici, FIOM-CGIL). The transposition of the EWC Directive in Italy clearly underlines the role and functions of both co-ordination and expertise attributed to the expert in the process of negotiation with management as part of the establishment of the SNB (Art. 5, n. 3 of the EWC Directive).

USPlastic

The business unit is engaged in producing panels and specialised plastic components. The EWC covers seven European countries: Netherlands, Spain, Italy, Germany, Austria, France and Britain. The European group is highly integrated along functional lines across companies and countries with global headquarters in Europe (Netherlands), where top functional management positions are filled predominantly by Dutch nationals. There is frequent contact between management and employee representatives, which have recently negotiated two European framework agreements on internet policy and the introduction of a 'pre-employment screening' or 'background checks' for the recruitment of employees. The employee side of the EWC is largely driven by the national activities of the Dutch employee representatives (three Dutch members sit at the EWC meetings), who represent the bulk of the company's European workforce. The transposition of the Directive into Dutch law recognises the role of the external expert as relevant in supporting the SNB during the EWC foundation process. The individual in question is a Dutch union official from the main representative trade union in the company (Federatie Nederlandse Vakbeweging, FNV). However, the expert within the EWC undertakes no co-ordination role.

The European industry federations in context

The European Metalworkers' Federation initiative

One of the first and most prominent initiatives developed by the European Metalworkers' Federation (EMF) was to strengthen the trade union role within the European company councils. The aim is to improve workers' involvement in the decision-making process and to foster co-operation between employee representatives at the European level. The tradition of industry rather than company-level bargaining is one of the factors that explain the openness towards international issues, which characterises the metalworking sector compared to other sectors in Europe. The relatively high number of agreements which have been negotiated in the metalworking sector since the implementation of the EWC Directive (667 agreements covering 221 enterprises) (Waddington and Kerckhofs 2003) has forced the EMF to strengthen the establishment of employee representation co-ordination at a European level. This primarily consists of implementing measures to monitor the existing EWCs, while at the same time enhancing networking and interaction for the promotion of collective interests. These elements were laid down in an EMF resolution entitled 'The role of the trade union co-ordinators in existing EWCs' (EMF 2000). As Luc Triangle, the chairman of the EMF-EWC Select Working Party within the EMF Company Policy Committee (ex Taskforce),[1] reported, at the heart of the co-ordination is the demand for regulating 'the political role of trade unions within the European structure of employee involvement at company level' (interview, Brussels, 11 April 2003).

This idea follows the approach developed by the EMF since the mid-1990s to increase the number of agreements which follow the EMF guidelines regarding procedures and content in the negotiation of EWCs. In an attempt to cope with the weak legislative framework provided by the Directive on the implementation of consultation and information rights at company level, there existed a general aim to enhance regulation by promoting co-ordination within EWCs. This involved a more effective articulation between European and national (local) union institutions. This approach promotes interdependence between the diverse union levels by setting up common guidelines at European level which are binding and, therefore, must be followed by the national union organisations, affiliated to the European industry federation, in the negotiation of the EWC agreements. These guidelines have been set up by the policy-making body responsible for EWC issues within EMF, which is the Select Working Party.[2] The adoption of the EMF guidelines for the establishment of EWCs contributed to a benchmark process of EWC agreements. This process affected all the industries within the metal sector, although with a higher intensity on those industries with the highest number of enterprises at the time of the introduction of the guidelines (such as engineering, electronics and the auto industry). Specifically, agreements should establish procedures and content of the negotiation; involve union experts in the negotiation; indicate frequency and number of meetings and pre-meetings per year among employee representatives and with management; identify the tasks and role of the Select Committee within EWCs (EMF 2000).

The most recent sector-based European Union strategy of benchmarking requires employee representatives and works councils at the local level to respect the framework of minimum standards agreed at the supranational union level. This implies that benchmarking is ensured through the monitoring of a non-homogeneous employee representation structure, which needs thereby to be co-ordinated. The 'core' of the co-ordination initiative consists of the presence at the EWC level of a trade union official with the title of co-ordinator. By anchoring a trade union perspective to the European structure of employee participation at company level, the EMF hopes to increase the interdependence between central and local union institutions within and around EWCs. This is because the EWC co-ordinator is 'the point of contact between the employee representatives within the EWC and EMF in guaranteeing that workers' European interests are safeguarded and the mutual dependency between (and among) local and European trade union levels reinforced regarding company issues' (EMF 2000:1). The mechanism of electing an EWC co-ordinator should facilitate such interdependence. The co-ordinator is indeed selected by the national union federation's affiliates and nominated by the EMF executive committee, so that the union's legitimacy as the 'voice' of national and local unionism is nominally ensured to the holder, who normally corresponds to the trade union expert mentioned in the EWC agreement.

While articulating central and local union interests, the EWC co-ordinator is engaged in encouraging employee representatives to organise their diverse interests and perspectives by facilitating networking and the exchange of information. As such, the co-ordinator fosters the social cohesion of the group which can potentially impact on cross-bargaining developments. Whereas EWCs are institutionally constituted as information and consultation forums with no formal negotiating role, networking may stimulate opportunities either to exchange bargaining-relevant information or to develop sophisticated arguments concerning the economic situation of the plants represented at the EWC. It is likely but not automatic that more interdependence with the European Union level can be assured when the co-ordinator comes from the country where the multinational company's headquarters are located.

The European Mine Chemical and Energy Workers' Federation initiative

The European chemical industry is a highly internationalised and competitive sector. Recent statistics from the European Mine Chemical and Energy Workers Federation (EMCEF) indicate that it accounts for about 30 per cent of global production, directly employs over 1.7 million people in Europe, and makes a wide range of products that are essential to other industry sectors and society. During the 1990s, the pressures stemming from financial markets were mostly passed on to a rationalisation of labour through downsizing, the result of which, in turn, has been clearly apparent in the sphere of industrial relations. The 1990s also saw employers and trade unions enter European social dialogue to discuss international initiatives that could improve and stimulate cross-national communication, especially on health and safety as well as environmental issues.

Evidence highlights a relatively feeble attempt by EMCEF to create a European dimension in their employee representation strategy. Whereas statistics indicate that more than half of the companies in the sector have EWCs, which reflects the highest level of agreements in comparison to the other industries, signs of weakness are nevertheless evident regarding how to implement representation rights at European level. Few initiatives have been set up to benchmark across the agreements. Specifically, it should be noted that procedures have been introduced at sector level in Europe regarding practical assistance on the content of the negotiations, such as establishing which companies are covered by the EWC agreement, how many members each country can send to the EWC, how members are elected or appointed, who is the expert, and how many meetings can be held per year, etc. Nevertheless, these procedures do not provide any guidance for the arrangement of the agreements that include, for example, the role of an external expert at meetings with management. In addition, rules on co-ordination have clearly not encouraged employees to initiate transnational networking within EWCs. Instead, these initiatives are left to the legal strength of the national context where the Directive is implemented or to the goodwill of the local representatives. The latter can independently endorse the initiation of the form of horizontal co-operation within EWCs. The outcome is that no form of articulation between the European and the local union level is fostered or formally indicated. Hence, the employee representatives' initiatives for networking and exchanging information within EWCs are nationally shaped, and this is reflected in the nature of the sector-based agreements which in most of the cases follow a company-based approach. As Reinhard Reibisch, the EMCEF general secretary, stated:

> The EWC agreements in the chemical sector are very much influenced by the country where the company is headquartered. For example, if you have got a French company the EWC is somehow reflecting French labour relations; the same if the company is German or Spanish or Italian.
>
> (Interview, Brussels, 14 March 2004)

In summary, there is little evidence of the advent of any model for a pan-European co-ordination of employee representation in the chemical sector.

Nevertheless, there exist some expectations concerning a specific role that the EMCEF could actually perform in this respect in the future. The congress held in Stockholm on 8–10 June 2004 announced the federation's objective to enhance cross-border communication regarding restructuring, industrial development, and information and consultation matters at an inter-industry level. It concerns the setting up of inter-industry committees for the establishment of common rules of co-ordination on employee representation, collective bargaining, industrial change and social dialogue matters. Regarding the co-ordination issue more specifically, the congress agreed to the creation of the EWC Statutory Committee. This committee includes thirty-three European delegates covering the current twenty-five EU member states, plus one national delegate from Norway, Romania, Bulgaria, Switzerland and Turkey. The committee will have the task to 'constantly monitor the performance of the information, consultation processes conducted by EWCs, with respect to the quality, the efficiency, and the real impact on the enterprise strategy and the union policies, and suggest appropriate measures' (EMCEF 2004).

As such, the committee will be involved in setting up guidelines for the negotiation of new agreements as well as the renegotiation of existing ones. One of these guidelines will cover the introduction of an expert/co-ordinator within the EWC. A general goal for the EWC committee is to link European and national union levels by broadening and deepening the influence of trade unions as well as increasing the number of union representatives within EWCs.

Co-ordinating employee representatives at European level in two sectors

Much debate on EWCs has considered the ability to communicate and participate in EWCs as problematic, leading to potential disparities of control and power in terms of both group and individual relations within them. This is because of 'cultural and language barriers' (Stirling and Tully 2004: 74) which risk precluding effective communication between EWC delegates and inhibiting their ability to create cohesion and coherent identities. The question of how far (and how) it is possible to create an organic collective identity from a heterogeneous range of individuals representing diverse constituencies within EWCs leads directly to the question of who represents the workforce constituency of each country represented within the EWC. This is in itself a central subject of discussion which necessarily includes trade union officials at both national and European levels and workplace representatives (Knudsen 2003). As such, constructing European-centred forms of regulation will necessarily be inclusive not only of employee representatives from different countries but also of diverse levels of trade union structure. In what follows, we highlight that horizontal co-ordination in the form of cross-national communication and exchange of information between employee representatives at company level is not accidental but formally fostered through the implementation of initiatives of articulation from the European industry federations.

When the research commenced, the diverse degree of influence of the European federations on employee representatives' co-ordination issues seemed strongly to affect the extent to which employee-side networking across borders could possibly arise and thereby promote transnational social integration. Cross-company comparison of EWCs in USMetA, USMetB and USPlastic illustrates that horizontal co-ordination is possible through the establishment of common minimum rules which facilitate the exchange of information regarding activities and developments undertaken at the company level. Thereby, it fosters regulation by implementing nego-tiation at local level with management or facilitates the elaboration of employee representatives' strategic responses to multinational capital. Responses by EWC representatives within USMetB, for example, illustrate the role and activity of the co-ordinator within the EWC as crucial in facilitating the exchange of information among employees.

In particular, local management in one subsidiary in Europe was con-fronted by local employee representatives who were clearly circulating data, gained from EWC meetings, suggesting that management was putting for-ward different functional reasons for obtaining legitimacy from local works councils for plant restructuring. During an EWC meeting, employee repre-sentatives were discussing and creating synergies on the possibility of resisting management attempts at restructuring through local plant-based negotiations. In this respect the expert/co-ordinator had a crucial role as the interface with management within the EWCs. This was also pointed out by a Belgian EWC representative within USMetA. The employee-side views were strongly affected by the complexity of co-ordinating resources to resist whipsawing by management at company level, due to the co-ordinator not attending official meetings with management. The latter contributed to generating a climate of competition or conflict between the participants in the EWC because of the company's challenge to close local plants some-where, and as a consequence leading to the dismissal of employees and the transfer of employment to somewhere else in Europe.

Hence, the role of the co-ordinator is crucial in order to plan better strategic responses to global company issues which affect labour at a trans-national level. The aim is to build up co-ordination at European level by conveying knowledge and achieving consensus from the bottom up for the creation of vertical interdependence. As an EWC representative in USMetA remarked, the crucial matter is to foster the creation of synergies among employee representatives and the experiences they possess from the local works council:

> The co-ordinator can build up some knowledge from what we say about our local experience as works councillors. I'll give you an example: you

must try to understand the 'numbers' locally because you learn where the problems lie and where future company restructuring will take place. This information we get from the local works councils and then it has to be co-ordinated at the European level.

Conversely, in USPlastic the absence of a clearly defined 'co-ordination' approach by the centre had the effect of constraining networks and the transferring of information to the country where the company's global headquarters are located. A good example is the way discussion on the closure of a plant in the Netherlands was handled at the EWC meeting. Dutch employee representatives and the expert alone – himself Dutch, from the FNV – intervened in the formal discussion which took place on the day of the meeting with central management. The nature of the conversation made clear the EWC's willingness to support the Dutch works councils in dealing with the social effects of the restructuring plan already decided by the company. Indeed, during the discussion, no possibility of reporting back was offered to the other EWC members unless the information they were providing could be of any benefit to the Dutch work councillors. Symptomatic of the lack of a co-ordinated approach was the expert's concern, during the meeting with central management, to direct attention towards the country-specific case, even though an EWC representative from Italy expressed anxiety that what had happened in the Netherlands could probably also occur in Italy in the near future. Thus, in USPlastic, networking was country-focused and most notably driven by domestic social concerns, with limited scope for the development of a 'transnational' employee representative orientation. As indicated, on the one hand this reflects the absence of specific initiatives towards co-ordination by the central union organisation in the chemical sector. On the other hand, as illustrated by Marginson *et al.* (2004), the fact that the company's global co-ordination direction is based in Europe, with the management side coming from the Netherlands and possessing a degree of knowledge relating to information and consultation procedures as well as experience in continental works councils-type institutions, has, to a varying extent, successfully encouraged the development of internal networking activity between management and domestic works councillors.

There is also another aspect to these differences in approach among European federations. It consists of the need to point out their relevance to how far EWCs can actively locate themselves at the interface of internal transnational corporate dynamics and external social and political relations within the trade union structures. This certainly reflects a different mode of connecting 'independent' and 'differentiated' employee representatives' response within EWCs. For example, in USMetB and USMetA employee representatives have well-established cross-border communication and exchange of information practices. As we have seen, even though management policy appeared more questionable in USMetA than in USMetB, in both cases co-ordination worked in a way to generate a climate of exchange of cross-national information. The outcomes of such networking have been used by local representatives either for negotiations with management at plant level or to elaborate strategic responses to global management at European level. Specifically, the latter provides the potential for the employee side to use information which has been gathered at the local works councils for pan-European purposes. This requires a strong co-ordination role, a job fulfilled by the co-ordinator. Conversely, at USPlastic networking was not as successful at drawing on international sources of communication and information from employee representatives. Although the continental European management policy facilitated higher interaction between management and employee representatives at European level, the lack of a direct intervention to articulate a response between central and local union bases contributed to a weakening of co-ordination between employee representatives and so inhibited the actors' ability to identify with the EWC. This is made clear by the difference across the three EWCs regarding the extent to which co-ordinated networking activity evolved as a reflection of the promotion of collective international relationships. In the case of the chemical industry, networking had a 'domestic' rather than an 'international' character, as found in the metalworking sector.

Although the analysis emphasises the sector-specific and industry federation effects as relevant to understanding the differences in EWCs' character and operations, there is no necessary one-to-one correlation between sector-based effects and EWCs. Other factors come into play, too, such as the national-based union orientations and identities. These factors concern the difficulty of aligning entirely common European-based initiatives and strategies with diverse national–local union choices.

National unionism and transnational solidarity

The problematic surrounding the scope for transnational solidarity contributes to the discussion around the extent to which local unions can fully engage with institutional superstructures for European cross-national labour movement collaboration. This lends support to literature which has raised concerns over the prospect of Europeanisation as a potential integrative factor for trade unions. This sheds light on the problematic assimilation of national trade unions strategies and choices to a European Union agenda (Hyman 2001). Research findings illustrate that much of the problem of building up cross-national solidarity relates to difficulties of articulating between the diverse levels of the trade union structure. An analysis in terms of the diverse union-based political and social identities and structures may be a useful explanatory tool, since it seems to shape different trade union orientations to European integration more generally. These orientations strongly impact on the diverse attitudes of employee representatives to the European policy initiatives regarding the role and functions of EWCs. In this regard, they are likely to affect the progress of European trade union co-operation more generally. How to overcome this obstacle is difficult to predict. However, we can speculate on the political willingness of the trade unions and national works council structures to initiate and sustain European strategies of effective cross-border forms of organisation and alliances within multinationals under a project fostering interdependence among diverse union levels. In this sense, articulation has the potential to affect the 'cognitive' preconditions of trade unions as learning organisations and hence increasing trust, as well as their transnational capability to protect European interests (Pulignano 2005b), constructing centred forms of trade union collaboration which prove capable of formulating a concept of 'transnationality' as a set of principles universally acknowledged. This would certainly imply achieving political integration while at the same time asserting diversity. This diversity should be addressed not only in sector-based patterns of cross-national co-ordination of employee representatives at European level more specifically, but in domestic-based trade union orientations to European policy more generally (Huzzard and Docherty 2005).

Research findings illustrate, for example, that German and Belgian respondents tended to have a more positive attitude towards the co-ordination of issues than their Italian, French, Spanish and Portuguese counterparts, who in turn were more positive than Dutch and Swedish respondents. This appeared to be a common feature across the chemical and metalworking sectors in spite of the differences in the two EIFs' policies and practices. The more favourable response from the German representatives overall seems to reflect the traditional mutually supportive relationship between the works councils and the German union movement (Klikauer 2004). Whereas problems of acceptance of the political role of the co-ordinator might exist because of the structural separation between the employee and the trade union pillars, the high level of unionisation of local works councils in Germany, on the one hand, and the crucial importance of works councils for union shop floor representation in German industrial relations, on the other, have generated more room for embedding European union policy into domestic union approaches. In Belgium the linkage between works councils and trade unions is directly ensured through works councils being an instrument for trade union policy. Conversely, the less positive attitudes among the Dutch employee representatives mirror the difficulty European trade union institutions have in persuading both the national union and the local works councils' members to follow European guidelines. This echoes the more independent role played by Dutch works council members (whether unionised or not) in respect of national trade union structure. Likewise, Nordic representatives, such as Swedish and Finnish, who typically are local trade union delegates (shop stewards), highlight the problematic attitudes towards the role of the co-ordinator within the EWC, which they reject. Because of the independence principle, in accordance to which shop stewards are left working alone, Swedish trade unions do not usually interfere in trade union activity at company level. Thus, as Kent Kärrlander, the general secretary of the association of Nordic chemical unions, argued, 'any rule or framework agreement which involves the trade unions engaging with company-level matters is regarded as unrepresentative of the will of the local works committees' (interview, Brussels, 22 April 2004).

If structural features of the domestic system of representation may explain the diverse national attitudes towards EWC practices, the views of respondents from Italy and Spain suggest that additional elements are also influential. The Italian employee representatives, for example, distinguish themselves from the Spanish and Portuguese counterparts by demonstrating reservations around co-ordination. More specifically, contradictions are inherent in the 'pluralism' across (and within) the national paths of unionism. Thus, it is stronger in the case of Italy and France where the presence of diverse union federations, often in political contrast one to the other, intensifies the difficulty of combining different national union orientations to a pan-European approach. Generally speaking, this reflects the widely diversified view within the southern European union movement regarding the performance and potential of the EWC. In Italy, for example, in accordance to the ideology (particularly strong in CGIL) that workers possess the right and the capacity to control production, EWCs are viewed as a weak mechanism of employee participation. Thereby, any attempt to use them as an effective instrument of employee representation at European level needs to be accompanied by a change in their constituency. This means that EWCs should be transformed into an effective instrument for negotiation.

Specifically, the bulk of disagreement lies in the lack of a bargaining function attributed to EWCs. This is not advocated as a crucial factor for the functioning of EWCs by the more moderate Christian Democratic wing of the trade union movement (CISL), which instead stresses employee participation as the highest expression of democratisation of the workplace. According to CISL, social democracy is guaranteed through employee participation. Therefore, any attempt to enhance the level of participation should be welcomed and fostered, irrespective of the bargaining role attributed to EWCs.

Within less pluralist contexts it is the affiliation of the national union to the European federation, as well as the active role played by the former in the industry federations, that determines the extent to which European trade union initiatives and policy orientations are better accepted by local works councils and union organisation. This is the case of Britain, where the degree of affiliation to the European federations and the intensity of activity of national trade unions vary according to industry-based factors. Therefore, we may expect these structural factors to directly affect the extent of articulation between European and local shop stewards. For example, in USMetA and USMetB the more active role played by the

Table 5.1 The different positions of unions and national systems towards EWCs

	Trade union positions	*National systems*
Germany	+	Dependency between works councils and trade unions
Belgium	+	Dependency between works councils and trade unions
Netherlands	−	Independency between works councils and trade unions
Sweden	−	Independency between works councils and trade unions
Portugal	+(−)	Union ideology
Spain	+(−)	Union ideology
Italy	−(+)	Union pluralism and ideology
France	−(+)	Union pluralism and ideology
United Kingdom	+	Deregulation and union weakness

Legenda: Positive (+); Negative (−); Nearly positive +(−); Nearly negative −(+)

British trade union Amicus within EMF can generally be seen as a positive signal to actively develop European policies on co-ordination at company level. But in a highly deregulated national context, such as the British, shop stewards in different subsidiaries may also find themselves in agreement to European regulation on company policy issues. This may especially occur when EWCs are seen as a means of improving employees' chances of working together and influencing management at the workplace (Waddington 2003). The outcome is that British national union officers see the co-ordinator as a trade union official who is likely to contribute to reinforcing bilateral regulation of the terms and conditions of the EWC agreement. This is a critical issue in Britain due to the fact that employers prefer external consultants, rather than union officials, to assist during the process of negotiation.

Table 5.1 attempts to give a concentrated account of the national variations in attitudes towards EWCs among unions and local representative structures.

Conclusions

This chapter has been concerned with analysing the contribution of EWCs to the procurement of a collective identity among employee representatives coming from different European countries. This has implied examining how far (and how) external factors such as trade union federations at both sector and national levels may help to determine or to inhibit delegates identifying with the EWC. We argue that co-ordination within EWCs may become a potential catalyst for the creation of alliances among employee representatives, on which cross-national trade union co-operation may potentially be systematically constructed. In so doing, our analysis draws from the experience of EWCs as possibly creating alternative and politically motivated dynamics as a way of forging new alliances among employees.

One should note, however, that these social dynamics are not produced in a vacuum but are often the results of initiatives undertaken by the trade union federations at European level. As such, these relationships are subject to evaluation, since they accentuate contested questions about the degree of articulation between the national, local and regional levels of trade union structure on the one hand and the extent to which sector and inter-company specific diversities and similarities impact upon such articulation on the other hand. As far as the former is concerned, the study has examined the sector-based trade union initiatives at European level by considering the extent to which these aim at co-ordinating national and local unions' diverse interests while articulating those interests with the centre and, thereby, pulling for a multi-tiered pattern of union co-ordination. The study demonstrates that this depends on the extent to which the different responses from the employee representatives are networked within EWCs and, therefore, on the interplay between the European and the national industry federations.

Comparative case study analysis illustrates that in the metalworking sector forms of well-organised horizontal co-ordination were more evident because of the higher engagement of EMF in the creation of inter-dependence with the national and local union base. As a result, local experiences of works councils could be used to promote networking and cross-fertilisation of experience while co-ordinating representatives' responses at European-regional level. Conversely, in the plastic industry the weak initiatives by EMCEF to articulate with the national level of the trade union structure constrained the development of network processes among EWC representatives to the country where the company is headquartered.

Whereas sector-specific factors are indicated as relevant in shaping the process of a more integrated union organisation at European level, difficulties for effective co-ordination nonetheless emerge. These difficulties mainly relate to the complexity of articulation between the European, the national and the local union institutions, and thereby reflect marked uncertainty and discrepancies in the breadth of creating interdependence as the synonym for transnational solidarity. The research explains such uncertainty by referring to the complications the European trade union organisations face in the attempt to align European policy initiatives with the diverse national (local) union contexts more generally. As indicated, these complications are primarily explained by the complexity surrounding the diverse national and even intra-union orientations in country-based settings. This diversity is usually reflected in different trade union functions in social (and societal) terms, which makes a broad achievement of employee solidarity uncertain. A second indicator is the weak regulatory framework surrounding the implementation of the EWC Directive, so that even when binding rules and guidelines exist to regulate the setting up of agreements, their effective implementation is left to the goodwill of country legislation where the Directive is implemented. Thus, some difficulties still exist, a fact that seems to have considerable salience in terms of explaining the degree of activity of the employee side within the framework of the EWC. These difficulties need to be taken into consideration by practitioners and policy-makers dealing with the functioning of EWCs, since they may contribute to questioning the effectiveness of the EWC as a potential conduit of transnational solidarity.

Acknowledgements

The research on which this chapter is based is funded by an award by the British Academy (SG-36170) on a project 'Multinational companies and employee representation: comparing and connecting local union responses'. Helpful comments came from the participants at the IREC 2004 conference in Utrecht, and from the editors of this book.

Notes

1 At the Congress in Prague in 2002, EMF renamed its internal structure. A 'Company Policy Committee' supported by the creation of a 'Select Working Party' has taken over the Taskforce's role and functions.
2 When we started the research, national EWC trade union experts within the EMF–EWC Select Working Party had already agreed to formulate concrete proposals for a joint position regarding employees' rights to information and consultation.

References

Crouch, C. (1993) *Industrial Relations and European State Traditions*, London: Clarendon Paperbacks.
De Vos, P. (1981) *US Multinationals and Worker Participation in Management. The American Experience in the European Community*, London: Aldwych Press.
Dølvik, J.E. (2000) 'European trade unions: coping with globalisation', in J. Hoffmann (ed.) *The Solidarity Dilemma: Globalization, Europeanization and the Trade Unions*, Brussels: ETUI, 83–118.
EMCEF (2004) 'The work and functioning of the proposed statutory EWC-Committee', Motion for Congress, 8–10, Stockholm.
EMF (2000) *Role of Trade Union Coordinators in Existing European Works Councils and Role of the National Organisations in this Respect*, policy paper, June, Brussels: European Metalworkers' Federation.
Hancké, B. (2000) 'European Works Councils and industrial restructuring in the European motor industry', *European Journal of Industrial Relations*, 6 (1): 35–60.
Hoffmann, J. (2000) *The Solidarity Dilemma: Globalization, Europeanization and the Trade Unions*, Brussels: ETUI.
Huzzard, T. and Docherty P. (2005) 'Between global and local: eight European Works Councils in retrospect and prospect', *Economic and Industrial Democracy*, 26: 541–68.

Hyman, R. (1999) 'Imagined solidarities: can trade unions resist globalisation?', in P. Leisink (ed.) *Globalisation and Labour Relations*, Cheltenham: Edward Elgar, 94–115.

—— (2001) 'The Europeanization – or the erosion – of industrial relations', *Industrial Relations Journal*, 32: 280–94.

Keller, B. (1995) 'European integration, workers' participation and collective bargaining: a Euro-pessimistic view', in B. Unger and F. Van Waarden (eds) *Convergence or Divergence? Internationalisation and Economic Policy Responses*, Aldershot: Avebury, 252–78.

Klikauer, T. (2004) 'Trade union shopfloor representation in Germany', *Industrial Relations Journal*, 35: 2–18.

Knudsen, H. (2003) 'European Works Councils: a difficult question for trade unions', in D. Foster and P. Scott (eds) *Trade Unions in Europe*, Brussels: Peter-Lang, 145–66.

Lecher, W. (1999) 'Resources of the European Works Council', *Transfer*, 5 (3): 278–301.

Lecher, W. and Rüb, S. (1999) 'The constitution of European Works Councils: from information forum to social actor', *European Journal of Industrial Relations*, 5 (1): 7–25.

Marginson, P. (2000) 'The Eurocompany and Euro industrial relations', *European Journal of Industrial Relations*, 6: 9–34.

Marginson, P., Hall, M., Hoffmann, A. and Müller, T. (2004) 'The impact of European Works Councils on management decision-making in US-based multinationals. A case study comparison', *British Journal of Industrial Relations*, 42 (2): 209–34

Martínez Lucio, M. and Weston, S. (2000) 'European Works Councils and flexible regulation: the politics of intervention', *European Journal of Industrial Relations*, 6: 203–16.

Pulignano, V. (2005a) 'EWCs and cross-national employee representative co-ordination. A case of trade union co-operation?', *Economic and Industrial Democracy*, 26: 383–412.

—— (2005b) 'Going global or European? Local trade unions politics in multinational contexts', paper prepared for the International Workshop 'Europeanisation and Organised Labour: An Unsolved Dilemma?', University of Warwick, 18–19 November.

Rehfeldt, U. (1998) 'European Works Councils: an assessment of the French initiative', in W. Lecher and H.W. Platzer (eds) *European Union – European Industrial Relations? Global Challenges, National Developments and Transnational Dynamics*, London: Routledge, 207–22.

Rivest, C. (1996) 'Voluntary European Works Councils', *European Journal of Industrial Relations*, 2: 235–53.

Schulten, T. (1996) 'European Works Councils: prospects for a new system of European industrial relations', *European Journal of Industrial Relations*, 2: 303–24.

Stirling, J. and Tully, B. (2004) 'Power, process and practice: communications in European Works Councils', *European Journal of Industrial Relations*, 10: 73–89.

Streeck, W. (1997) 'Neither European nor Works Councils: a reply to Paul Knutsen', *Economic and Industrial Democracy*, 18: 325–37.

—— (1998) 'The internationalisation of industrial relations in Europe: prospects and problems', *Politics and Society*, 26: 429–59.

Tuckman, A. and Whittall, M. (1997) 'Cultivating change: flexibility and competition in a European multinational', in E. Bax (ed.) *Management at a Crossroads*, Groningen: Groningen University, 309–26.

Waddington, J. (2003) 'What do representatives think of the practices of European Works Councils? Views from six countries', *European Industrial Relations Journal*, 9: 303–25.

Waddington, J. and Kerckhofs, P. (2003) 'European Works Councils: what is the current state of play?', *Transfer*, 9: 322–40.

Wills, J. (2000) 'Great expectations: three years in the life of a European Works Council', *European Journal of Industrial Relations*, 6: 85–107.

6 Regional clusters of communication

Between national and European identities

Monica Andersson and Christer Thörnqvist

> We have two Englishmen in our select committee; one of them is easy to understand, the other's from Liverpool.
>
> (Swedish EWC representative, SCA)

> You can't expect a middle-aged woman who has been cleaning for ten years to sit opposite to the CEO of the world's largest cleaning company and express herself in a foreign language.
>
> (Swiss EWC representative, ISS)

Identity in working life is a many-sided feature; there are many barriers to overcome if an EWC is to develop a common, 'European' identity among its members. The cultural hindrances, including differing national political interests, are covered by several chapters in this book. Hence, this chapter highlights another important aspect, in fact the basic tool for human communication, namely language. As discussed by Stirling and Tully (2004), there is a major risk that linguistic barriers develop from being only obstacles for communication, to a matter of inclusion, in fact, to what decide power relations within the EWC. Moreover, a recent overview of EWCs and EWC studies gives the impression that the linguistic problem is not yet very well researched at all (Hall and Marginson 2005). The chapter deals with different aspects of, and preconditions for, identity shaping in two EWCs, both of Scandinavian origin. One is the Swedish group SCA, the other the Danish group ISS. The sources of the study are semi-structured interviews with EWC representatives from all over Europe, in total fifty-one people, complemented with observations from EWC meetings we have attended.[1] Of these fifty-one persons, thirty belonged to the SCA EWC, representing nine different countries, and twenty-one were members of the ISS EWC, representing fourteen countries.[2] It should be added that the gender differences are remarkable: in ISS, the share was equal, with eleven men and ten women, while in SCA twenty-seven interviewees were men and only three women.

The next section introduces the companies and the EWCs, while the following sections discuss issues connected to the shaping of international identities, such as why the interviewees became EWC representatives, their views on EWC membership and how to make the EWC work, trade union contacts and finally social and informal contacts. First, however, we shall briefly outline our approach to 'identity' and 'language'.

The study of how EWCs attempt to create the capacity to overcome national self-interest and develop into countervailing organisations with a transnational perspective is as old as the idea of EWCs itself (cf. Lecher 1999; Miller 1999; Wills 2000). Still, the research on identity-shaping in working-life organisations at large is for natural reasons much older, and it has sometimes been rather problematic to adapt the study of 'EWC identities' to already existing theories. In the words of Hogg (2000), an 'organisation' consists of internally structured groups connected in a complex network of subgroups, or inter-group relations, relations that are in turn characterised by differences in power, status and prestige. An EWC is no exception and its network of subgroups must first of all be focused at two different levels: first, at a European or even global level, as a cross-national group of representatives, shaped by different industrial relations systems, judicial systems and so on; and second, at national level, where each subgroup is constituted of individual members differing from each other regarding knowledge, position, abilities, values, beliefs and so on.

The 'upper' level is relatively easy to get a grip on. If problems in making an EWC work smoothly depend on, for instance, a clash between northern European consensual and southern European confrontational traditions *vis-à-vis* management, these will most certainly either show up in documents such as minutes, statements, etc., or be discovered by interviews with important representatives. The national or local level is more difficult to deal with, however. The subgroups at European level are formed by various individuals who do not necessarily all fit the national stereotypes. There are several other influences on how individuals think than simply the trade union tradition they belong to; therefore this chapter focuses on individual motives and abilities for EWC engagement. Language and individual communication is just one such feature, but in our opinion, an important one. The degree of support for interpreting and translation, flexibility in the working language(s) and training provision all have a considerable impact on the ability to create a workable communicational framework for formal as well as informal contacts. As argued by an EWC co-ordinator, cited in Miller *et al.* (2000: 315), the best way to break down cultural hindrances is 'not by talking about serious trade union matters, but by actually socialising, speaking to people, getting to know people'.

The two companies and their EWCs

SCA is a manufacturer of absorbent hygiene products, tissue and fluff products, packaging solutions, publication papers and wood products, with about 42,000 employees. The company's first EWC agreement was arrived at in autumn 1995. ISS is concerned with services and is in fact the world's largest company in the cleaning industry, with some 260,000 employees worldwide. The first EWC agreement here was concluded in summer 1995.

There are fundamental differences between manufacturing and services. Most of all, manufacturing is generally more capital- and knowledge-intensive, which implies more participation, networking and empowerment in many organisations. Moreover, trade union density is normally higher in manufacturing companies, which, as we shall see below, is important for EWC work. By contrast, the kind of services ISS offers its customers are more often small-scale and adapted to local demands, and the employees are, on the whole, much less skilled, with lower formal education (Andersson and Thörnqvist 2003: 83–4). When we started our fieldwork, ISS had for a long time had an HRM problem: the workers did not develop any professional identity or feelings for their jobs and labour turnover was high (Venneslan and Ågotnes 1994: 112, interview with ISS's HR manager Martin Christensen in October 2001). During our investigation period this was changing for the better. A remaining problem, however, for both HRM and EWC work, is that the 260,000 employees in ISS are spread over about 75,000 workplaces; i.e. the average number of ISS employees per workplace is about 3.5. In addition to that, only 53 per cent of the employees are hired on full-time contracts.

The organisation of SCA is quite different. When our study began, the company operated in three different business areas: Hygiene, Packaging and Forest products.[3] One of these areas, Hygiene Products, underwent a major change in 1995, the year the EWC agreement was reached, when its headquarters moved to Germany following an amalgamation with a large German company. Swedish trade unionists feared that the moving of the headquarters might weaken possibilities for collaboration across borders. It was felt that in the long run this might, at worst, lead to employee participation solely at local level (interview with Christer Larsson, head of EWC related issues for the Swedish Paper Workers' Union, October 2001). It is, however, still – a decade later – difficult to see any such effects.

In SCA the EWC is strictly an employee-side body, while ISS has chosen a joint management and employee model. Trade union representatives are also associated with ISS's EWC, even though they are not employed by the company, a form of representation that is prohibited at SCA. The most peculiar feature of the SCA EWC is that it is divided into three different EWCs (at the time of writing actually on its way to becoming four), due to organisational changes within the group. Each business area has its own EWC, each led by its own executive committee, and the three of them are united under a 'pan-EWC' – also with a special executive committee at the top. According to the SCA agreement, the chairman of the pan-EWC and its deputy should represent different business areas and different countries. Also at business area level it is recommended that the chairman and the deputy should come from different countries, if possible. This structure certainly facilitates EWC work, in particular communication within the EWC.

The SCA agreement recommends two meetings per year, of which one should be with the pan-EWC. In practice, such a meeting has only taken place every second year, but on the other hand the executive committee of the pan-EWC meets more frequently, normally three times per year, and the business area EWCs meet up to three times a year plus occasional extra-ordinary meetings. Another facilitating feature is that the company arranges language courses in English for EWC members. SCA Hygiene Products invites each representative to undertake a week of English training per year. All SCA EWC representatives are offered a three-week-long English train-ing course at the beginning of an EWC mandate period, with follow-ups in accordance with individual needs and interests. It should be noted that native English speakers are supposed to take part in these courses too. The reason is, as hinted in the quote that introduced this chapter, that they often speak fast and in dialects that are hard for people from abroad to under-stand. One result of the language training SCA offers is that the EWC meetings are less dependent on interpreters than, for example, at ISS.

After this introduction of the two companies and the differences between them, in the following sections we will look more closely into what con-stitutes the representatives' identities.

Reasons for EWC engagement

When asked about their motives for personal engagement with EWCs, an open question with no form of scale, an overwhelming majority of the representatives highlighted the importance of international cross-border issues at large and often a great personal interest in such matters. 'I'm interested in international issues and rather good at English,' a Swedish delegate from SCA laconically noted. A Dutch member of the SCA EWC was even more laconic: 'I'm interested in people,' he simply offered. A French delegate (SCA) stated that his main reason for EWC involvement was 'to try to contribute to implementing workers' know-how and under-standing into the group strategies', and get improved working conditions for the workers in return. Regarding the desire to understand the full scope of the company, many of our interviewees mentioned their interest in other countries' unions and ideas: 'I'm interested in international matters and want to get contacts in other countries,' an ISS member from Austria said. Likewise, a German representative with the same attitudes, also from ISS, exemplified that she 'wanted to know more about what was going on in other countries' works councils [*Betriebsräte*]'.

Another, rather common, answer to the question of EWC engagement was 'I was elected.' 'My colleagues convinced me,' as a German ISS repre-sentative expressed it, or in the words of a Danish ISS representative, 'It was very difficult to say no when they asked me.' In most cases, however, we have reason to believe that this was merely a way to treat the issue in a modest manner; attendant queries revealed a much deeper interest in EWC issues. 'If I didn't think I could do a good job for my colleagues all over the group, I would not have joined in; everybody must get fair treatment when plants are closed down or merged,' a Norwegian SCA representative explained, which might be a good illustration of why he 'let himself be talked into' the task. A rather similar reason was offered by a British ISS representative, who explained that he became an EWC member because he 'was "chasing management" with so many questions of different kinds that finally both my colleagues and myself thought it best if I was elected to the EWC'. The following edited quotes are, in our opinion, both representative and illuminating:

> I was always interested in global working, so I said to my colleagues, 'We have to look up in Austria, and look at the big global players.' The unions lag behind there ... and we have to do something ... In Austria employees ... have no 'feeling' for globalisation. It is our, *my* job to get them interested ... I always say – think global, not local. By the help of the unions we must put pressure on the Austrian government to make the legislative framework work.
>
> (Austrian representative, SCA)

> Globalisation was my trigger. We [the Swedish Paper Workers' Union] had reason to catch up with what was going on within the group in other countries and map the decision-making processes.
>
> (Swedish representative, SCA)

> For me it was really clear: I was in the German PWA, it was the biggest paper company in Germany and it was bought by SCA in 1996. At the time SCA negotiated over the EWC agreement. And OK, as we were bought by SCA, we were invited to the negotiations, and because I was the chairman of the central works council in Germany, it was rather obvious that I was sent to the EWC. The problem was that I had not spoken a word in English. I have learnt English during these years, I had to.
>
> (German representative, SCA)

> The conclusive reason for my engagement was actually the language. Most of my workmates were scared off by the need to speak and read English, but I've been living abroad, in South Africa, for many years.
>
> (Swedish representative, SCA)

The two last quotes pinpoint the problem of language, to which we shall soon return. First, however, it should be mentioned that there were respondents who openly stressed that they saw it as their task to look after national interests. A UK representative (SCA) expressed his motivation as to 'see my [sic!] managers, to try to communicate the problems that we have ... This is a way of getting information from the shop floor to the top managers.' The same interviewee further highlighted face-to-face communication with management, but never mentioned any need for, or importance of, an international perspective within the EWC. Rather the contrary: he spotted a national conflict within the EWC, especially in connection with the election of a new chairman for the pan-EWC. 'Honesty is necessary,' he said, and as if he wished to explain himself he continued by saying that 'everything behind the scenes is not good'. Two interviewees actually seemed to have no serious interest at all in EWCs or international employee representation, but we shall return to them below.

The 'right' qualities

A question that tells us much about how people think of their own identities is what, in their minds, characterises a 'good' EWC representative. We asked our respondents what they thought were 'the most important qualities an EWC member should have'. Such a question is on the one hand very open-ended, but on the other it reveals much of the respondent's own views and experience. The answers in general focused on two features: an understanding of cross-national issues and language abilities. In both companies we studied, the group language was English; hence, 'language abilities' meant an ability to communicate in English. The native English speakers were not very accommodating on this point. Even though both companies were of Scandinavian origin, and one had German headquarters for one of its business areas, it was 'the other' representatives who should learn better English, not the English speakers who should learn new languages. We could also find a small, perhaps insignificant, difference between the two companies: ISS members were often more 'direct', i.e. stressing shop floor issues more directly than, for instance, language issues. The most important qualities are 'motivation and organisational abilities', as it was expressed by a Belgian ISS representative who continued by saying that the most important task for his EWC was 'to work better on the floor'.

Language was the means of reaching different cultures, according to several of our interviewees, but it was just a means; cultural differences in ways of thinking had to be addressed in the light of language. For instance, a Swedish SCA representative expressed the view that good knowledge of English was highly important, but since the company was of Swedish origin it was important to be familiar with 'the Swedish state of things too'; and a German ISS representative emphasised that a 'good' EWC member must have good contacts with management, i.e. communicate in German with the national management, but still be able to read English to understand what the German national management actually decided. Several of our respondents, however, were not too keen on English as a working language. We found a big difference between countries on this point. A Dutch representative from the SCA said that 'the Netherlands is a trading country, therefore we *have* to speak other languages; we are not so proud of our own language, which is actually an advantage in the EWC work'. People from other countries with more 'international' languages found it hard to share that view, though. A Swedish SCA member tried to bridge the problem by saying that 'language is most important and we must have a common language for all informal contacts', but, he continued, 'it must be possible to express oneself in the native tongue too, to make sure that everybody is really able to give their opinion in a correct way'. Another expression of how important language is, is revealed by the following quote:

> One reason why language skills are so important is that ISS now has business activities in more or less every country in Europe, not only within the EU. If all these countries should be represented in the EWC, we must accept that a lot of important information and exchange goes on outside the formal meetings, in the bar or at coffee breaks, and such a situation demands good knowledge in probably more than one foreign language.
>
> (Swiss representative, ISS)

The right to express oneself in one's native tongue was often emphasised by representatives, in particular from France. Language abilities were, from their point of view, not at all important in shaping the activities of EWC representatives. Yet four of the five German interviewees spontaneously, without being asked, excused themselves for not speaking English, and also said that they wished to improve their English during their time in the EWC. By contrast, in the interviews in French, none of the four interviewees mentioned any interests of that kind.

Regarding issues other than language, it was the 'international thinking' that was found to be most important. The connection between the two issues was, however, more or less always present. An Austrian representative for SCA expressed it as follows: 'The representative must think not locally, but in a European manner; thus he or she must have the will to learn languages and different cultures.' Others mentioned the need to have good contacts with national trade unions and/or management. The following quotes are illustrative:

> He or she must have a clear vision of defending the workers' interest in increasing the 'conscience' in the country, and an ability to have a fruitful dialogue with the management, instead of just receiving information. All the representatives must also share the same goals – similar ideology.
>
> (Spanish representative, SCA)

> The EWCs must be more involved in 'traditional' trade union practices, since an EWC is the best, maybe the sole, means to bridge cultural distances between countries.
>
> (Swedish representative, SCA)

Besides decent language skills, the representative must have a 'social sensibility'; you must care for your colleagues, so that when you face top management you speak their mind instead of 'excusing' yourself for your existence.

(Norwegian representative, SCA)

A good member of the EWC must have much knowledge of both trade union work, the field of business and the employers' view.

(Swedish representative, SCA)

Interestingly, the latter view was shared by at least three of the Swedish SCA representatives and expressed in similar terms.

Expectations of the EWC and how to make things work

One way of approaching national and international features of the representatives is to ask them about their expectations of the EWC work and of how they expect to reach their goals. The international view and its connection to national issues were very salient in the majority of the answers. The SCA representatives in particular stressed the risk of 'social dumping' and the EWC's role in preventing it through different forms of levelling between countries, for instance by means of similar bonus systems. In the ISS case, the fear of social dumping is, for obvious reasons, not as conspicuous; ISS is a service company, and thus the employees are not at risk of cleaning jobs being moved to other countries. On the other hand, there is a perceived risk that the failure to preserve the protections of the Posted Workers' Directive, and the final outcome of the EU Services Directive on labour standards in Europe, open the workforce up to another form of social dumping through labour immigration, and some of our ISS respondees underlined this aspect.

Several of our respondents in both companies expressed a vision that the EWC could be a means against social dumping, emphasising the cross-national contacts. As an Austrian representative (SCA) put it, 'Even if the wage negotiations are national, we might in the longer run get the same sort of bonus system within the whole group.' On the attendant question, of whether it was possible to reach such a goal, he answered that a precondition would be more regular contacts between the members to make them able to understand each other, meeting at least four times a year. A similar point of view was taken by a Finnish ISS representative:

One thing I have learned this far is that so many countries have much worse working situations than we have in Finland. If we are ever to be able to avoid similar situations, however, we must talk more, not only in meetings. When we do that we can get more things to happen even in countries with bad situations.

(Finnish representative, ISS)

Regarding expectancies, several ISS members also mentioned that there was an actual 'continuity problem' with 'two or three new faces at every meeting'. A much bigger problem, though, was that management changed too often. In four years, the HR manager responsible for EWC issues had changed three times, and a fourth one was on his way. Currently, he too has left his position and a fifth HR manager is being appointed. Another problem stressed by many ISS members was the lack of any introductory programme or introductory information for new representatives. Because of the group's rapid growth, such a programme would be very useful, but the size of the company was at the same time seen as a major obstacle in making such a programme work in practice.

The following quotes provide useful insights into the expectations of EWC members in the companies concerned:

> The most important task for the EWC is to equalise differences between countries; our discussions must aim to get a better understanding of national peculiarities.
>
> (French representative, SCA)

> We must have more frequent meetings if we are to be able to make our countries aim for the same targets.
>
> (German representative, ISS)

> Mutual trust and many informal contacts are the most important within the EWC. In the contacts with management it is very important that the EWC has a certain status, which I believe we have; as an EWC representative, I can get management to listen to me. Actually, the EWC representatives are discussing international marketing strategies with top management in a way that their factory managers are not even close to, and that gives us status.
>
> (Swedish representative, SCA)

> The EWC is a great means when you have a factory manager who never listens to the trade union. When you cannot reach him from 'below', through unions, the EWC gives the workers a chance to instead reach him from 'above', through contacts with his superior managers. We have seen several examples of this.
>
> (Norwegian representative, SCA)

> A very important item is health and safety, and another one is money. Money means, for example, when we are talking about bonus systems. Negotiations about money are not a task for the EWC; yet we have talked about it and we have signed an agreement about the bonus system in Stockholm. I think this will be more and more a task for EWCs. For the future, I hope we will be able to get more and more negotiations to

set minimum standards in different sectors. Sometimes management *wants* to negotiate things with us, but I think our EWC is not yet prepared for it.

(German representative, SCA)

EWCs and trade unions

In the previous sections, we have discussed the EWC representatives' view of their role. Here we examine the critical issue of the connections they have with trade unions. National versus international identities and interests is a rather complex issue for trade unions. On the one hand, trade unions have a long tradition of international co-operation and international organisations reaching back more than a century (cf. Annand 2001). On the other hand, unions are formed in national contexts to face national or local challenges.

Several interviewees underlined the importance of connections with national trade unions and international trade union federations. The two companies differed in one important organisational way, however; while SCA does not allow trade union representatives who are not employed by the company on the EWCs, ISS have seats reserved for union federations in its EWC select committee. For example, two persons from outside the group had seats; one was a lawyer from KAD, the Danish cross-occupational union for unskilled women workers (Kvindeligt Arbejderforbund); and the other one was the head of UNI Property Services section. UNI, the successor of FIET, is the international trade union federation for employees in commercial, clerical, professional and technical occupations. UNI Property Services has its headquarters in Switzerland. Consequently, it is a very important link between EWCs and trade unions in the cleaning business.

During our interview with this key EWC representative in January 2002, several problems regarding the connections between EWCs and 'ordinary' trade unions were explored, and the great importance of such connections for a successful EWC was emphasised. 'As a trade union officer myself,' the head of UNI Property Services said, 'I have a clear vision of all ISS members being organised in national trade unions.'

> A reason for this is that only a few European countries have developed national works councils within transnational groups; thus too many EWC members have big problems in spreading the EWC information in their own country. A consequence of this is that many local managers do not feel obliged to follow the recommendations or statements their own group managers make at EWC meetings – far too often I hear EWC representatives saying that when they approach management back at their workplaces they are just met by something like: 'Yeah, yeah, that's what group management says, but down here, *I'm* the boss and responsible for how things are made' ... that's why we must get local branches of the EWCs in close connection with trade unions, to make

sure that the HRM philosophy is at least not less favourable for the workers in practice than group management states.

(Head of UNI Property Services, ISS representative)

However, he made it clear that this was easier said than done. Among other things, he pointed out that the introduction of EWCs has created a manpower problem for unions and other bodies for employee representation. Within a few years, between 20,000 and 30,000 new employee representatives had to be found all over Europe. Finding that many EWC representatives might not only be hard in countries with weak trade union traditions, but it might be a problem in, for instance, the Nordic countries too, despite their long and strong corporative traditions and high union density. Actually, the strong Nordic trade unions might be a problem in themselves: why involve themselves in EWCs when there already exist well-functioning organisations for employee representation?

This is perhaps a crucial point for the making of an international identity: it is not necessarily the countries with weak trade union traditions that are the problem. The very strength of Scandinavian trade unionism is in danger of creating a kind of 'moral hazard' in terms of their international orientation. This was vividly demonstrated by the Laval episode, a labour dispute in the Swedish construction industry arising from the presence of Latvian contract labour in Vaxholm outside Stockholm in 2004 and 2005 (Woolfson and Sommers 2006). Accordingly, some Swedish unionists responsible for international matters have complained that the Swedish unions neglect the EWC question and that the debate of employee influence in transnationals is far too silent (Kärrlander 2000). A rather remarkable example of how easily international co-operation can turn into national chauvinism was when the local trade union branch at the Swedish multinational Electrolux tried to extend the employee co-operation within the group in 1977, i.e. long before EWCs were on the agenda. Several French factories had recently been merged into Electrolux and the trade union branch therefore found it important to develop contacts with French unions at the new Electrolux plants. Accordingly, the local union board visited some factories in France early in 1977, but perceived French trade unionism as a confusing, and confused, mix of small, independent or even competing organisations. Their conclusion was that the only possible solution was therefore to invite them to Sweden with a view to teaching the French unionists how trade union activities 'should best be performed' (Åkerman 2003: 203–7). The Swedish unionists did not learn anything about the industrial relations framework in France before deciding what should be done; actually, they neither knew about the French employers' hostility to union activities at the workplaces, nor understood the connections between French unions and the *Comité d'entreprise* system for employee representation.

We are left with a paradox: on the one hand, a good EWC representative should preferably have a thorough experience of national or local trade union work; on the other, s/he risks being too narrow-minded from the same experience! This raises an empirical question of how much trade union experience EWC members have. Table 6.1 shows how many years the representatives have held positions in a trade union. Some of them might have been members much longer, but that is less important when it comes to trade union experience.

Members of both companies' EWCs are in general very well used to representing employees in trade unions. Only three representatives are not members of a union, and among the rest all but six hold or have held some kind of position. In addition, several had also been engaged in works councils, such as German *Betriebsräte* or French *Comité d'entreprise*. Almost two-fifths had been trade union representatives for ten years or more. The 'record' was held by a Dutch EWC member at SCA and a Belgian at ISS; both had been trade union representatives since 1962, that is for forty years. The Dutch representative had also been chairman of the local union branch and member of the *ondernemingsraad* (works council) for twenty-five years. The second most experienced EWC member in each company was a Swedish representative for SCA who had been chairman of the local union branch for twenty-eight years, and an Irish ISS member who had held positions in her trade union for twenty years.

Yet, at the time of our interviews in 2002, ISS had two Dutch EWC members who had both been elected from among middle management. Neither of them belonged to a union. One of them held a rather 'neutral' view of EWCs and trade unions in general. The other, however, was outspokenly hostile to trade unions. To our question on whether he belonged to a union, he forcibly answered: 'Definitely not!' explaining that he was not interested in the EWC, but there were three positions to fill up and so he more or less had to accept the task. 'I don't see any good things coming from the EWC, and then it is hard to be motivated … If I could find anyone else, I would let that person have this mission,' he said. However, such views were atypical.

A complementary question asked about trade union contact persons to assist in handling EWC issues. Table 6.2 shows the results of that question.

Table 6.1 Duration of positions held in trade unions by EWC representatives

Years	SCA	(%)	ISS	(%)	In total	(%)
0	5	(16.7)	1	(4.8)	6	(11.8)
<5	5	(16.7)	4	(19.0)	9	(17.6)
5–10	4	(13.3)	9	(42.9)	13	(25.5)
>10	14	(46.7)	5	(23.8)	19	(37.2)
Not member	1	(3.3)	2	(9.5)	3	(5.9)
No answer	1	(3.3)	0	(0.0)	1	(2.0)
In total	30	(100)	21	(100)	51	(100)

Table 6.2 Number of EWC representatives with a special trade union contact

TU contact	SCA	(%)	ISS	(%)	In total	(%)
Yes	22	(73.3)	14	(66.7)	36	(70.6)
No	3	(10.0)	7	(33.3)	10	(19.6)
No answer	5	(16.7)	0	(0.0)	5	(9.8)
In total	30	(100)	21	(100)	51	(100)

A clear majority of the EWC members affirmatively answered that they have special trade union contacts to assist in these issues.

On the follow-up question: 'What kind of support do you request from your trade union in your EWC work?' the answers spread over a wide landscape of items including legislative support (Spanish rep. SCA); spreading information between different companies and workplaces (Swedish rep. SCA); as interlocutor and help to compare different work agreements (Swiss rep. ISS); helping to understand, for example, the German or the Austrian organisations (Swedish rep. SCA); providing contacts with the EU in Brussels (Austrian rep. SCA); and providing support during mergers or downsizings (German rep. SCA). A French representative in SCA explained: 'It depends on the delicacy of the situation: the more ticklish the subject is, the better it is to have a trade union to handle or help handling the issue, and this far, I've got all the help I've needed from my union.' A Swedish SCA EWC member stated that the most useful help he got from his trade union was the contact with the international trade union federations, which, he argued, was important to avoid the EWC having strained relations with the internationals, 'instead of having them with us'.

The social contacts

As we have seen, the need for language skills is highlighted by a vast number of our interviewees; at the same time, however, many of them also emphasise that it must be possible to express oneself in one's native tongue during meetings. This gives a hint that the language problems are maybe more a question of *how* to communicate with each other *outside* the meeting, i.e. during coffee breaks, in the bar or at dinner. Hence, we asked our respondents how important they found such 'social activities', including every possible situation they had to communicate with each other outside the conference room. The results, on a four-grade scale, are shown in Table 6.3.

On the fixed scale, a vast majority answered 'very important'. There is also a significant difference between the two companies. ISS representatives who did not speak English well enough to communicate with the other EWC members found the social events just 'boring'. Many respondents, however, confirm the strong link between the importance of social activities and the knowledge of language. 'The social activities are so important because we

Table 6.3 The importance of social activities for the EWC

	Very important	Rather important	Less important	Not important	'Don't know'	No answer	In total
SCA (#)	26	0	0	0	0	4	30
SCA (%)	(86.7)	(0.0)	(0.0)	(0.0)	(0.0)	(13.3)	(100)
ISS (#)	14	2	0	3	1	1	21
ISS (%)	(66.7)	(9.0)	(0.0)	(14.3)	(5.0)	(5.0)	(100)
In total	40	2	0	3	1	5	51
(%)	(78.4)	(3.9)	(0.0)	(5.9)	(2.0)	(9.8)	(100)

Note:
The question read: 'How important are the social activities for a successful EWC?'

seldom meet and do not speak the same language,' a Swedish EWC member said, and a Swiss representative for ISS stated that it was the key to cross-country communication. The EWC members who answered that social activities were not important were people who did not speak English well enough to chat with others without an interpreter. The sole exception among the 'rather' and 'not important' answers was the Dutch representative for ISS who, as mentioned above, did not find EWC activities at all important in any way.

A majority of the comments were, however, just 'enthusiastic', without pin-pointing any special feature, except the 'informality', the 'chance to speak more freely', the 'lack of pressure you have in the meetings', 'build up relationships', 'the possibilities to make personal contacts', and so on. The possibility of learning more 'basics' from other countries was often mentioned, and how important that was to understand nationalities. A Swedish SCA representative said that it was the only way to get to know about daily life in other countries: – 'What about your supermarkets? How much is the milk?' Another aspect was brought up by a Belgian ISS member: 'At coffee breaks and dinners we go into fruitful discussions,' he said, 'but we cannot bring these discussions up on the agenda the day after, no matter how important or good they are; at worst, we therefore have to wait one year to have it up on the agenda,' which, he argued, 'feels extremely long'.

The social contacts led to another important question: what contacts exist between meetings? How often were members of EWCs in touch with other members, and from which countries? Language barriers were very important here. Table 6.4 shows contacts 'within' and 'across' language borders. The language groups are English (Britain, Ireland, the Benelux countries and Scandinavia); German (central and eastern Europe); and French (southern Europe).

The result is maybe not quite as bad for ISS as it seems at first sight. The Swiss chairman is bilingual, and in addition to German and French speaks both English and Spanish fluently; hence, he communicates with people from all three groups, and all communication with him is counted as internal in

Table 6.4 Contacts within the EWCs

	Within the 'language group'	Outside the 'language group'	In total
SCA	77	30	107
ISS	52	0	52
In total	129	30	159

the table above. Still, besides communication with him, *there is no regular communication at all across the language barriers.* The result is, in the worst case, a 'regionalisation' of identities instead of an 'internationalisation' of identities.

Conclusion

In the introduction to this chapter we stated that an EWC, like any large organisation that is not strictly hierarchical, consists of a complex network of subgroups, of inter-group relations, which in turn have different power resources, status and prestige. At a European level, there are representatives from different countries with different industrial relations systems, judicial systems, etc. Below that, at national level, there are numerous individuals, all with different knowledge, skills, abilities, values, beliefs and so on. Most of them have been elected because of their engagement in trade unions or national works councils and thus, in some way, represent a national system. Yet, as this chapter suggests, this is not the whole picture. For instance, it is not possible to say that the two Dutch ISS members who were elected from middle management are representative of the system of trade unions and *ondernemingsraad* in the Netherlands.

Rather, the focus here has been on the individuals' backgrounds and interests, suggesting that they have much in common despite national 'peak-level' differences. Some of the main findings are that EWC representatives are in general very interested in international matters, and therefore think and act beyond narrow national interests. Moreover, a vast majority of our interviewees have long experience of trade union work. On the one hand, they are thus 'impregnated' with national views of how to handle issues, but on the other, many of them claim, explicitly or implicitly, that it was the national trade union work that made them realise how important cross-national contacts and actions were.

In sum, the EWC representatives in both company groups are in general very keen to learn more about other countries and to forge closer contacts with people from other parts of the company. The major obstacle seems to be language. The best way to get to know other representatives, but also to get important information, is informal contact during coffee breaks, in the bar or at dinner in the evenings; yet in all such informal contacts language barriers can separate people (which is most obvious in the ISS case). Even though professional interpreters are always present at the meetings, it is not practically possible to use them to make informal contacts during or between meetings.

One risk is that, rather than genuine internationalisation, the EWCs may experience a regionalisation, where most contacts take place within different regions: For example, Nordic Europe with the UK/Ireland; central Europe and Latin Europe. This potential 'regionalisation' of identity is important for the development of EWCs. In ISS, with its more widespread representation over countries and languages, this was particularly apparent. Here, cross-country contacts in the company's EWC had to go through either the multi-lingual Swiss chairman or through the international trade union federation UNI, also with a language-skilled official responsible for handling EWC issues. It is possible to find differences in attitudes between different country representatives in both companies, but thanks to the better communicative situation in SCA such cultural differences are much easier to deal with when shaping a more coherent European identity. Paradoxically, the more 'formal' structure of the SCA also benefited the development of 'informal' contacts; the system with three smaller EWCs with frequent meetings connected under a common pan-EWC makes it easier to both make and maintain contacts with other people. One possible way to promote EWC contacts in ISS could be to undertake a similar dividing-up into three smaller EWCs, one for each of the three distinct communicative groups. Group management financial constraints may not permit this, however. Even in the world's largest cleaning company, it is only possible to use brooms to sweep; it is still not possible to fly on them.

Acknowledgements

The authors are grateful for help and comments from our informants, from the editors of this book, from the HRM people at SCA and ISS, and from Arne Kristoffersson and Charles Woolfson.

Notes

1 The interviews were undertaken in 2001 and 2002 and were made either face-to-face with the respondents or over the phone. All respondents were contacted about one week before the interview, when they also received a written questionnaire. The interviews were conducted in Scandinavian languages, English, French, German and, with help from interpreters, Spanish. Most interviews took about one hour, though some were considerably longer, even more than three hours. Further, the interviews covered many aspects of EWCs and EWC representation, and therefore only a few of the questions are used in this chapter.
2 In SCA, the home countries of the interviewees were Sweden (13), the UK (4), Germany (4), the Netherlands (2), France (2), Austria, Norway, Italy and Spain. In ISS, they were from Germany (3), Switzerland (3), Belgium (2), Denmark (2), France (2), the Netherlands (2), Austria, Ireland, Finland, Sweden, Slovenia, Spain and the UK.

3 To be exact, there were four areas, since North America constituted a 'business area' of its own, solely on geographical grounds, which, however, is less important for a study of EWCs.

References

Åkerman, J. (2003) *Lokala fack iglobala företag: Electrolux verkstadsklubb iMotala och koncernfacket 1925–1985*, Stockholm: Arbetslivsinstitutet, Arbetsliv i omvandling 2003 (6).

Andersson, M. and Thörnqvist, C. (2003) 'The making of EWCs: a comparison of European Works Councils in four Scandinavian transnationals', in D. Fleming and C. Thörnqvist (eds) *Nordic Management–Labour Relations and Internationalization – Converging and Diverging Tendencies*, Copenhagen: Nordic Council of Ministers, Nord 2003 (15): 79–101.

Annand, R. (2001) 'The European industry federations – key players in a European industrial relations system', in S. Jefferys, F. Mispelblom Beyer and C. Thörnqvist (eds) *European Working Lives: Continuities and Change in Management and Industrial Relations in France, Scandinavia and the UK*, Cheltenham and Northampton, MA: Edward Elgar, 248–66.

Hall, M. and Marginson, P. (2005) 'Trojan horses or paper tigers? Assessing the significance of European Works Councils', in B. Harley, J. Hyman and P. Thompson (eds) *Participation and Democracy at Work: Essays in Honour of Harvie Ramsay*, Basingstoke: Palgrave Macmillan, 204–21.

Hogg, M.A. (2000) 'Social identity and self-categorisation processes in organizational contexts', *Academy of Management Review*, 25 (January): 121–40.

Kärrlander, K. (2000) 'Svenskt fack försummar EU', *Dagens Arbete*, 15 May.

Lecher, W. (1999) 'Resources of the European Works Council – empirical knowledge and prospects', *Transfer*, 5: 278–301.

Miller, D. (1999) 'Towards a "European" Works Council', *Transfer*, 5: 344–65.

Miller, D., Tully, B. and Fitzgerald, I. (2000) 'The politics of language and European Works Councils: towards a research agenda', *European Journal of Industrial Relations*, 6 (3): 307–23.

Stirling, J. and Tully, B. (2004) 'Power, process, and practice: communications in European Works Councils', *European Journal of Industrial Relations*, 10 (1): 73–89.

Venneslan, K. and Ågotnes, H.J. (1994) 'Transnationalization and participation', in B. Schiller, K. Venneslan, H.J. Ågotnes, N. Bruun, R. Nielsen and D. Töllborg, *The Future of the Nordic Model of Labour Relations – Three Reports on Internationalization and Industrial Relations*, Copenhagen: Nordic Council of Ministers, Nord 1993 (36): 93–164.

Wills, J. (2000) 'Great expectations: three years in the life of a European Works Council', *European Journal of Industrial Relations*, 6 (1): 85–107.

Woolfson, C. and Sommers, J. (2006) 'Labour mobility in construction: European implications of the Latvian construction company Laval and Partners' dispute with Swedish labour', *European Journal of Industrial Relations*, 12: 49–68.

7 Ethno-, poly- and Eurocentric European Works Councils

How does German involvement influence their identity?

Helen Bicknell

The ontological claim of much academic research is that European Works Councils (EWCs) should ultimately assume some kind of transnational, European identity. However, even qualified EWC observers have so far had little success in identifying this rare European specimen (Marginson and Sisson 2004: 238). National identity and intercultural differences are proving to be stubborn obstacles. Lecher *et al.*'s (1999) typology describes EWCs as symbolic, service providers, project-orientated or participatory. This has gained considerable acceptance in EWC literature describing the wide divergences in EWCs' effectiveness. However, these categories offer few explanations as to why EWCs develop in certain directions, nor do they help explain the role national identity plays as a force affecting the trajectory an EWC may follow.

Marginson (2000), drawing on Levinson's (1972) work on transnational employee solidarity, uses the terms ethno-, poly- and Eurocentric to describe different EWC typologies. Similar terms (ethno-, poly-, region- and geo-centric) were also used by Perlmutter (1969) to describe how companies internationalise. This chapter attempts to develop the concepts of ethno-, poly- and Eurocentrism further as a tool to help explain the role national identity plays in many EWCs. Within the German context, these classifications demonstrate why one particular national input may nevertheless result in several possible outcomes. The 'centrism' approach examines a wider range of national influences, not just country of origin of the controlling undertaking, to see how these affect EWCs in practice.

German influence on EWCs is particularly important because of its strong industrial relations traditions as well as the size of its economy. Despite its current structural, growth and reunification problems, the German economy is still the largest in Europe and continues to flourish, particularly in the export sector, where most EWCs are to be found. According to the latest European Trade Union Institute's (ETUI) figures (Kerckhofs and Pas 2004), Germany is the home base for 26 per cent of companies in Europe which are legally obliged to have an EWC (572 out of 2,169), but only 14 per cent of the current 737 companies which have in fact signed EWC agreements are German-based. However, not only the home base of the company is relevant when considering German influence. Of the

2,169 companies covered by the directive, there are 1,702 MNCs with subsidiaries registered in Germany (78 per cent).

The relevance of these figures for EWCs is even greater than the mere numbers of companies or their subsidiaries indicate. The decisive qualitative factor is the way the German dual system of industrial relations operates. The German transposition of the EWC Directive (EWCD) foresees the appointment of EWC representatives as coming from the highest level of works council representatives within the enterprise.

In this chapter, theoretical arguments are supported by quantitative and qualitative research on German influence in EWCs, framed within the concepts of ethno-, poly- and Eurocentrism. After explaining the research methods and concepts, the 'centrism ideal types' are outlined, as well as the areas of German national identity that seem most relevant for EWCs. These are German industrial relations culture, company and managerial structures, the perceptions of German works councillors and trade unionists towards EWCs, and finally, issues of language, culture and German attitudes towards European integration. The connections between these national influences and the kind of EWC which may result are then discussed.

Methods and concepts

The analysis of German identity in EWCs will primarily deal with what Streeck (1997a: 16) refers to as 'industrial citizenship'. This investigation examines how German works councillors perceive EWCs and their expectations of them. Do EWCs improve strong, national workplace representation structures or are they perceived as a threat? Is the 'highly symbiotic' relationship between German trade unions and their works councillors (Müller-Jentsch, 2002) enhanced or weakened by this supranational institution?

Data used to answer these questions are based on questionnaires and qualitative interviews conducted between 2003 and 2004 and Kerckhofs and Pas' ETUI 2004 database. In-depth, qualitative interviews were carried out with twenty-five representatives from different EWCs from various industrial sectors. Twenty-two of the interviewees were German (eight worked for German-based companies), two were British and one was Dutch. Approximately 400 questionnaires were sent out and answers were received from 128 EWC representatives, sixty-four from Germany and sixty-four from the rest of Europe. These replies came from a total of sixty-two EWCs, twenty of which were German-based. Thirty-three of the German representatives were from German-based companies, and thirty-one were from foreign-owned MNCs.

National identity, particularly with respect to diverging industrial relations systems, has often been recognised as an obstacle to the development of EWCs as transnational organisations by EWC 'pessimists' such as Streeck (1997b) or Schulten (1996). Marginson *et al.* (2001) suggest that EWCs are greatly influenced by 'country of origin' and 'country of location' factors as well as company-specific conditions, such as the sector, the international focus of the business and its management structures. However, they conclude, in agreement with Vitols (2003), that 'in general, EWCs seem not to be primarily an extension of national systems' (Marginson and Sisson 2004: 234).

In order to link the above-mentioned origin, location and business-specific factors to national identity, the concepts of ethno-, poly- and Eurocentrism prove helpful. Marginson (2000) also relates these concepts to Lecher *et al.*'s (2001) typology of symbolic, service-provider, project-orientated and participatory EWCs. Marginson (2000) develops the concepts of ethno-, poly- and Eurocentric EWCs drawing on Levinson's (1972) analysis of transnational collective bargaining by trade unions. He describes EWCs as 'polycentric' if the national representatives merely attempt to use EWCs to further their own national interests. Marginson and Sisson (2004) describe such EWCs as belonging to the 'symbolic' category. Those EWCs which are dominated by home country representatives and are more active are described as 'ethnocentric' and correspond to the 'service-provider' or 'project-orientated' categories. Only those which take on a new, European identity 'distinct from that of the structures of representation in the home country' (ibid.: 234) can be called 'Eurocentric' or would become what Lecher's typology considers 'participatory'.

However, by relating EWC 'ideal types' to Perlmutter's (1969) concepts of ethno-, poly-, regio- and geocentrism based on the analysis of the company's international growth strategy, a slightly different picture emerges. Perlmutter's basic premise is that companies have a 'strategic predisposition' towards international development, depending on the structure of the company, the way it develops internationally (by growth or acquisition), its management and organisational structures. Adapting Perlmutter's ideas to EWC developments results in the following 'ideal types' as illustrated in Table 7.1.

Table 7.1 Ethno-, poly- and Eurocentric EWCs: 'ideal types'

EWC 'ideal types'	Description
Ethnocentric	Home country representatives dominate proceedings and deal with management. Non-home country representatives are marginalised. EWC may be regarded as either not necessary or ineffective by home country representatives from inclusive workplace representation systems. Non-home country representatives may benefit from access to information.
Polycentric	EWC is a mutually beneficial information exchange platform for all representatives. Home country representatives try to actively include other representatives in meetings and positions of responsibility. Management may try to 'play off' countries against each other, but this can be resisted through 'trust', 'talk' and 'training'.
Eurocentric	EWCs develop a clear European identity. High levels of internal trust and communication between members, office-holders and management. A common European agenda is planned.

These descriptions of EWC 'ideal types' vary from Marginson's, making 'polycentric' EWCs more international than 'ethnocentric' EWCs. They serve well, however, to structure the results of this investigation which indicate that the most ethnocentric (and also symbolic) EWCs in Germany are those where German representatives dominate proceedings, and regard EWCs as having little added value. Those EWCs which could better be described as polycentric fitted the service-provider or project-orientated typologies. Very few EWCs could be described as Eurocentric. The most Eurocentric were well-established EWCs which had close links to national and European-level trade union organisations and were found in large, internationally orientated companies.

German 'industrial citizenship'

> Co-determination constitutes one of the central pillars of Germany's economic order, and must be retained and developed further as an element of the social market economy.
>
> (Kommission Mitbestimmung 1998, author's translation)

Co-determination or *Mitbestimmung* entered the German industrial relations landscape in 1849.[1] Today's dual system provides for works councils to participate in company-level decision-making procedures from workplace to group level and includes co-determination at supervisory board levels in companies with more than 500 employees. Collective bargaining takes place between trade unions and employers associations at the sectoral level. Although co-determination is often criticised by conservatives and liberals, a recent attack by Michael Rogowski, the president of the German Industrial Employers' Association (BDI), calling it 'an error of history' led to considerable public debate (Manager-Magazin.de 2004). An opinion poll organised in response to this statement showed that 82 per cent of the population were in favour of co-determination, viewing it as necessary, motivating and positive for entrepreneurial development (Hans-Böckler Stiftung 2004).

In Germany works councillors are elected by the whole workforce, irrespective of trade union membership. Works councillors' rights and duties are clearly defined in the Works Constitution Act (WCA).[2] Co-determination rights cover areas of social policy and personnel issues, as well as financial and economic matters, and must take place in an atmosphere of mutual trust and goodwill towards the company. Regarding collective bargaining a main principle is that once agreements have been reached, they are binding for all workers covered by the agreements, regardless of whether they are trade union members or not (Traxler and Behrens 2002). However, in recent years, the boundaries between the company and the sectoral level have become increasingly blurred and weakened due to the use of 'opening clauses' in collective agreements, and there has been an increase in workers and companies not covered by any collective agreements at all (Bispinck and Schulten 2005). Although trade union membership in Germany is quite low, at just under 30 per cent, collective bargaining coverage is much higher, at around 61 per cent (ibid.).[3] In large companies close to 80 per cent of works council chairpersons are likely to be union members (Niedenhoff 2002).

Most companies with over 200 employees (the threshold for one full-time representative) have works councils and are covered by sectoral collective bargaining agreements. For companies with more than 1,000 employees the coverage rate is almost 100 per cent (Hans-Böckler Stiftung 2003). As German EWC representatives are chosen from the highest level of workplace representation in the company, this means that they are invariably highly experienced, 'professional' works councillors. Thus, in most German-based companies with an EWC and in some foreign-owned companies with large German workforces as well, the EWC representatives are often members of the national supervisory board, the group works council (*Konzernbetriebsrat*), and other important company committees, with strong national legal rights to information, consultation and co-determination and close contacts to national trade union organisations.

It may be assumed that work councillors in large companies are well informed about their rights to instigate an EWC. Therefore, if they decide not to request one, this could be because they perceive no 'added benefit' due to the lack of co-determination rights for EWC representatives. This hypothesis could apply to many companies based in Germany which are large enough to be affected by the EWCD. These 'non-existent EWCs' may be the most 'ethnocentric' of all, because their representatives may have deliberately chosen to by-pass this European institution, regarding it as inferior to their national system. This would concur with the Euro-pessimists' assessment that 'EWCs are neither European, nor works councils' (Streeck 1997b).

Effects of German company and managerial structures

Many case study comparisons of EWCs in practice categorise them using the 'country of origin' principle (Lecher *et al.* 2001; Marginson *et al.* 2001). They also include sector considerations as well as the international orientation of the business (Whittall 2000; Wills 2000; Hancké 2000). As mentioned, some researchers have concluded that EWCs do not seem to be extensions of national systems. However, this does not mean that national identity plays no role in the way EWCs function. A different picture of national identity emerges by examining the particular roles played by the works councillors, and how they work within the EWC, given the company structure and its business focus. The role of German national identity seems very relevant, given the roles played by German EWC representatives, and even if the companies' headquarters are not based in Germany.

As was shown in Table 7.1, the 'ideal type' ethnocentric EWC will be dominated by the home country's culture. Decisions will be made at national committees, and foreign EWC representatives will, at best, be able to receive information and have some access to the home country's management team at EWC meetings. The majority of EWC seats are often held by German representatives who also control key EWC offices, but who view its functions as being very much secondary to their main work as national works councillors. One interviewee from a German cement company described it very bluntly:

> Well, we're a German company, in the building industry, and we didn't want any old country coming along and taking the butter off our bread. Our partners are here in Germany, and so we will speak German. And the majority of seats will be held by Germans ... We want to work together, co-operate, but we said: we are a German company, we bought your sites, and now they should be pleased that they have still got their jobs.
>
> (German rep., German Cement 2, 2004)

Some Article 13 agreements were even signed by the German works council with the German management without involving the foreign representatives in the EWC negotiations.[4]

Privatisation and rapid growth through international mergers and acquisitions have dramatically changed the structure of many traditional German concerns in recent years. Growth through acquisition usually means larger foreign subsidiaries and the need to integrate different intercultural business traditions and organisational systems. An EWC which has a more even spread of representatives will either have to learn to communicate and understand the 'foreign' way of doing things, or will be doomed to 'symbolism'. Therefore, given these recent business changes, learning how to become polycentric has become a major task for many German EWC representatives. The results of this research show that the representatives welcome this in principle, although in practice they are often frustrated through problems of language, culture or communication. Cultural difficulties due to different industrial relations cultures were cited by 20 per cent of the questionnaire respondents as being the most negative aspect of their EWC. Communication problems between EWC members and management were cited by 16 per cent, while language problems were mentioned by 7 per cent of the respondents. While email and direct telephone communication was usually possible, some EWCs are still being hampered by basic technological barriers:

> We are really at the absolute bottom as regards communication possibilities. When I want to speak to my Spanish colleague, I send something to the union – and they pass it on to her. The English girl – I send

things to her husband, and then she tells him what to reply, and he sends it back to me. That is how we communicate. Otherwise, sometimes I phone up on Sundays, using the cheap rates, from home. So that is about how it works. It is that bad.

(German rep., UK Nutritional Company, 2005)

Cultural problems between management and the EWC can be quite basic – 'The most important thing is that we try and get [the company] to understand that England belongs to Europe' (German rep., UK Airline, 2005) – or specific, because of different trade union and workplace representation traditions:

When I think of countries like France or Belgium, where the idea of trade unions has been brought into the institution and not the attitude, 'I'm from [the Company]'. Yes ... this trade union mentality and these different ideologies – trying to incorporate them all into the group. I don't think this is such a good idea. But of course, that is what happens sometimes, in practical terms.

(German rep., Swiss Chemical, 2005)

You can learn the language, but the culture ... it takes generations!

(Dutch rep., Dutch Bank, 2004)

Yes, a common voice – on a cultural basis. That is sometimes rather difficult in Europe ... the Swedes have a different temperament to the Spanish – that is a fact.

(German rep., American Automobile, 2005)

When companies are undergoing international restructuring, the EWC is also challenged and has to accommodate these changes. This may involve redistributing the seats or even renegotiating the whole EWC agreement. Apart from problems which some countries may have about losing seats, the EWC also has to accommodate new representatives, increasingly from eastern European countries with very different industrial relations systems, languages and cultures. Nevertheless, these upheavals sometimes have a positive effect on the way the EWCs function, giving them a serious 'project' to work on. This research revealed several German-based EWCs that have responded to the eastern European enlargement by relinquishing German seats to their new colleagues. This alone should tend to make their EWCs less ethnocentric. The main reason given for this decision was to avoid increasing the number of EWC plenary session members, in order to enable them to operate more effectively.

If companies have been very multinational for many years, it is easier for an EWC to become Eurocentric. The most Eurocentric of the EWC representatives who were interviewed and who replied to the questionnaires were from companies which have very international structures and have been operating internationally for many years. One of them remarked: 'I would say they [EWCs] are not just useful, but an important precondition in order to push the idea of Europe forward' (German rep., American Automobile, 2005).

The managerial structures of a company and managerial attitudes towards EWCs are also important factors determining the way EWCs are likely to function. If all the top managers, as well as most of the EWC representatives and its 'office holders', come from Germany it is unlikely that the EWC will be anything other than primarily ethnocentric. If the management team is more international, then a poly-, or Eurocentric outcome is more likely. Several surveys have demonstrated that company managers often find the EWC a useful forum to help them focus on and develop their European strategy (Vitols 2003; Hall 2003). High levels of managerial support were reported by the representatives from those EWCs which could be described as 'Eurocentric' or approaching this description. This was demonstrated by high levels of communication between management and the EWC, especially its select committee, support for EWC training and other facilities. In these EWCs the representatives reported that they had developed beyond information and consultation forums to become negotiation partners.

Views and expectations of German industrial relations actors towards EWCs

As mentioned earlier, if German representatives see so little value in an EWC that they do not even wish to request its establishment, then these 'non-existing EWCs' must also be included in the assessment of the influence of German identity on EWCs. However, at present we can only speculate on why so many companies in Germany have not yet formed EWCs. It may be assumed that, in the great majority of cases, this is not because the German representatives are unaware of the directive or of their possibilities of initiating a Special Negotiating Body. Such 'non-EWCs' could therefore be regarded as 'ultra-ethnocentric' EWCs.

This section includes data obtained from the EWC representatives who replied to the 2004 questionnaire which assessed how the active EWC representatives view this institution, and whether the German representatives are more or less positive about EWCs than the representatives from other countries (see Table 7.2). In the survey, 90 out of 128 respondents (70 per cent) all agreed that EWCs have an important role to play as European industrial relations actors. Of course, it could be argued that there would be a built-in bias, as only EWC representatives who had a positive attitude towards EWCs would reply to such a questionnaire. Nevertheless, apart from the fact that the response was highly positive, it is interesting to see that the German respondents were *more* positive than the 'rest of Europe'

Table 7.2 EWCs as European industrial relations actors?

	Yes	Perhaps	No	Don't know	No answer	Total (n = 128)
Germans (n = 64)	73%	19%	3%	3%	2%	100%
Rest of Europe (n = 64)	67%	11%	11%	5%	6%	100%

group: 73 per cent of German representatives versus 67 per cent from the rest of Europe replied 'yes, they have an important role to play', and 76 per cent of German representatives in German companies answered that 'EWCs have an important role to play as industrial relations actors', compared to 71 per cent from non-German companies.

Another question considered whether the representatives' own EWC had been particularly important to date. Again, the attitudes of the German respondents were more positive than the others, with nearly 72 per cent of the German respondents considering that their EWCs had performed a 'very useful role so far', and a further 25 per cent saying that they had performed a 'quite useful role so far'. The non-German respondents were less convinced of the usefulness of their EWC to date, with only 48 per cent answering that their EWC had been very useful and 34 per cent saying it had been quite useful. Slightly more non-Germans than Germans considered that the EWC had not been useful (nearly 11 per cent as opposed to 6 per cent).

Within the group of German EWC representatives, the representatives coming from German-based companies were more positive about the usefulness of their EWC so far than those from non-German companies. Of those from German companies, 76 per cent considered their EWC to have played a very useful role, compared to 68 per cent of German representatives from non-German companies. Only one respondent from each group considered that their EWC had not played a useful role so far. Thus the German practitioners seem to be less sceptical than some EWC 'pessimist' researchers once suggested (Streeck 1997b; Keller 1995).

In the qualitative interviews, the attitudes of the German representatives on the role of the EWC as an industrial relations institution were investigated in more depth. Here, the connection between the German system of industrial relations and their expectations of the EWC became more apparent. Three of the fourteen respondents interviewed in 2004 felt that their EWC lacked any real influence. Decisions were made elsewhere and the EWC had no particularly constructive role to play, even if it was seen to be valuable or useful for other reasons such as improving international understanding and communication channels. One of the respondents saw no need for the EWC at all: 'Our company says, we are only present in three countries and otherwise we only have small sales office, so why do we need an EWC?' (German rep., German Construction 1).

EWCs were regarded as having sufficient power by other representatives in German-owned companies; the German respondents felt that the EWCs fitted well into the established workplace representation institutions, adding an international dimension to existing, well-functioning German structures:

> Everyone concerned receives the information at the same time. So those employees who are concerned are informed all at the same time and can deal with what is necessary for them at the national level. We last had this combination of group works council and EWC meeting, for example, the last time on the 17th March to discuss a common topic.
>
> (German rep., German Chemical 2)

A very 'German' result from the interviews was that representatives in German companies bemoaned the lack of co-determination rights for EWCs. Their perception of a European Works Council is moulded by their experience of works councils in Germany, and they are unhappy with the lower level of co-determination at the European level: 'if the contents of the German co-determination could be adopted into the EWCD, that would be an ideal combination' (German rep., American Automobile, 2005).

Learning about the other European systems and having made contact with them through the EWC was not only seen as being positive, but also seemed to make many of the German interviewees really appreciate German co-determination rights. Most of them were definitely in favour of EWCs receiving more co-determination rights, and several had improved their foreign colleagues' rights by pushing forward some 'German' practices, in particular allowing foreign representatives to visit other sites within their own countries and awarding them more time off to fulfil their EWC duties. German EWC representatives were usually very sensitive about not wanting to interfere with other countries' systems, although sometimes this meant that they had not even discussed topics important to the EWC development, such as the different national procedures for nominations or elections to the EWC.

As already mentioned, the German industrial relations system is not just works councils, but the close interaction of works councils, with their designated duties and responsibilities, working together with their respective sectoral trade unions. The official position of the German Trades Union Confederation, the DGB, is to support European integration and to encourage EWCs to positively use their influence in transnational enterprises to promote social dialogue within Europe (Einblick 2005).

The main sectoral unions in terms of membership numbers which cover companies that have EWCs are the IG Metall (metalworking sector), Verdi (service sector) and the IG Chemie (chemicals). Other relevant unions for EWCs are the IG-Bauen-Agrar und Umwelt (building and construction sector) and the Nahrung-Genuss und Gaststätten (NGG, food and catering sectors). All of these unions have information on their websites for EWCs and have at least part-time administrators responsible for EWCs in their sectors. The support given varies greatly, in terms of both resources and methods used. However, none of them are over-staffed. The most favoured method of support once an EWC is operating is to have a union co-ordinator responsible for several EWCs within a sector, giving advice and helping to promote 'best practice', as well as website information.

The issue of EWC training is quite complicated. While most unions were reasonably active in the mid-1990s, offering training courses to encourage works councillors to initiate EWC negotiations and providing trade union support wherever possible, ongoing training of international groups is really beyond their mandate or capabilities. Most German unions have now set up guidelines, have produced brochures about European industrial relations and publish best-practice examples of actual EWC work.[5] At the European level, there is little training available for normal EWC representatives.

Thus it seems that while German trade unions are supportive of EWCs in principle, in practice such support is hampered by their lack of sufficient resources and personnel.

'German identity': between ethno- and Eurocentrism

So far, we have seen that German EWC representatives are usually both trade union members and full-time works councillors. They are deeply embedded within the German system of industrial relations. The concepts of ethno-, poly- and Eurocentrism can be applied not only to managerial but also to EWC structures. The research results have shown that German representatives have a fairly positive attitude towards EWCs in general and their own in particular, even though they may regret the lack of co-determination rights available to them at the European level. Let us now continue our search to see how German influence affects the functioning of EWCs.

In order to influence EWC structures and functions, representatives must first ensure that they are well represented on the EWC, in particular by occupying its functional posts, as chairpersons or 'EWC secretaries'[6] or members of the select committee. Waddington's (2003) study points out that the actual distribution of seats and the nationality of 'office holders' are revealing indicators of national influence on EWCs. Even within a French model EWC, German representatives can still exert a strong influence depending on how the EWC secretariat is set up and who draws up the EWC agenda (Altmeyer 2003). The chairperson and select committee will usually meet together, and ideally with management, before any issue of transnational importance has been decided on.

This research identified fifty-four (out of sixty-two) EWCs who reported that they had at least one full-time works councillor from Germany on their EWC. The exact distributions of the German seats are shown in Table 7.3.

Table 7.3 shows that among these fifty-four EWCs, 25 per cent had one full-time German representative, 17 per cent had either two or three, 20 per cent had four, and 21 per cent of them had five or more full-time

Table 7.3 Number of full-time German representatives on EWCs (*n* = 54)

No. of full-time German reps on EWCs	No. of EWCs	
	Total	*%*
1	14	25
2	9	17
3	9	17
4	11	20
5	2	4
6	4	7
10	2	4
11	1	2
15	1	2
19	1	2
Total 232	54	100

German representatives. The largest number recorded in this survey was nineteen German representatives at Continental AG (which had nineteen full-time German representatives on the EWC out of a total of thirty-two representatives).

In the survey, thirty-two companies gave details about their select committees. Thirteen of them had one representative per country on the select committee. Twenty-five of the select committees had at least one German representative, and nearly half of these (eleven) had more than one representative from Germany on the select committee.

Table 7.4 shows the German influence on the select committees of the fourteen companies interviewed in 2004. On the basis of these figures, plus other statements given in the interviews, the degree of ethno-, poly- or Eurocentrism will be considered.

As Table 7.4 shows, the first four EWCs had no select committee. German Construction 1 and German Cement 1 justified this by the small size and predominantly German (ethnocentric) orientation of their companies. German Chemical 1 officially had no select committee, but the Austrian chairperson regularly visited the German headquarters to speak to the head of human resources, and at the same time met with the German works council chairperson and EWC vice-chairperson. This meant that although the EWC was 'officially' chaired by a non-German representative, the German national chairperson was always closely involved with all EWC-related discussions. Therefore, all these three companies seemed to have ethnocentric EWCs, with power and decision-making processes closely linked to or identical with national German procedures. The German tourism company had only recently established its EWC and had not yet established a select committee. For the time being, all procedures were being dealt with by the German EWC chairperson. Belgian Food only had Belgian select committee members.

Table 7.4   Number of German representatives on select committees

EWCs interviewed	No. of representatives on select committees	No. of German office holders
German Construction 1	no select committee	0
German Chemical 1	no select committee	0
German Cement 1	no select committee	0
German Travel	no select committee	0
Belgian Food	3	0
German Construction 2	3	2
German Chemical 2	3	2
German Cement 2	3	1
German Metalworking	6	2
UK Hotel	5	1
French Chemical	7	2
Swiss Insurance	7	1
German Chemical 3	6	2
Dutch Bank	7	rotation system

The next three EWCs had small select committees with three persons. German Construction 2 and German Chemical 2 both had long-standing, Article 13 EWCs, and had their largest workforces in Germany. Both chairpersons interviewed had been involved with their respective EWCs from the start. They had tried to ensure their EWC included and involved all national groups and were generally positive about the role their EWCs had played so far. However, as we have seen, two out of three select committee members were from the home base. This was explained by practical considerations (lack of possibilities for non-German representatives to attend regular meetings in Germany). These EWCs think of themselves as polycentric, yet still retain some ethnocentric predispositions.

In the next group, there are five companies which had select committees with between five and seven members, but with no more than two German 'office holders'. Two of these companies are German-based, three foreign-based. All of these companies had more than the stipulated one EWC meeting per year; most had three or four meetings per year. They all had well-established EWCs and worked closely with national trade unions. All the German-based companies in this group and the French company were very polycentric in their attitudes. German Chemical 3 was moving beyond polycentrism to Eurocentrism. This was being intensified through common intensive training courses organised by the IG BCE and the European Union. They were developing new EWC structures and ongoing project groups together with management in-between meetings. These project groups matched the international divisional structure of the company.

Swiss Insurance had a UK chairperson (who was a fully seconded trade union official). He regarded the EWC as an important institution, but was not very satisfied with the way their EWC worked. UK Hotel had a full-time

German works councillor as its chairperson, despite initial attempts by management to insist on the chairperson being a native English speaker! The German chairperson tried very hard to make this EWC as 'European' as possible, but often experienced intercultural problems when dealing with the UK-led management side. The Swiss Insurance and the UK Hotel chairpersons were both concerned and sometimes disappointed about the lack of interest in the EWC work shown by some of their EWC colleagues. They felt that the EWC was sometimes taken more seriously by management than by the representatives. So, generally, German representatives on German-owned, polycentric EWCs seemed to be more satisfied with their EWC activities than representatives on foreign-owned polycentric EWCs with less German influence.

Finally, the EWC of the Dutch Bank must be considered. Not only is this EWC different from all the others because of its system of rotating office holder seats among all the EWC members, it also has regular, usually monthly, EWC or group committee meetings. This avoids the problem identified by Waddington (2003) of two-tier layers of knowledge and communication among EWC representatives. The Dutch chairperson emphasised that the EWC members continuously worked together with management on project committees, etc., and were involved with all international decision-making processes from the earliest stage. The only national group of EWC representatives which did not agree with this strategy was the French (active trade union) group. All the other questionnaire respondents from this company were very convinced that their EWC worked effectively and played an important role in their company's international strategy. This EWC (with the notable exception of the French participants) certainly seemed to be operating very 'Eurocentrically'.

One method to increase the profile of EWCs and help them to become 'project-orientated' or even 'participatory' has been the increased use of framework agreements. Many EWCs have begun to increase the obligations of their companies via their European (and sometimes even worldwide) workforce by signing framework agreements or joint texts. Carley's list in Hall and Marginson's (2004) EIRO report show seventeen examples of such agreements which were signed between 2002 and 2004. In this research, twelve out of the sixty-two EWCs investigated reported a total of twenty-nine framework agreements. The incidence was significantly higher in the non-German based companies. This could imply that the German representatives are fighting harder in foreign-owned companies to achieve more encompassing and codified rights for the EWC than in German-owned companies, where presumably they feel adequately protected by national rights and agreements. However, generally there was a high amount of interest in framework agreements by German EWC representatives. This policy is actively supported by German trade unions such as the IG Metall. This fits well with the German system of works councils signing company agreements.

An example of how the EWCD is less compatible with German under-standing of co-determination is the fact that German delegates seemed reluctant to fully exploit their possible powers to call 'extraordinary meet-ings'. One German chairperson brought up this point in the interview, when he said that the EWCs did not really need more power but they did need to make better use of their possibilities to demand extraordinary meetings. Demanding extraordinary meetings is regarded as quite confrontational and does not concur with German understanding of works councils acting in trust and co-operation. The German delegates would prefer more defined rights and obligations both for themselves and for management, reflecting their national identity.

The influence of language and culture

The more varied the national and cultural mix of the EWC representatives, the more difficult it is for them to operate effectively together. EWC representatives who either share a common language or speak a common second language with some degree of fluency usually have far fewer problems than when all communication has to pass through an interpreter. As Stirling and Tully (2004: 75) point out, communication ability is not just concerned with exchanging information but is 'inextricably linked with questions of power and control'. The ability to speak the 'company language' often determines which EWC representatives are able to exert the most influence. In this research, all the non-German chairpersons in German companies were from countries which were both linguistically and culturally quite close to Germany – such as Austria, Holland or Denmark. However, the most problematic cultural factor, cited again and again by interviewees and questionnaire respondents con-cerned the different industrial relations structures prevalent across Europe.

In order to understand how influence can be exerted in an international environment, the actors need to be aware of underlying cultural differences which are sometimes difficult to perceive, such as Hofstede's (1980) 'power distance' or 'uncertainty avoidance' factors. These cultural differences are usually entrenched in a complex mesh of institutional, political, religious and social practices. It is often very difficult for individuals to appreciate the extent to which 'national culture' affects their thoughts, decisions or actions. These differences only become apparent in an international environment. When 'cultures clash', as may be expected within any international group, the result may be a retreat to positions of national 'safety zones', or an offensive attack leading to open dissent and confrontation, or an exchange of views leading to a new level of understanding and co-operation. To reach a positive outcome, the actors concerned must be able to differentiate between problems which may be due to 'national', cultural effects, and those due to objective differences of opinions or approaches.

As already mentioned, language is a key, not only to communicative ability but also to power and control. Just as it is almost impossible for an international manager to not speak English nowadays, it is also difficult for EWC office holders if they are not communicatively competent in English, as well as the language of the home base. Even if translation and interpretation facilities are provided at the official EWC meetings, this is not always the case for the select committee meetings, working groups or communications between meetings. This is an issue which causes severe communications problems for some EWCs, and in particular for representatives who are 'excluded' from the main language(s).

If the company is large and German-based, the EWC representatives, or at least its office holders, are usually communicatively competent in English. As workers in large companies often have several full-time officers to choose from, it is usually those with more international interests, experience and/or language abilities who tend to be nominated for EWC posts. In smaller companies with fewer full-time officers this choice may not exist. Therefore, if the chairperson is German and the company language is German it is very difficult for any non-German speakers to gain much influence on the EWC. This was the case in several smaller 'ethnocentric' EWCs. However, in German Construction 2, where the EWC had been established for over ten years, the chairperson reported that they had recently elected a Spanish representative to the select committee and that, since then, more interpretation and translation facilities had been made available to accommodate the ensuing communication problems. In German Construction 1, the representative had been surprised that management had been willing to cover 'extra' translation and/or interpreting costs. But in the German Travel company, the EWC representatives had agreed to hold meetings without interpreting facilities, in order to save costs at a time when the company was undergoing severe economic difficulties. The justification was that most of their staff was fluent in German and English, but there were non-German representatives on their EWC who had to rely on non-expert, 'whispered' explanations. Such arrangements definitely do not comply with the EWCD provisions.

Given the role of English as an international business language, it is theoretically possible that a German-dominated ethnocentric EWC could operate in English, but this is unlikely. The delegates' ability to communicate in one or more common languages is an important prerequisite for an EWC to operate effectively, in either a poly- or Eurocentric way. Negotiating training and other facilities to improve the EWC internal communication channels is an important task, but learning languages is a time-consuming undertaking which has to be directly invested in individuals, who may later leave the EWC. Some of the older interviewees thought the problem would solve itself over time, but this will remain an ongoing problem.

A final aspect of national culture which must be mentioned is the way Germans view themselves as Europeans. On the one hand, all the German representatives interviewed felt that European integration was important and that they enjoyed the possibility of playing a role in this process within their companies. Their contact with the industrial relations systems of other European countries made them very aware of the advantages of their own system, in particular compared to their colleagues from the UK and Ireland. They sometimes had difficulties understanding the motivations and dynamics of their colleagues from France, Italy and Spain with pluralist unions. They also sometimes felt that their Scandinavian colleagues seemed to keep their distance. Thanks to the national facilities available to them German works councillors were usually well equipped, able and willing to play an active role in their respective EWCs. However, on the other hand it was important for them not to act in a dominating way. They were often wary of being seen as the 'leaders' and tried instead to pull the strings from behind (either as vice-chairs or select committee members), and tried to include the others as much as possible.

Conclusions

The influence of German identity on EWCs is complex, but of great significance because of the fact that German representatives are actively involved in over three-quarters of all EWCs, often as 'office holders'. The concepts of ethno-, poly- and Eurocentrism are useful in understanding the different ways German identity can impact on how EWCs function. While there are definitely still some ethnocentric EWCs (which may also include many German-owned companies without EWCs), this research reveals an increasing number of German representatives taking a polycentric approach to their EWCs.

Good communications and the growth of trust relationships between EWC representatives can counteract managerial attempts to play subsidiaries off against each other. In Eurocentric EWCs, the representatives regard the EWC as being even more important than the national forums, because it is here that they first receive information about international decisions, which are then implemented at the various national levels. German influence does not automatically promote Eurocentric EWCs. This is because in large German companies major decisions are made at the national level and the representatives have more powers here through their national rights. Eurocentric EWCs are very unlikely to develop unless strong industrial relation actors play a leading role, and strong support is provided by either trade unions and/or management.

The most important influences seem to be

1 the structure of the company;
2 the role played by the dominant industrial relations system(s) of the office holders;
3 the individual abilities and national characteristics of the key players.

The different ways the three factors mentioned above interact means that German influence does not always result in the same outcome. Table 7.5

summarises some of the main factors that influence the way EWCs function. Not all of these factors are national. Table 7.5 should not be interpreted in a deterministic way; the idea is to illustrate how various factors
are likely to affect the nature of the EWC.

The main conclusions which can be drawn are that most EWCs which
have a high level of German influence are either ethno- or polycentric.
Because of the size of many companies in Germany, its encompassing
industrial relations system and the large percentage of German-based companies covered by the EWCD, it is possible that there are more German-
dominated ethnocentric EWCs than ethnocentric EWCs dominated by
other national cultures. It has also been hypothesised that 'ultra-ethno-
centrism' may be a reason for the non-existence of many EWCs in German-
based companies. This research indicates that the structure of the company,
its managerial structures and the precise roles played by the German
representatives, particularly 'office holders', are important factors determining whether EWCs have a strategic predisposition to become either
ethno-, poly- or Eurocentric.

Recent economic and political developments are causing German-based
EWCs to become more polycentric. This is partly a result of the increasing
number of European mergers and acquisitions. These, in turn, are a direct
consequence of economic and monetary integration, as well as attempts to
increase European competitiveness by privatising former 'national cham-
pions'. Although polycentrism can mean that national representatives or
management try to use the international forum to promote national interests, the increased use of framework agreements shows that many EWCs are
trying to achieve common standards, or even raise standards of workplace
representation or working conditions in countries which do not have such
encompassing industrial relations systems as Germany. German representatives who have been working in well-established EWCs and who receive
trade union support are often keen to participate in these EWCs and promote activities which reflect and complement the German system. They
bemoan the lack of co-determination rights and complain that information
is often received 'too late'. However, they often seem reluctant to make full
use of their rights to call extraordinary meetings.

Eurocentric EWCs are still a rare breed. It is usually necessary for the
company to be a large and long-established transnational enterprise, with
an international management structure and a well-established EWC. The
representatives need to have a high level of cohesion and trust, which in
turn is usually a consequence of team training, high levels of managerial
support and excellent communication possibilities. So far, few German (or
other) representatives seem willing or able to relinquish their national culture and structures in order to move into this new European trajectory, with
all the risks this may incur. However, in the few cases where a Eurocentric
approach has been observed, nearly all the EWC representatives (including
the Germans) seem to find it advantageous.

Table 7.5 Influence factors and their ethno-, poly- and Eurocentric effects

Influences	Ethnocentric EWCs	Polycentric EWCs	Eurocentric EWCs
Company structure	Organic growth	Recent growth via mergers and takeovers.	Long-established transnational company.
Managerial structures	Top management all from home country.	Some foreign managers.	International team.
Size of EWC	Small (fewer than ten).	Average (ten–thirty).	Average or large (more than thirty).
Seat distribution	Most representatives from home country.	Mixed according to size and geographical distribution.	Mixed according to size and geographical distribution.
Select committee (SC) members	No select committee or majority of members from home country.	Majority of members from home country.	International mix reflecting seat distribution.
Number of meetings and contacts with management	One EWC meeting per year. Information often not timely.	One to four EWC meetings per year. Regular SC meetings. Occasional extraordinary meetings. Information sometimes too late.	Three or more meetings per year. Regular SC meetings and project groups. Continuous flow of information and consultation.
Managerial support	EWCs seen as an 'unnecessary' cost factor.	EWCs can be useful forums, particularly to help implement managerial decisions. Basic facilities and training provided.	EWCs can add value to company's international business strategy. Continuous training and facilities provided.
Industrial relations system	Representatives of home country regard national system as superior to EWC rights.	Different IR systems have different strengths and weaknesses. Framework agreements can help raise standards of low-level systems.	National systems less important as representatives concentrate on common European issues.
Language	Home country language spoken. Translation and interpretation only provided at main EWC meeting.	Translation and interpretation facilities provided as required.	Translation and interpretation facilities provided as required. Most reps are able to communicate in English.
Culture	Home culture is seen as superior to others.	EWCs are seen as important forums for learning more about other cultures.	Representatives identify with a common European culture.

Notes

1 For historical overviews of the German dual system of industrial relations see Jacobi *et al.* 1998; Hyman 2001; Müller-Jentsch and Weitbrecht 2003.
2 The German term for WCA is the *Betriebsverfassungsgesetz.*
3 Both union density and collective bargaining coverage have declined by almost 10 percentage points in the past ten years. Coverage is much lower in the eastern states, with only 23 per cent of companies participating in collective bargaining agreements. Total number of DGB members on 31 December 2004 was 7,013,037.
4 The EWC at Lufthansa is an example of this type of agreement.
5 However, this information does not always filter down to the representatives, as observed from talking to EWC representatives at training seminars between 2003 and 2005.
6 This is the common term for the main employee representative in the French model, joint employer–employee EWCs.

References

Altmeyer, W. (2003) 'Work in progress' *Die Mitbestimmung*, int. edn 08/2003, Düsseldorf: Hans-Böckler Stiftung.

Bispinck, R. and Schulten, T. (2005) 'Deutschland vor dem tarifpolitischen Systemwechsel?' *WSI Mitteilungen*, 8/2005: 466–72.

Einblick (2005) 'Neuausrichtung der Lisabon-Strategie', Vol. 7/05, DGB.

Hall, M. (2003) 'Survey highlights business benefits of EWCs', *European Industrial Relations Observatory On-line*, Ref: EU 0301204F.

Hall, M. and Marginson, P. (2004) 'Developments in European Works Councils', *European Industrial Relations Observatory On-line*, Ref: TN0411101S.

Hancké, B. (2000) 'European Works Councils and industrial restructuring in the European motor industry', *European Journal of Industrial Relations*, 6 (1): 35–59.

Hans-Böckler Stiftung (2003) 'Betriebsräte nach Branchen und Betriebsgrößen', Düsseldorf. Online. Available HTTP: http://www.boeckler.de/cps/rde/xchg/SID3-D0AB75D88F1923/hbs/hs.xsl/256_15877.html

—— (2004) 'Zur aktuellen Kritik der Mitbestimmung im Aufsichtsrat', Düsseldorf. Online. Available HTTP: http://www.boeckler.de/pdf/mitbestimmung_2004.pdf

Hofstede, G. (1980) *Culture's Consequences. International Differences in Work-related Values*, London: Sage.

Hyman, R. (2001) *Understanding European Trade Unionism*, London: Sage.

Jacobi, O., Keller, B. and Müller-Jentsch, W. (1998) 'Germany: facing new challenges', in A. Ferner and R. Hyman (eds) *Changing Industrial Relations in Europe*, Oxford: Blackwell.

Keller, B. (1995) 'European integration, workers' participation and collective bargaining: a Euro-pessimistic view', in B. Unger and F. van Waarden (eds) *Convergence or Divergence? Internationalisation and Economic Policy Responses*, Aldershot: Avebury, 252–78.

Kerckhofs, P. and Pas, I. (2004) *European Works Council Database 2004*, Brussels: ETUI.

Lecher, W., Nagel, B., Platzer, H.-W., Fulton, L., Jaich, R., Rehfeldt, U., Rüb, S., Telljohann, V. and Weiner, K.-P. (1999) *The Establishment of European Works Councils*, Aldershot: Gower.

Lecher, W., Platzer, H.-W., Rüb, S. and Weiner, K.-P. (2001) *European Works Councils: Developments, Types and Networking*, Aldershot: Gower.

Levinson, C. (1972) *International Trade Unionism*, London: Allen and Unwin.

Manager-Magazine.de (2004) 'Arbeitnehmer sollen Aufsichtsräte verlassen', SPIEGELnet GmbH. Online. Available HTTP: http://www.managermagazine.de/unternehmen/artikel/0,2828,druck-322915,00.html (accessed 10 December 2005).

Marginson, P. (2000) 'The Eurocompany and Euro industrial relations', *European Journal of Industrial Relations*, 6 (1): 9–34.

Marginson, P. and Sisson, K. (2004) *European Integration and Industrial Relations*, Basingstoke: Palgrave Macmillan.

Marginson, P., Hall, M., Hoffmann, A. and Müller, T. (2001) *The Impact of European Works Councils on Management Decision-making in Anglo-Saxon Multinationals: A Case Study Comparison*, Coventry: Industrial Relations Research Unit, University of Warwick.

Müller-Jentsch, W. (2002) 'Works councils – a German story', *Die Mitbestimmung*, int. edn, 08/2002, Düsseldorf: Hans-Böckler Stiftung.

Müller-Jentsch, W. and Weitbrecht, H. (2003) *The Changing Contours of German Industrial Relations*, Munich: Rainer Hampp-Verlag.

Niedenhoff, H. (2002) *Mitbestimmung in der Bundesrepublik Deutschland*, Köln: Deutscher Instituts-Verlag GmbH.

Perlmutter, H. (1969) 'The tortuous evolution of the multinational corporation', *Columbia Journal of World Business*, January/February: 9–18.

Schulten, T. (1996) 'European Works Councils: prospects for a new system of European industrial relations', *European Journal of Industrial Relations*, 2 (3): 303–24.

Stirling, J. and Tully, B. (2004) 'Power, process and practice: communications in European Works Councils', *European Journal of Industrial Relations*, 10 (1): 73–89.

Streeck, W. (1997a) 'Citizenship under regime competition: the case of the "European Works Councils"', Jean Monnet Chair Papers No. 42, European University Institute.

—— (1997b) 'Neither European nor Works Councils: a reply to Paul Knutsen' *Economic and Industrial Democracy*, 18 (2): 325–37.

Traxler, F. and Behrens, M. (2002) 'Collective bargaining coverage and extension procedures', *European Industrial Relations Observatory Online*. Ref: TN0212102S.

Vitols, S. (2003) 'The beginning of a beautiful friendship?' *Die Mitbestimmung*, int. edn, 08/2003, Düsseldorf: Hans-Böckler Stiftung.

Waddington, J. (2003) 'What do representatives think of the practices of European Works Councils? Views from six countries', *European Journal of Industrial Relations*, 9 (3): 303–25.

Whittall, M. (2000) 'The BMW European Works Council: a cause for European industrial relations optimism?' *European Journal of Industrial Relations*, 6 (1): 61–83.

Wills, J. (2000) 'Great expectations: three years in the life of a European Works Council', *European Journal of Industrial Relations*, 6 (1): 85–107.

8 Still learning from Europe

Spanish participation in European Works Councils

Holm-Detlev Köhler and
Sergio González Begega

In spite of several scholars' negative opinion with regard to the quantitative and qualitative advances of European Works Councils (EWCs), there is a certain evidence that these bodies have become a potential institutional basis for dealing with European firm-level social dialogue in depth. Difficulties, however, in the development of a European common identity for labour representation within EWCs seem to be among the most important barriers concerning EWCs' future, hindering further progress in European firm-level social dialogue experiences (Köhler and González Begega 2004a).

The lack of a common European identity (with regard not only to industrial relations but to the whole social and political European integration process) is a direct outcome of the diversity in EU members' institutions and in national actors' mindset, practices and expectations (see Featherstone and Radaelli (2003) for an outlook of the general obstacles being faced by the political and social Europeanisation dynamics). In short, the key issue for the development of a European industrial relations arena is how to build common institutions and co-ordinated practices and attitudes at the European Union (EU) level on top of the very different national industrial relations traditions (for a conceptualisation of the different national systems in the EU see Ebbinghaus and Visser (1992) and also Platzer and Kohl (2003) for a revision after the eastern enlargement; for a general discussion of EU identity problems, see Offe (1998)).

Regarding EWCs, the identity problem is materialised in the different nationally conditioned expectations of employee representatives towards the operation, purpose and agenda of these transnational information and consultation bodies (Lamers 1998). Some authors have argued that if EWCs do not succeed in developing a common European mindset, there will not be an 'integrated European system of representation but international extensions of the national system of workplace representation in the company's country of origin' (Streeck 1997: 331).

The aim of this chapter is to contribute to the description of the expectations and experiences of Spanish labour actors with regard to EWCs, to highlight the EU identity formation problems to be overcome, and, as far as possible, to identify the positive contribution (if there is any) coming from

Spain to develop a common identity for EWCs. We will evaluate the Spanish case, analysing the meaning and significance of the EWC process for the Spanish industrial relations institutional and agency structure, and we will also focus on the obstacles and possibilities identified by the Spanish actors for the development of this common identity.

Usually, opinions on the Europeanisation of industrial relations come from the analysis of the political and economic problems of the EU's core continental members. With regard to EWCs, most of the assessments derive from the experience of French-, German- or Nordic-owned companies, basic on well-defined institutions and practices for information and consultation. In these countries, the practice of national works councils, supported by a highly developed trade union structure, provides a strong basis for EWCs' operation.

However, this core-focused perspective misses minority representations' opinions on EU construction. Questions then arise about EWC practice in countries whose national industrial relations arrangements do not provide a strong institutional platform. This is the case of Spain, where a strongly regulated legal industrial relations framework does not correspond with the reality of labour relations practice. Our chapter also aims to fill the void about the contributions of southern Europe to this discussion.

We will start by providing a short review of the Spanish industrial relations system and its main features. The difficulty of co-ordinating national institutional diversity at EU level is particularly visible in the Spanish participation in EWCs (Traxler 2002; Marginson and Sisson 2004). This participation is characterised by an adversarial industrial relations tradition, the fact that Spanish representatives typically join EWCs from a minority position as employee representatives in subsidiaries, and a limited experience in the setting up of EWCs in Spanish-based multinationals (Aragón *et al.* 2001; Köhler and González Begega 2004a).

Following this, we will present Spanish industrial relations actors' assessments and their expectations on European firm-level dialogue. Later we will evaluate their proposals to meet the co-operation and co-ordination requirements of these bodies, identified as basic preconditions to mobilise EWCs' potential. And finally we will assess whether there is any positive contribution coming from the Spanish experience in order to help the consolidation of a European mindset for EWCs.

The Spanish experience with EWCs

The Spanish industrial relations system

Before analysing the Spanish participation in EWCs, we consider it necessary to briefly outline the main institutional pillars of the Spanish industrial relations system and to identify its main actors after the fall of the Franco regime in 1975 and the subsequent democratic transition.

Many authors consider the Spanish industrial relations system to be immature and still in the process of formation. In spite of a radical modernisation during the last twenty-five years, it is still characterised by the weight of its institutional legacy (Crouch 1993). The process initiated in 1975 has implied the progressive retreat of a centralised and interventionist state, conceived as the regulator of all the spheres of activity, public and private, and the beginning of a transition that finally led to the entry of Spain into the European Economic Community in 1986. In parallel, a process of privatisation of publicly owned industry has reduced the importance of the state in the economy.

The first decade of political transition after the enactment of the constitution of 1978 was marked by the development of a detailed legal framework for industrial relations and the progressive stabilisation and adaptation of the social partners to the new democratic framework. Four main trends characterise this transition to a democratic industrial relations system:

1 the intention of the state to develop some kind of *trilateralism* and a spirit of social partnership at the national level materialised in the so-called Moncloa Pacts from 1977[1] and in the 1980 Workers' Statute, the constitutive law of the new democratic industrial relations;
2 the interest in consolidating and institutionalising the major trade unions, Union General de Trabajadores (UGT) and Comisiones Obreras (CCOO) and the employers' association, Confederacion Española de Organizaciones Empresariales (CEOE);
3 the markedly political attitude of the social partners during the democratic transition;
4 the extremely high unemployment and industrial dispute rates.

On this basis, an industrial relations system emerged defined by the following features: *omnipresent* labour regulation affecting all spheres of activity; a *dual* structure of employee representation through trade unions and works councils; a low trade union density between 15 and 20 per cent of the workforce; a government interest in promoting social dialogue between the social partners; and a high coverage level of collective bargaining, between 70 and 80 per cent, due to the automatic extension of collective agreements (*erga omnes* clause).

Works councils in Spain are union action and collective bargaining bodies. They have information and consultation rights, and also duties regarding the monitoring of the implementation of some legal, health and safety, training and disciplinary issues at shop floor level, but no co-determination rights. They also have strike initiative rights, but compared with works councils in Nordic and central Europe, participation is limited.

The dual collective bargaining structure, through trade unions and works councils, is highly complex and fragmented at multiple levels: firm, industry, regional, industry-regional, etc. The fragmentation itself, the stance of the employers' association in favour of decentralisation of negotiation, the consecutive reforms oriented to make the labour market more flexible, both from left wing (1982–96) and right wing (1996–2004) governments, have brought about an effective trend towards the decentralisation of collective bargaining to the company level. Recent labour reforms from 1997 onwards, however, attempt to compensate for this trend, reserving certain topics for inter-professional and sectoral collective bargaining (Köhler and González Begega 2002).

The Spanish participation in firm-level Europeanisation of industrial relations

In Spain, from the very beginning, law and not tripartite agreement was the preferred choice for implementing the EWC Directive. After the preparation of the law through consultations between the government and the social partners and its endorsement by the Spanish Economic and Social Council, the EWC Directive was transposed through the Law 10/1997 on information and consultation rights of employees in Community-scale firms and groups, 24 April 1997.

The direct influence of the directive on the Spanish industrial relations system was kept to a minimum, since EWCs were fitted into existing arrangements. As the impact on national industrial relations depends mainly on the institutional framework, particularly whether representation bodies similar to works councils already exist, in Spain the EWCs fitted very well into the industrial relations framework, mirroring the legal position of shop floor works councils. The legal outcome of the process of transposition also set up protection mechanisms for EWC representatives and reserved to the trade unions the key role of appointing the members of special negotiation bodies and EWCs.

There are relatively few multinational companies headquartered in Spain, and the Spanish transposition of the directive has not attracted non-European firms to establish their EWCs under the Spanish legal framework.[2] Therefore there are relatively few Spanish EWCs. Before the EU enlargement, by May 2004 Spain headquartered thirty-six companies covered by the directive. After May 2004, following several assessments made of the number of additional companies headquartered in Spain which come within the scope of the directive as a result of employees in the ten new member states, it was estimated by the CCOO that around fifty-six Spanish firms are covered by the directive. But what requires analysis is why only seven of the original thirty-six companies have set up an EWC[3] (CES 2004). This represented only 19 per cent of the covered firms, while the corresponding figure for the European Economic Area is around one-third. Furthermore, with one of these seven firms moving its European headquarters to Hungary (see note 2) and with twenty additional eligible companies after the enlargement, figures dropped to a poor 11 per cent.

Since we do not argue that Spanish trade unionists and workers' representatives in multinational companies are slower off the mark exercising their rights than their colleagues in other countries, the explanation for the significantly lower Spanish figure may lie in the features that determine Spanish participation in EWCs.

Possibly the first limitation for the development of EWCs in Spanish firms is the structure of the national industrial and labour market. Spain is dominated by a small and medium-sized nationally limited firm structure, and the bigger companies tend to make use of outsourcing, subcontracting and diversification practices, which hinder the setting up of clear negotiation processes. This *pocket firm structure* restricts trade union activity and limits interest towards EWCs.[4] If we use this term to define relatively small multinational firms, with a workforce just over the directive thresholds and exhibiting frequently low trade union density, the setting up of an EWC becomes a very difficult task and is not a priority, either for the management or for workers' representatives. If what we define by pocket multinational is a fair-sized company, but with very limited international operations, there will be no EWC for other reasons. The weight of the domestic operations of the firm explains why the creation of an EWC is not a priority, because management and workers' representatives can solve their problems at local and national level.

The second characteristic that limits the setting up of EWCs in Spain is that large Spanish multinational companies, mainly privatised firms belonging to the financial, energy and communication sectors, have orientated their internationalisation not to the European Union but to Latin America. As a consequence of these two characteristics, Spanish employee representatives have mainly experienced EWCs from their position as workers in subsidiaries, and this has conditioned their problems and prospects (Aragón *et al.* 2001).

Beside these two characteristics, Köhler and González Begega (2004a), in one of the few studies published in Spain on EWCs, found four additional reasons rooted in the Spanish industrial relations tradition to explain why the remaining covered firms have not even started to set up an EWC:

1 The relatively low trade union presence in Spanish multinational firms effectively stops workers from going ahead and initiating the process of negotiating an EWC.
2 The lack of a structure of collective bargaining and of works councils at the national level: in Spain, the arenas for collective bargaining are essentially regional and industry-regional,[5] and there is not a comprehensive structure of *single* bodies for representation at the national firm level. As a result, the move to create EWCs is not stimulated, but actually hindered, by this lack of national firm-level committees and the practical absence of communications between workers in different plants across the country. This lack of national bodies for the co-ordination of

plant-level work councils also disrupts the relationship between workers and their representatives in EWCs and leads to a misunderstanding of the functions of EWCs in the workforce. The employees usually regard the activities of the EWC as distant and not very useful. As workers fail to understand these bodies, EWCs are underdeveloped in Spain.

3   The non-existent multinational culture among Spanish managers and social partners: from a Spanish point of view, the internationalisation of the firm is something that started at the beginning of the 1990s. Spanish firms, in a short period of time, had to assume new structural obligations deriving from their new international engagement. Their late internationalisation is frequently based on an *ethnocentric* model of development, with a closely monitored human relations management function (see Bartlett and Ghoshal 1989). This model, which is an outcome of the survival of national practices and structures, partially explains why Spanish multinational firms have found it easier to implement their practices in Latin American markets than in the European Union. As a result of the late internationalisation of Spanish firms, the trade unions have only recently recognised the significance and implications of global, and indeed European, operations. They started to commit themselves seriously with EWCs and to improve their skills in this area only when feeling the special consequences of the link between transnational restructuring and EU enlargement, both for Spanish-owned firms and for multinational subsidiaries in Spain. Delocalisation, transfers of production and job cuts due to international competition are now on the agenda of Spanish trade union officials and have probably been the bitter reason for their new interest in European industrial relations (Köhler and González Begega 2004b).

4   The adversarial tradition of the Spanish industrial relation system itself, based on the definition of the social partners as adversaries, as opposed to the Continental and Nordic consensual models which inspired the EWC Directive.

From a Spanish employer point of view, an EWC, with its information and consultation guaranteeing character, implies the danger of a loss of business control. In general, Spanish managers are eager to limit the role of EWCs and to retain managerial control of the processes of information and consultation. This attitude has effectively blocked one of the possibilities of initiating the setting up of EWCs, namely management starting the ball rolling and leading the negotiating procedure, and has contributed to spreading a passive climate towards EWCs among Spanish actors.

Characteristic Spanish corporate attitudes can reasonably be described by a predisposition on the part of management towards pursuing a *damage limitation* approach with regard to EWCs (see Hall *et al.* 2003 for a similar approach in Anglo-Saxon management). The general determination of human resource managers in Spanish firms is to prevent the establishment of an EWC and, once it has been established, to avoid a proactive approach, blocking its development or policing its limits.

These cultural attitudes, alongside structural factors (as the mentioned lack of communication channels at national level between plants of the same firm), suggest that the Spanish representatives may be (or feel) less comfortable within EWCs than their counterparts from Continental and Nordic Europe, who have a more developed experience of consensual industrial relations and works council co-ordination at national level.

On the whole, there are a range of problems stemming from the immaturity and lack of confidence characterising Spanish industrial relations. Besides, trade unions do not seem to understand the functions of EWCs well and tend to misinterpret them in the light of their national practices.

Spanish trade union officials argue that the cause of the under-development of EWCs in Spanish multinational firms is the lack of a culture of dialogue among the managers. This may be true, but it is also certain that the trade unions have not made enough efforts to change that situation, taking advantage of the possibilities for dialogue and confidence offered by EWCs. Probably, as a consequence of the particularities of the Spanish industrial relations system, EWCs have not been considered a trade union priority. Furthermore, unions' federative structure, by industry and by region, built to fit the Spanish structure of collective bargaining, is a source of weakness for the strategy of trade unions. It blocks the access to national and foreign multi-industry and multinational firms, and it reduces their ability to force managers to accept and support EWCs.

As argued elsewhere, countries like Spain with relatively few domestically based multinational firms suffer additional disadvantages, such as the possibility of being left in a secondary position in EWCs of foreign-based firms and bearing the costs of learning to understand the culture of industrial relations of the parent company (CCOO 2003; Ferner 1997).

The lack of Spanish multinational companies directly engaged in the process of Europeanisation of industrial relations at the firm level is also harmful for the quality of the participation of employers and trade unions in other processes at sectoral and interprofessional level. Undoubtedly, leading the process of setting up an EWC as a worker representative of the parent company is not the same as simply joining the EWC as a representative of a subsidiary, when all important decisions have already been taken.

EWCs from the perspective of Spanish labour and employers

As already indicated, the views of Spanish employees and trade union officials on EWCs and the Europeanisation of industrial relations have changed significantly in recent times. The European level is starting to be perceived as the natural arena for solving those transnational challenges that cannot be dealt with in national arrangements.

In the following paragraphs we will refer to the opinions and expectations of the actors with regard to EWCs, as they are shaped by the conditions of their participation in these bodies. Following Waddington (2003) we have distinguished the opinion of trade union officials from that of EWC representatives, mainly because the former often have a broader perspective about the process and because frequently they are more capable of linking EWCs and worker representation at transnational level, on the one hand, with the erosion of national borderlines for trade union action, on the other hand. Therefore, we will begin with their opinion, then we will evaluate that of EWC representatives, often more connected with practical problems, and finally we will consider the stance of the Spanish employers' association.

Trade union officials

Spanish trade union positions about EWCs have changed significantly over the last few years. As Spain has experienced the consequences of the eastern enlargement of the EU in a special manner, becoming an 'old periphery' area, the European level is achieving increasing importance in the minds of the Spanish trade union officials. Since 1999, the two major trade union confederations, CCOO and UGT, have followed the ETUC line in demanding a revision of the directive to reinforce information and consultation provisions, to clarify the concept of supranational issues to be dealt with by EWCs, and to include a clear status for trade unions. Further development of EWCs requires a clearer set of rights.

Although they consider the revision of the directive a priority, they also coincide with our argument to underscore the significance of the day-to-day practices of EWCs. The creation of a common European mindset in EWCs becomes a basic component in their objective of avoiding traumatic delocalisation, transfers of production, through these bodies.

Being aware of the limits of EWCs, there is little talk of transnational bargaining as an EWC function, but they do discuss transnational firm co-ordination on non-wage issues such as labour conditions, health and safety, flexibility and productivity, environmental policy or corporate social responsibility. Both the CCOO and the UGT are co-ordinating their participation in European structures quite well, defining common strategies and standpoints and sharing joint objectives, as this interviewed Spanish trade union official states:

> We have been working at EMCEF on two or three new objectives for EWCs' basic competencies. The EWCs must go further in their information and consultation rights; we have to define clearly what we understand by these two terms ... we must have a real right to participate ... Talking about a European agreement on wages is a utopia ... but I don't want a German wage, what I want is to converge

on working conditions to compete on an equal basis ... not being
forced to accept cutbacks in production because we have a lower level
of productivity.

(Spanish trade union official)

Spanish trade union officials point out two basic obstacles for the development of this kind of European identity in EWCs. They complain about
the problem of diversity in EWCs and their functioning as mere fora for
national interest representation. To the well-known institutional and cultural diversity, they add the problem of a lack of unionisation and discipline, which might be a particular Spanish difficulty not to be found in
those countries where EWC representatives are well linked to union
organisations.

National diversity in the EU affects all dimensions of the Europeanisation of industrial relations, from tripartite social dialogue to transnational
co-ordination of collective bargaining policies. The Spanish trade union
officials are well aware of this and base their evaluation of the problems and
potentials of EWCs on this argument.

The first consequence of this national institutional and practice diversity
in EWCs is a lack of mutual confidence among representatives from different countries. The absence of a co-operative attitude sometimes leads to
open struggles for dominance in the distribution of seats. In case of imbalance between a dominant national group and several minority delegations, a
well-known situation for Spanish representatives, the latter may opt to
develop passive attitudes, concentrate on national action, and effectively
block transnational co-operation.

Trade union officials regret the lack of interest of representatives from
well-developed industrial relations systems with a prominent position in
EWCs, concerning the problematic situation of minority groups and their
engagement in identity-building. They usually point out the fundamental
role of the European industry federations in helping the development of
EWC identity, but in their opinion there is the problem that some national
trade unions do not actively support these organisations. Those from well-
developed industrial relations systems often perceive the European level as
no progress at all compared with their home system, while those from less
developed systems often feel disappointed and opt for non-constructive
attitudes.

In fact, the only European industry federation with a real transnational
mandate from its members is the European Metalworkers Federation ...
We have to overcome the reluctance of national trade union organisations to transfer powers and resources to the European level, and this
will have direct consequences in the promotion of good practice in
EWCs.

(Spanish trade union official)

Therefore, in their opinion, the key factor blocking the development of a common identity within EWCs is the existence of an unbalanced power distribution in labour representation. In their view, the recent enlargement introduces even more diversity into European industrial relations. For an already feeble process, the enlargement means even more heterogeneity in addition to the traditional European north–south divide.

> Globalisation has come to stay ... it is very difficult to establish common positions and interests between such different countries. At first they will be absolutely delighted to receive transfers of productive capacity from western Europe and it will be very difficult to achieve some basic solidarity between us and them.
>
> (Spanish trade union official)

They consider that the Spanish participation in EWCs will be harmed, as the redistribution of seats will have negative effects on the old national minority representations. In fact, the enlargement is expected to cause further fragmentation of EWCs. What would be the consequences of this further fragmentation? We may state at least two: (1) if the EWC was already controlled by a national majority group, the enlargement could reinforce its position, hindering alliances between minority delegations; and (2) if the EWC had a balanced representation, the enlargement would introduce more heterogeneity and it would become increasingly harder for worker representatives to come to common standpoints.

> We must try to persuade them to avoid practices of social dumping ... we must know one another ... Also, multinational firms shouldn't get into a labour cost comparative strategy inside the European Union.
>
> (Spanish trade union official)

To complete this mainly pessimistic evaluation, trade union officials identify a second, maybe particular Spanish, problem in giving EWCs an identity, regarding the deficiencies in the relationship between representatives and trade unions and the risk of the appearance of some sort of company trade unionism inside EWCs.

In Spain, the mechanism for choosing EWC representatives depends on the membership of a plant works council. In theory, EWC representatives are selected among the different plants of the firm in the country. Nevertheless, we have found that it is a common habit to send representatives from dominant plants in terms of workforce size, seniority or trade union density rates; these representatives are frequently unaware of the specific situation of the other plants they represent on the EWC. The absence of structures at national level for the co-ordination of shop floor work councils causes a gap between the local and the European level of workers' representation.

As the directive points out, it is not necessary to be a member of a trade union to participate in the EWC as an employee representative. Nevertheless, in practice almost every Spanish EWC representative belongs to one of the two main Spanish trade unions or secondarily to a regional trade union, such as the Basque ELA-STV.[6]

Union membership partially determines the point of view of the delegates and theoretically solves intra-firm communication gaps through an external mechanism of trade union co-ordination (similar to the activity of the European industry federations, but at national industry level). However, the scarcity of resources available, the existence of several trade union confederations involved in this co-ordination and the vertical weakness of the federal structure of the Spanish trade unions, all cause the practical ineffectiveness of most of these efforts.

The Spanish trade union officials are aware of the potential EWCs have for management in developing a corporative culture and excluding trade unions from firm-level industrial relations.

We have detected dichotomies and micro-political struggles between trade union co-ordinators and EWC representatives. Although this may seem odd, because as we have already said the mechanism for appointing EWC delegates is headed by the trade unions, the fact is that some trade union officials talk about a problematic unionism among EWC representatives. This problem must be considered in addition to a growing presence of non-unionised EWC delegates in the service sector, related to what trade union officials understand as an attempt of the management to 'tame' the representation of employees at both local and European firm level.

> It is very difficult for us to manage a complicated one hundred or one hundred and fifty EWC map ... Sometimes we don't have information about an EWC because its representative, even if he is a member of our trade union, doesn't report anything back to us ... Sometimes our representatives participate in the meetings of the EWC and simply say whatever they want ... One way or the other, what we need is to co-ordinate their activities ... but it is very difficult ... really, personally I don't know more than half of the representatives I co-ordinate.
> (Spanish trade union official, responsible for the co-ordination of EWCs)

This concern often places EWC representatives in the middle of gunfire between trade unions and firm management. Trade union officials in Spain argue that this problem will only be overcome with the revision of the directive along the lines proposed by the European Trade Union Confederation.

> We need a revised directive that recognises our right to participate in EWC meetings ... but we also need to discipline the activity of our representatives in EWCs ... it is very difficult for non-unionised

representatives to recognise that they represent the whole workforce of a country ... they must also have a general view of the company ... sometimes it is very complicated to co-ordinate and be informed because firms have many resources to discipline and 'tame' their employees.

(Spanish trade union official)

To conclude, quoting a statement of another trade union official, the construction of a common identity for EWCs is now more complicated than ever:

It will be necessary to overcome the domination of EWCs by representatives of the home country of the firm and reduce power imbalance among national delegations in order to create a real European body ... An important transformation of trade union attitudes will also be necessary to go beyond national concerns ... this kind of attitudinal change in the strongest national trade unions would help minority representations to adopt a more committed disposition towards EWCs.

(Spanish trade union official)

EWC representatives

Worker representatives share the major part of trade union officials' opinion about general problems of EWCs. First, because almost every Spanish EWC delegate is also a member of a trade union and is co-ordinated by a trade union official. And second, because several trade union officials are full members of EWCs themselves.

Without going deeper into cultural particularities, we will now show some of the practical problems hindering a better EWC practice from the point of view of the Spanish representatives.

First, their condition as employees of a subsidiary firm determines their expectations and opinions. In many cases they joined the EWC without having taken part in its setting-up negotiations and frequently without knowing the exact meaning and the specific extent of their participation. As one Spanish EWC representative told us, in the beginning he was there 'just because we had to be there ... and without knowing very well why and what for'.

Second, they refer to several difficulties that obstruct the operational practice and reduce their interest in effectively participating in EWCs. Obviously, as Lamers (1998) argues, the assessment of these bodies depends on the expectations and hopes the interested parties have. In the Spanish case, attitudes and expectations depend on an already mentioned adversarial industrial relations tradition. Therefore, the incorporation into these bodies of dialogue at European level, inspired on the co-operative industrial relations model, implies a novelty and poses positioning and understanding problems to actors used to acting in other environments.

We have found several complaints on the functions and practice of EWCs among the Spanish representatives. Some of them coincide with weaknesses identified by the literature of European industrial relations and others depend on specific national factors:

1   The presence of dominant national groups in EWCs, generally from the home base of the firm, makes it difficult to gain access to the information and consultation rights on an equal basis for all members.
2   The language constitutes an insurmountable problem, hindering the establishment of informal and more frequent contacts between formal meetings. The lack of knowledge of the industrial relations traditions represented on the labour side in EWCs also poses a major communication barrier:

> Our relations inside the EWC depend on personal affinities ... we have simultaneous translation to all the languages at the meetings, but it would be more interesting to have the possibility of establishing informal relationships with our colleagues ... language is a huge barrier that prevents us from establishing direct contact with other representatives.
>
> (Spanish EWC representative 1)

> We have a big problem with language ... but also with our different ways of doing things.
>
> (Spanish EWC representative 2)

3   Many representatives are not totally sure of the objectives and competencies of EWCs. The Spanish word for consultation (*consulta*) can be easily misinterpreted in terms of entailing workers' approbation or reprobation rights. In fact, the boundaries between information and consultation on the one hand, and bargaining on the other, are more diffuse in practical terms in the Spanish industrial relations system than in those of the other continental EU member states.

Whatever representatives understand about competencies of EWCs they would like to obtain bargaining rights:

> As the EWC has no bargaining capacity we can only support local actions and decisions taken by plant works councils ... it would be interesting to provide EWCs with true negotiating power, but for the moment this is not possible.
>
> (Spanish EWC representative)

As they work at the local as well as the European level, EWC representatives can easily compare what they obtain in material terms from both. Therefore, for some the shop floor level is still the important one, while to date 'EWCs are more or less decorative European elements'.

Bad experiences on delocalisation with inoperative EWCs strengthen these opinions. But on the other hand there are also other representatives that recognise EWCs potential, with awareness of the existence of positive examples of EWCs' in dealing with corporative restructuring.

It is hardly surprising that those representatives with a more positive evaluation were members of EWCs that were able to agree on its practical function and government with the management, for example establishing additional meetings or a stable and functioning steering committee. Many representatives stressed the importance of these permanent bodies in developing common labour-side positions and in generating confidence among EWC members.

The Spanish employers' association (CEOE)

The CEOE serves as an advisor for the Spanish firms covered by the directive. Their experts basically coincide with our analysis and explain the lack of Spanish-based EWCs as a result of a

> lack of interest both from trade unions and management ... As a result of the very small size of the Spanish firms covered by the directive, they found it very difficult to implement an efficient EWC because of costs ... In the last five years we only have had five or six Spanish firms interested in EWCs and we don't think this situation is going to change after the enlargement of the European Union.
>
> (CEOE official)

As to the regulative basis of EWCs, the CEOE also supports the UNICE position. Considering the revision of the directive, CEOE's experts argued when the deadline for revision came in 1999:

> We are against the revision of the directive and we consider that in this case, the real revolution is to observe the normative ... If we want a well-functioning transnational information and consultation system to communicate certain strategic issues to the workforce, like delocalisation, transfer of production, organisational changes, new policies of human resource management or general goals of the firm ... we don't need to alter the directive in an unknown direction ... because it is really working fairly ... but to promote an organisational change to alter the view some firms have about their EWC ... We can't change the directive until it is fully implemented.
>
> (CEOE official)

Possibly as a consequence of the limited number of Spanish firms with EWCs, CEOE officials have always been against going beyond and extending EWCs' rights. Conditioned by the Spanish authoritarian and paternalistic industrial relations tradition, they see EWCs neither as valuable bodies for corporate management nor as possibilities to enable information and participation of employees and to help in building up new firm communication channels. Instead, they consider that even the soft participation rights enacted by the directive are slightly inappropriate, since worldwide increased competition makes them unsuitable.

On the other hand, CEOE officials support our considerations about the significance of the practical dimension of EWCs, when arguing that their successful development depends less on further European legal norms than on a genuinely co-operative mindset:

> EWCs only function well in those companies with a previous willingness. Those without this frame of mind consider EWCs as purely formalities, both by managers and employee representatives.
>
> (CEOE official)

The very limited direct experience of the Spanish employers' association with the construction of European firm-level industrial relations has blocked any evolution towards a new co-operative approach. Once again, the Spanish particularities cause the appearance of specific attitudes and expectations towards EWCs. The CEOE defends a classical, non-constructive employers' organisation position, reinforced by the difficulties it had to face participating in EWC processes as a representative of multinational firms, although without fundamental prominence in them. As a result, there are few positive conclusions in CEOE's evaluation of EWCs. This might be seen as an additional confirmation of the importance of a practical and informal way of developing EWCs in day-to-day relations between worker representatives and management.

Conclusion: learning from EWCs but unable to contribute decisively for the time being

Proposals and evaluations from the Spanish experience with EWCs are oddly contradictory. On the one hand, this participation is limited, although it is also true that this typically minority participation is enriching the development of EWCs.

Like other national representations in EWCs, Spanish delegates came up against more negative than positive experiences. There is no significant contribution in terms of best practice except in isolated cases, where these representatives also hold positions of responsibility at European level (for example, the EWC co-ordination function in a European industry federation) and to a smaller extent where they are national trade union officials; or, in some recently privatised firms, where the works councils have a consolidated tradition in co-determination rights at board level.

On the other hand, labour-side answers underline the pedagogical potential of EWCs, as they have turned out to be a useful source of knowledge for Spanish trade union officials and worker representatives, helping them in joining and understanding the process of Europeanisation of industrial relations.

But even in positive assessments, Spanish trade union officials and representatives question whether EWCs could be evaluated as functioning bodies providing employees with valuable information on transnational issues such as investments, delocalisation and corporative restructuring, first because management attitudes pose practical limits for information and consultation, and second because there is a lack of articulation between workers and their representatives in EWCs.

Although EWCs are helping Spanish workers to be more aware of the significance and the implications of being employed in a multinational firm as opposed to national or local undertakings vaguely dependent on distant foreign companies, the absence of communication channels linking trade unions, EWC representatives and workers hinders a positive evaluation of the process.

Representatives and trade union officials coincide in the identification of a consensual orientation as a basic precondition for a positive EWC development. They also argue that a revision of the directive is needed to improve the provisions of information in terms of quality, quantity and timeliness and to develop genuine consultation processes. Probably both premises must be linked if EWCs are to represent the first step in the construction of a European industrial relations system at company level.

Spanish representatives also mentioned the classical communication and practical problems in EWC practice (material resources, existence of further meetings, development of an active steering committee) and the need to train EWC members in language and economic and industrial relations skills. There is also some kind of hidden accusation to national majority groups of ignoring minority representations and hampering the development of positive labour-side dynamics.

In spite of these complaints there is no evidence that employee-side actors from dominant countries are less committed to developing an influential role for EWCs based on mutual understanding and confidence. On the contrary, our findings in several French- and German-based multinationals suggest that they are more likely to have the necessary resources and skills to play a positive leading role in the EWC. Unfortunately, difficulties in having access to information and consultation rights usually refer to limitations among Spanish employee representatives themselves.

For the time being, several shortcomings are conditioning the Spanish participation in EWCs. The process of building a common European identity for these bodies is being led and effectively developed by national dominant groups within the EWCs, coming from those industrial relations systems which inspired the process. They have more experience in addressing issues of worker participation at corporative level, and sometimes this makes minority delegations feel like guests in somebody else's house.

As we have already argued, presently the EWC process has a pedagogical component for the actors of industrial relations in Spain. Trade union officials and EWC representatives are still learning to act at the transnational level. Their case demonstrates to the new eastern European members of the EU that it is possible to join and learn from these bodies, and probably this is the main positive conclusion we can obtain from the Spanish experience with EWCs. Except for some isolated cases, the development of a genuine Spanish contribution to EWCs' identity will take considerably longer.[7]

Notes

1 The Moncloa Pacts, signed by all the political parties with the support of the social agents, started a period of national social and economic pacts, headed by the government and lasting until 1985.
2 There are only two non-EU based companies headquartered in Spain with an established EWC, General Electric Consumer Industries-GE Power Control Iberica and Tudor Exide Technologies-Grupo Praxair. The former started to move its European headquarters to Hungary in May 2004.
3 Grupo Repsol-YPF (2001); Cia. Roca Radiadores S.A. (2000); Cia. Grupo Praxair (2000); General Electric Power Control Iberica (1999); Altadis S.A. (2003); Sociedad Anonima Industrias Celulosa Aragonesa (SAICA) (2004); Banco Bilbao Vizcaya Argentaria (BBVA) (2004). The other Spanish financial sector giant, Banco Santander Central Hispano (BSCH), does not have an EWC to date, but this is expected to change after the takeover of British Abbey National.
4 After the enlargement, the majority of the new Community-scale companies headquartered in Spain are not major undertakings, either in Spain or in their overseas operations, and have relatively few workers. None have started the process of setting up an EWC and it is unlikely that they will do so soon.
5 And also at workshop level, as a result of the process of decentralisation of collective bargaining experimented by the EU economies in the last decade (Köhler and González Begega 2002).
6 We can find exceptions to this general trend only in the less unionised service sector.
7 All the interview references included in this text belong to fieldwork developed during 2003 and 2004 for a research project financed by the Spanish Department of Science and Technology. This fieldwork was carried out through semi-structured interviews with social partner officials, managers of multinational firms and EWC representatives in Spain, and also ongoing EWC documentation such as agendas, minutes and other texts provided by our interviewees.

References

Aragón Medina, J., Estrada, B., Rocha, F. and Sanz, F. (2001) 'Los Comités de Empresa Europeos en España', *Cuadernos de Información Sindical*, 14, Madrid: CSCCOO.
Bartlett, C. and Ghoshal, S. (1989) *Managing across Borders. The Transnational Solution*, London: Century Business.
CCOO (Comisiones Obreras) (2003) 'Informe de conclusiones sobre el Seminario M.I.E.R.' (Medidas innovadoras frente a las reestructuraciones), Barcelona, 20–21 February.

CES (Consejo Económico y Social) (2004) 'Diez años de la Directiva de Comités de Empresa Europeos: Avances y nuevos retos en 2004', no. 67, Madrid: CES.

Crouch, C. (1993) *Industrial Relations and European State Traditions*, Oxford: Clarendon Press.

Ebbinghaus, B. and Visser, J. (1992) 'Making the most of diversity? European integration and transnational organisation of labour', in J. Greenwood, J. Grote and K. Ronit (eds) *Organised Interests and the European Community*, London: Sage, 206–37.

Featherstone, K. and Radaelli, C.M. (eds) (2003) *The Politics of Europeanisation*, Oxford: Oxford University Press.

Ferner, A. (1997) 'Country of origin effects and HRM in MNC companies', *Human Resource Management Journal*, 7 (1): 19–37.

Hall, M., Hoffman, A., Marginson, P. and Müller, T. (2003) 'National influences on EWCs in UK- and US-based companies', *Human Resource Management Journal*, 13 (4): 75–92.

Köhler, H.-D. and González Begega, S. (2002) 'Las relaciones industriales en España', in L. Pries and M. Wannöffel (eds) *Regímenes de regulación en la globalización*, Bochum: Bochum University Press, 109–36.

—— (2004a) '¿Hacia un sistema de relaciones industriales europeo? La experiencia de los Comités de Empresa Europeos (CEUs)', *Cuadernos de Relaciones Laborales*, 22 (1): 7–36.

—— (2004b) 'Towards a new enlarged industrial relations model? Extracting useful conclusions from the Spanish experience with European Works Councils', paper presented to the IREC 2004 Conference Utrecht, 26–28 August.

Lamers, J. (1998) *The Added Value of European Works Councils*, Haarlem: AWVN.

Marginson, P. and Sisson, K. (2004) *European Integration and Industrial Relations*, Hampshire: Palgrave Macmillan.

Offe, C. (1998) 'Demokratie und Wohlfahrtsstaat: eine europäische Regimeform wider den Streß der europäischen Integration', in W. Streeck (ed.) *Internationale Wirtschaft, nationale Demokratie*, Frankfurt and New York: Campus, 99–136.

Platzer, H.-W. and Kohl, H. (2003) 'Labour relations in central and eastern Europe and the European Social Model', *Transfer*, 9 (1): 11–30.

Streeck, W. (1997) 'Neither European nor Works Councils: a reply to Paul Knutsen', *Economic and Industrial Democracy*, 18 (2): 325–37.

Traxler, F. (2002) 'European Monetary Union and collective bargaining', Working Paper 207/02, Barcelona: Institut de Ciències Politiques i Socials.

Waddington, J. (2003) 'What do representatives think of the practices of EWCs? Views from six countries', *European Journal of Industrial Relations*, 9 (3): 303–25.

9 Interest representation and European identity

A twofold challenge for European Works Councils

Volker Telljohann

In this chapter we analyse the conditions under which a European collective identity is likely to develop within European Works Councils (EWCs). The arguments are based on the results taken from a case study-based project[1] designed to draw up a qualitative inventory relating to the operation of EWCs and outcomes produced so far by these new European employee representation bodies. To this end the research project studies the 'inner life' of EWCs: that is, the structures and processes of communication, patterns of interaction within EWCs and between EWCs as well as other actors in the industrial relations system. These cover not only formal arrangements, but also informal information and communication networks.

As a consequence the project set out to undertake a qualitative investigation into the entirety of the processes of communication and interaction that condition and affect the constitution as well as the shape of EWCs. This involved a systematic study into the subjective dimension of the interests, motives, expectations and perceptions of the actors involved and of the barriers to socio-cultural interaction characterising the operation of the EWCs.

In the chapter we try to answer two closely related questions:

- What are the conditions under which an EWC can become a genuine European body of employee representation?
- Under what conditions is a European collective identity likely to develop within EWCs?

Through a field analysis of forty cases carried out in 2002–3, the project also aimed to provide some suggestions for improving the effectiveness and efficiency of EWCs (Telljohann 2005a, 2005b).

While at the beginning of this contribution we intend to briefly discuss the most relevant research results regarding the general functioning of EWCs, in part two the chapter analyses the role of EWCs in the context of restructuring processes. In the final section, we try to identify the prerequisites for identity-building processes within EWCs.

The functioning of EWCs

The research results show that in most cases there is a need for EWCs to improve their functioning (Weiler 2004). In particular, it seems to be important to guarantee a functional information and communication system, both within EWCs and between EWCs and the other actors, such as works councils and outside union structures in the various countries. With regard to the functioning of EWCs, it appears that the temporal dimension has a certain importance. In some of the EWCs that have existed for some time, an evolutionary trend can be observed, this involving a learning process, which has led to an improvement in their functioning.

The results of the case studies also show that there is a strong need for training in order to develop the individual capabilities of EWC members, to provide them with skills to deal with the specific demands arising from their role as European-level representatives. There is a particular interest among the delegates to receive information about the various industrial relations systems and, in particular, about the bargaining systems in the various countries represented in the respective EWCs. As regards the qualification processes, the trade unions seem to play an important role for EWCs. Most EWC members stress the general importance of trade union support for the efficacy and efficiency of EWC activities.

With regard to the co-operation between EWCs and national trade unions, it can be observed that the latter are investing both politically and in terms of resources in the EWCs of TNEs based in the home country and less so in the EWCs of foreign groups. The objective behind this choice probably consists in maintaining control within the scope of the industrial relations at group level. Especially in countries characterised by a one-tier system of interest representation, it may happen that trade unions have an influence on EWCs similar to the one they exert on national bodies of interest representation. In these cases the EWCs risk being relegated to a mere extension of the respective national industrial relations system. The dominant influence of the home country's industrial relations culture can contribute to undermining the internal cohesion of the EWCs.

In general, the level of integration of the EWCs into the national systems of industrial relations is still very weak. The bodies of employee representation and the decentralised union structures remain essentially outside the EWC experience. This relative isolation may lead national structures of interest representation to question the legitimisation of EWCs. Therefore, the EWCs will have to develop measures aimed at improving their relationship to national systems of industrial relations.

There are also critical aspects with regard to the relationship between the EWC and management. This relationship is determined by the quantity, quality and timeliness of the information processes, on the one hand, and by the presence or absence of consultation processes, on the other. In most cases we can observe a management strategy that could be defined as minimalist. In these cases management tries to meet its obligations without conceding any more than is necessary. Especially when this involves restructuring, research shows that with regard to information processes both their quality and their timeliness are considered as inadequate. Management is determined to maintain its prerogatives and, consequently, tries to limit the EWCs' scope for action. In other cases management tries to manipulate and control the EWC in order to reach its strategic objectives. Some case studies have indeed shown that management's interest in the EWC was based on using this new body as an instrument for supporting the creation of a *corporate identity* and, in particular, achieving consensus with regard to its competition strategies at a European and global level. When the EWC does not have its own well-defined strategy, this kind of approach may lead to internal divisions and, consequently, to the subordination of the EWC.

Last, in a minority of cases there exists a management strategy that can be defined as constructive. The relationship between the EWC and management is characterised by the fact that management shows it is willing to grant some entitlements that go beyond the parameters set by the EWC Directive. This management attitude can be the result of common interests, for example in the field of labour policies and corporate social responsibility. In these cases management voluntarily accepts the EWC as a counterpart. In other cases, especially in cases of restructuring, it is the EWC, in co-operation with trade unions, that succeeds in forcing the management, through collective action, to accept the EWC as a counterpart. However, it has to be said that in these cases the involvement of the EWCs is limited to the management of the effects of the restructuring processes.

If, as happens in many cases of restructuring, management tries to bypass the EWC, then in other cases also the EWC itself appears to be incapable of using its albeit limited rights. As they do not take on a proactive role, in most cases the EWCs are characterised by substantially passive behaviour. Indeed, it appears that the right to information and consultation is only partly used. There are only a few cases in which real consultation has taken place. In general, the EWCs studied appeared to be incapable of identifying common objectives and developing a shared strategy. As a consequence, they have never interpreted their right to consultation in a radical way, i.e. by developing autonomous proposals that differ from those of the management. There are various explanations for such passive behaviour. In general, it is the result of a lack of internal cohesion due to diverging interests and the different industrial relations cultures and traditions present within the EWCs. In certain cases, the passive behaviour of delegates can also be put down to an inadequate training for EWC members.

As a consequence, among the EWCs analysed there was no example where an EWC had become a truly European-level representative structure. There are, in fact, also delegates criticising this under-use and the passive role of EWCs. These delegates underline the need for a qualitative leap in the EWCs' activities, often demanding the conferral of a negotiation function on the EWCs. Such a qualitative leap seems to be necessary in order to maintain the motivation of the individual delegates, on the one hand, and to improve the legitimacy *vis-à-vis* employees and the national bodies of interest representation, on the other.

To lay claim to a negotiating function, as a growing number of EWC members do, presupposes a certain level of internal cohesion which, in general, can only be developed in the mid or long term, as it is the outcome of intercultural learning processes. A negotiating function would also imply a thorough preparation and the development of an adequate strategy in order to achieve the possibility of negotiating with central management. Taking on a more active role is necessarily linked with the claim for resources and rights that are indispensable for sustaining the autonomy of EWCs.

On the way to becoming a real European-level body of interest representation the EWCs will not only encounter the resistance of management but, first of all, they will have to overcome the problem that consists in developing common objectives within the EWC. Therefore, they will have to try to overcome the obstacles deriving from the different national industrial relations experiences. In most EU member states, the company-level employee representative bodies have stronger rights and, in most cases, members consider the respective national co-determination and/or bargaining systems to be far more effective than the EWC. As a consequence, they are sceptical about devolving functions and competences to the supranational level. This is particularly true for Nordic countries such as Sweden and Denmark (Knudsen 2005). Critical positions may also arise among delegates who come from countries characterised by a two-tier system of interest representation (Germany), where the company-level structures of interest representation do not have a bargaining function.

Restructuring processes and the role of EWCs

So far we have dealt with the functioning of EWCs, the interactions, the tools at their disposal and the rights they can make use of. Furthermore, we have dealt with the content of the EWCs' activities, relevant in regard to the evaluation of the concrete role of EWCs. It has emerged from existing research that a critical point in general concerns the future prospects of EWCs. The basic challenge seems to involve an improvement of the EWC activities that allows for a shift from a passive towards a more active role.

In the following we intend to examine cases in which the EWCs have succeeded in taking on a negotiating role. We shall analyse what the prerequisites were in these cases for being successful in defining strategies based on common objectives. In this context the most relevant indications seem to come from EWCs that were actively involved in restructuring processes.

Forms of involvement of EWCs in restructuring processes

Enterprise restructuring and the deregulation of employment conditions through cost reductions, increased efficiency and the application of short-term performance criteria represent a widely diffused response to global competition. As the employees of transnational enterprises are particularly exposed to the risk of restructuring processes that in general have an impact on employment levels as well as on working conditions, in a growing number of cases EWCs see this as an important challenge. Consequently, there exists an EWC emphasis on becoming truly involved in such restructuring processes.

Although the rights of EWCs are formally limited to information and consultation, in recent years there have been several cases of a more far-reaching involvement on the part of these European bodies of interest representation. Research reports have shown that since the end of the 1990s there have been a number of cases where EWCs have participated in transnational restructuring processes and which to varying degrees have been successful. In his overview report, Carley (2001) lists four cases (Danone, Deutsche Bank, Ford, General Motors) in which the EWCs had a negotiating function within the framework of company restructuring processes, and two other cases (Vivendi, SLdE) in which the EWCs took on a strongly influential role in regard to company globalisation and expansion strategies.

In other cases, EWCs also managed to encroach upon the field of negotiations. In the case of Deutsche Bank in 1999, a joint position on job security was signed in which the group committed itself to arrangements that went well beyond those set down in the EWC Directive (Carley 2001).

Restructuring processes in the automotive industry

The most advanced examples of EWC involvement in restructuring processes are found in the automotive industry. A significant example is the agreement signed between the Ford EWC and central management on the spin-off of the car component producer, Ford Visteon (Klebe and Roth 2000). The agreement, which applies to Visteon plants in Germany, the UK and France, ensured that employees transferred to the new company still enjoy previously existing rights. In this agreement, Ford also commits itself to purchasing Visteon components for at least nine years in order to guarantee sales of the new company.

With regards to the General Motors Europe (GME) case in 2000, an agreement was signed between management and the European Employee Forum (EEF) on the consequences of the alliance with Fiat. In this example, the EEF succeeded in obtaining the following rights:

- continuous and timely information must be provided about developments within the alliance;

- the alliance must not lead to workforce reductions, plant closures or the worsening of working conditions;
- existing collective bargaining agreements must stay enforced;
- workers subject to transfer should have the right to remain and return;
- current national or EU-wide representation bodies and unions should be recognised in any new enterprises that may be formed.

In 2001 another important framework agreement on restructuring initiatives was signed between the EEF and the GM management. In this agreement, management committed itself to avoiding forced redundancies in relation to the planned restructuring initiatives and to maintaining vehicle production in Luton (UK). This agreement is probably one of the most important signed at European level as it 'provides for a concrete set of rules to be applied in specific circumstances; and a framework for lower-level action' (Carley 2001: 53).

Faced with a deep crisis in competitiveness in 2004, GME presented another restructuring programme that provided for a reduction of the labour costs valued at €500 million a year. The initial plan provided for delocalisation processes, with the closing down of at least one manufacturing plant, a reduction in employment levels and a cut in wage levels. In order to maximise the results of the restructuring plan, the group tried to force the various plants to compete with one another. As had already occurred in 2000 and 2001 with the help of the European Metalworkers' Federation (EMF), a day of European-wide industrial action was organised to oppose company strategy. The day of protest, which saw the participation of the plants situated in Germany, Sweden, Great Britain, Belgium, Poland and Spain, demonstrated a certain compactness among the various national representative bodies. The demonstration of solidarity between the different plants and the co-ordination role taken on by the EMF had the effect of making management accept the need to negotiate with the workers' representatives at European level. These negotiations led to the signing of a framework agreement on 8 December 2004 between the central management of GM Europe and the EEF that called off the announced plant closure and dismissals. The framework agreement laid down the foundations for the subsequently more detailed negotiations at national level.

The difficulty in developing a strategy and reaching agreements shared at European level is demonstrated by the protests of the workers' representatives in Great Britain and in Belgium who, in the final stages of the talks, made a formal protest to the EMF. They claimed that their German colleagues from the Bochum plant had infringed the principle of transparency. Indeed, at Bochum divergent orientations appeared within the trade union, the works councils and among the blue-collar workers, criticising the results of the talks with management. This example shows the EWCs' difficulty in developing a shared strategy at European level.

In 2004 and 2005 in the German automotive industry there were several cases in which companies threatened to transfer production and/or address

future investments towards countries with lower labour costs. In some cases
it is a matter of competition between plants inside the old EU; in most
cases, however, it involves plants in the new member states or even outside
Europe. Always it is the management taking the initiative: they ask for cost-
cutting in order to improve or regain competitiveness on the international
level. This argument is not only used for groups such as General Motors
Europe that have had to deal with large losses in recent years, but also
groups like Audi, BMW and Porsche that in 2004 achieved decidedly positive results. The leading role played by management, which finds itself in a
strong position as it can make aggressive use of a global-level benchmarking
policy, is answered by the defensive stance of trade unions and works
councils that in the main generally try to hedge the negative effects of
global competition.

In the negotiations on the restructuring processes in the automotive
industry it can be observed that the EWC was involved only in the cases of
Ford and General Motors. All the other cases[2] were exclusively dealt with at
national level. During the restructuring process of 2004–5, the GME-EEF,
which as long ago as the year 2000 had taken on the negotiating role (Telljohann 2004), even signed a framework agreement that represented a
common point of reference for the subsequent negotiating processes at
national level. The case of General Motors has shown that in order to
develop a strategy based on a form of European-wide solidarity a close co-
operation between the union federations and the EWCs is essential, together with an integration between the representation bodies at European,
national and company levels. The positive experience of the EEF is also due
to a high degree of internal cohesion. According to the president of the
EEF, some working principles have become consolidated over the years.
These include transparency, frankness and loyalty. As regards the co-
operation with the EMF, it is worth observing that for the first time a
monitoring group has been set up at the EMF with the task of accompanying restructuring process. According to the EEF president, this group's
work has significantly improved the standard of co-operation between the
EEF and the EMF.

In the case of General Motors, the protest and strike activities involved
various European countries. From the union standpoint, the strikes and
protest actions chiefly had the function of demonstrating the existence of
solidarity between the blue-collar workers, at both national and European
level. In the cases of the other car-makers, national strategies persist that,
from the point of view of a European-wide co-ordination, could be considered inadequate. It is indeed likely that the agreements will also have
some repercussions outside Germany and thus, according to the orientations of the EMF, it would have been worthwhile at least to have preliminary
discussions at the European level (European Metalworkers' Federation
2005a). Last, the attempt to find isolated solutions at the level of the single
plants or at the national level fosters the tendency towards competition

between the individual productive sites or between the various national contexts.

If we consider Ford and GME the two most advanced experiences of involvement of EWCs in restructuring processes, it is interesting to note that both experiences have taken place in TNEs with headquarters outside Europe. It is, in fact, likely that in the case of restructuring processes in EU-based TNEs the respective national trade union organisations are interested in controlling the process. In these cases EWCs are often dominated by the delegates of the home country who, in certain cases, consider the EWC an appendage of the national industrial relations system and for this reason prefer not to see the EWC involved. In general, these clearly dominating home country structures do not exist in TNEs with headquarters outside Europe. Consequently, this probably makes it easier for European bodies, such as the EWCs and the European trade union federations, to take on a co-ordinating function in the event of restructuring. This means that in the case of TNEs with headquarters outside the EU the 'country of origin factors' (Hall *et al.* 2003) seem to be less relevant and EWCs have more freedom to develop a really European strategy of interest representation.

The cases of Ford and GME proved the importance of the time factor. They showed that the EWC is not a static institution but a dynamic reality that has the chance of developing and moving from one phase of development to another as the internal and external conditions of action may change in the course of time. That means that EWCs can develop from service EWCs to European bodies of interest representation able to carry out European-wide actions and negotiations in co-operation with the EMF.

Restructuring processes in the household appliances industry

The household appliances industry has also been exposed to massive restructuring processes in which there are cases where EWCs have taken on an active role. In the cases of Electrolux and Whirlpool, the EWCs succeeded to a certain extent in developing autonomous activities aimed at influencing strategic management decisions. Electrolux and Whirlpool are TNEs that have been going through restructuring processes since the mid-1990s. Therefore, these cases are of particular interest as they also show how the role of EWCs can evolve in the course of time.

In the case of Electrolux, the EWC was involved in the restructuring process in the second half of the 1990s, but without having a negotiating role. In 1997, top management reported to the EWC a lack of competitiveness compared to general international standards in the sector. The management argued that the lack of competitiveness was a hindrance to the consolidation of production and employment at group level. A particular challenge consists in the fact that the sector is characterised by a major production overcapacity, the stagnation of main markets, falling prices, a tendency for consumers to look to the low-end product ranges and, finally, the entry of new non-EU producers. Consequently, management announced its intention to carry out a group restructuring process involving the closure of numerous industrial plants and major employment cuts. The Electrolux management pointed out to the EWC that though the actual size of the job cuts had been accurately defined (twenty-five production units and fifty warehouses, totalling 12,000 fewer workers), it had not yet been decided which plants to close and where. Management told the EWC members that Electrolux intended to close down the less competitive plants and to concentrate production and investments in the others. The EWC members were thus urged to table national debates in the various countries in order to increase the efficiency and the competitiveness of their own plants. As a matter of fact, a sort of European-wide 'auction' was started that actually caused major internal competition between the countries, during which each plant sought to prove that it had achieved a certain standard of efficiency and productivity to assure the group's competitiveness benchmarks. As a result, on this occasion there were major disagreements between the national representatives of the EWC, evidently and predictably committed to defending their respective national positions.

From the delegates' point of view, the involvement of the EWC in the restructuring process revealed several weaknesses. Although the management informed the EWC on a regular basis with regard to the planned restructuring measures, the EWC did not succeed in actually influencing management decisions. The main shortcomings were probably the insufficient internal cohesion of the EWC and the lack of co-ordination between the EWC and the external trade union organisations, especially the EMF. In this case, the involvement of the EWC thus represented a merely formal act. The EWC was limited to a subordinate role *vis-à-vis* management interests as management succeeded in making an instrumental use of this European body.

In 2005 the Electrolux central management announced a new phase of restructuring. This time, management's plans focused particularly on production sites in Germany and Italy. According to their restructuring plans the production sites at Nuremberg (Germany) and Parabiago (Italy) would be closed. Furthermore, they planned to downsize the Scandicci (Italy) plant. These plans implied job cuts of 1,750 redundancies in Nuremberg, 650 at Parabiago and 200 at Scandicci. The restructuring processes were supposed to contribute to an increase in competitiveness in order to penetrate new markets. While planning cutbacks in the western European countries, Electrolux invested €65 million in order to upgrade the plant in Hungary, to open a new plant in Russia producing washing machines, to enlarge the Polish factories, where part of the German production is to be transferred, and to finance an industrial project in Mexico, where from 2006 onwards a million refrigerators a year will be made. That means that Electrolux intends to transfer production to low-cost countries without offering alternative plans in order to safeguard the interests of employees in the western European plants.

In order to support the demand for negotiations, in July 2005 employees at the Italian and German Electrolux group plants organised a strike that stopped production from a minimum of one hour to a maximum of four hours. The employees' objective consisted in avoiding closures and upgrading the plants. The strikes in Germany and Italy were supported by the respective national metalworkers' trade unions as well as by the EMF.

The EMF decided to co-ordinate the work of the various national trade union organisations in order to ensure a sustainable future for the European household appliances industry. As a result of this decision a European-wide action day was organised in October 2005 in order to protest against the restructuring plans of the Electrolux group based on a strategy characterised by social dumping which plays one production site off against the other. On this occasion about 20,000 Electrolux employees in Italy, Germany, Sweden, Hungary, France, Spain and Belgium participated in a variety of information and consultation activities. In the various countries national metalworkers' unions in co-operation with the EMF organised different types of action involving picketing, strikes, protest demonstrations, information meetings and plant-level personnel meetings. The actions were meant on the one hand to demonstrate that unity exists among the Electrolux employees throughout Europe and on the other to ask the central management for negotiations at European level. The position of the EMF consisted in demanding 'socially responsible solutions taking also into consideration the repercussions on the industrial fabric of the regions and an industrial strategy based on innovation and high technology with a view to securing the future of Electrolux in Europe' (European Metalworkers' Federation 2005b). The central management, though, rejected European-level negotiations.

Comparing the experiences in the late 1990s with the experiences in 2005, we can say that an important learning process has taken place in the case of Electrolux. The main difference consists in the fact that the EMF in 2005 took on an active role of co-ordination involving all national trade union organisations and company-level structures of interest representation, including the Hungarian representatives. Furthermore, alternative proposals focusing on the upgrading of the western European plants and processes of product innovation were developed.

In the case of Whirlpool, the Whirlpool Europe Employee Committee (WEEC) had to face a first phase of restructuring in 1997 and a second one in 2005. The WEEC has not yet taken on a negotiating function but, according to both the Italian representatives of the WEEC and the central management representative, its intervention has at times influenced management decisions. What best lends itself to corroborating the previous statement is the role of the WEEC in the restructuring that took place in Germany and France. In the former case, in 1997 an extraordinary meeting was called to inform the steering committee about the closure of the Calw plant in Germany. Following the announcement in which it was stated that

Whirlpool intended to close down the plant, the WEEC served as an amplifier for the German claims in Europe. Indeed, the WEEC participation in a seminar organised by IG Metall and financed with European Commission funds, specifically concerning the closure at Calw, gave greater international visibility to the German situation and resulted in protests at several European plants within the group. A European-wide strike could not be organised seeing that in several countries, such as Sweden, national legislation did not allow for solidarity strikes to be called. Furthermore, WEEC released an official communication protesting against the closure of the plant in Germany. By means of a targeted information strategy by the WEEC, all the European plants were nevertheless involved. In every country some initiatives were chosen that were deemed to be appropriate for informing all the workers about the closure in Germany. Among the most significant initiatives were the publication of several specific articles in the local Italian press, the protest by the German workers before the main group head offices in Italy and a solidarity strike organised by the Trento (Italy) facility. According to the Italian WEEC delegate, the international protest did not prevent the closure of the plant but, by making the matter public domain, pressed the company, interested in safeguarding its own image, 'into reaching the best possible agreement'. Last, the agreement underwritten in Germany provided for a solution based on the relocation of staff to other factories in Germany, on the one hand, and the use of an early retirement scheme, on the other. According to the Italian member of the WEEC, the German representatives have positively evaluated the role that the WEEC has managed to take on within the scope of this restructuring process.

It can thus be argued that the WEEC has in some way managed to develop a common position in regard to a case of restructuring. In the implementation of the actions at European level it then had to adapt to the existing constraints in the various countries involved. In most cases these constraints regarded legal problems within the scope of the national industrial relations systems. The fact still remains that the WEEC on this occasion had managed to take on an active role and in some way also an incisive one. In this case it was the WEEC itself that had won this role. Inside the WEEC it was the German IG Metall that pushed to take on a more active role in defence of employment levels.

In 2005, despite a positive European scenario, Whirlpool presented a restructuring plan involving the dismissal of around 1,000 workers in Italy. The Italian trade unions feared that this cutback of personnel was a precursor to a more extensive relocation plan. The restructuring process was limited to the Italian plants, protest demonstrations were also limited to Italy and the WEEC did not take on a role in this phase of restructuring. It is, however, likely that the production site for dishwashers in Neunkirchen, Germany, with about 550 employees, will be at risk when the Wroclaw plant in Poland reaches its full production capacity. It can, therefore, be envisaged that the WEEC will have to face the problem of restructuring processes again in the near future. The risk is, however, that the Whirlpool management will argue that single plant closures and cutbacks in employment relate to respective national contexts and are therefore not the subject of discussions at the WEEC level.

To conclude, it can be observed that not only are EWCs requesting support from the trade unions, but the unions are increasingly recognising the usefulness of the EWCs as a source of information and, at times, as a platform for European-wide co-ordination (Köhler and Begega 2005). The EWC can help them to organise European-wide actions, as has happened, for instance, in the cases of Ford, General Motors, Fiat, Electrolux and Whirlpool, where the union, in this case the EMF, called industrial action in response to the strategic choices of central management (Klebe and Roth 2000; Erne 2004; Rehfeldt 2004). Furthermore, in several cases the EWC, in close co-operation with the union, has signed agreements. By recognising the potential of this new body of representation at European level, it seems that there is an ongoing trend among the trade union organisations to try to increase the added value of EWCs. It should be stressed, however, that the most advanced agreements were signed in TNEs based outside the European Union. The future will have to show whether the European trade union federations will be able to promote important experiences of European-level negotiations, also in EU-based TNEs.

Prerequisites for developing a European-wide strategy

The above-mentioned examples show that in several cases the EWCs have succeeded in going beyond information and consultation procedures. In most of these cases trade unions are successful in using EWCs to generate common positions and to achieve concessions from management in safeguarding jobs, working practices and conditions. In this context, Ford and GME have to be considered the most relevant illustration. In these and the other cases (Danone, Deutsche Bank) the agreements signed at European level deal with company development factors as well as employee-side factors. Especially, the EWCs at Ford and GME have shown that there is room for manoeuvre and that the chance to really influence decisions is much greater at a higher level than at a local level where works councils are mostly confronted with implementation discussions only. Furthermore, evidence indicates that EWCs are not necessarily simply vehicles for international competition between labour regimes (Hancké 2000). On the contrary, in the case of the first restructuring process during the 1990s at Electrolux, management succeeded in involving the EWC in a strategy based on competition between the various plants in the countries represented by the EWC. The EWC was unable to develop a European-wide common strategy and as a consequence local interests prevailed, giving rise to internal competition. Faced with pressure from central management, the EWC members did not make full use of the mechanisms provided for in the EWC agreement, and they did not succeed in developing an adequate partnership with the EMF.

The development of a European-wide strategy in 2005 as a result of the co-ordinating role of the EMF seems to show that a learning process had taken place in the meantime.[3] It is important to note that European-wide actions have been shown to be possible in the case of a TNE based in Sweden where EWCs in general are considered reluctant to delegate competences to the European level (Hammarström 2005; Huzzard and Docherty 2005; Knudsen 2005). However, it is not yet clear whether in the case of Electrolux it will be possible to go beyond the level of European-wide actions and to develop a common strategy of interest representation and negotiation, as has happened in the case of GME.

Particularly at the European level, as the various cases have shown, it seems indispensable that there is a close co-operation between EWCs and European trade union federations when facing the necessity to develop a European-wide strategy in response to transnational restructuring processes (Telljohann 2003: 43). According to Rehfeldt:

> the EWC by itself will always have great difficulties when it tries to define the common interests of the workforce in different European plants and in different economic situations. Union intervention will always be necessary in order to facilitate a compromise between different interests and different strategic approaches.
>
> (Rehfeldt 2004: 189)

Trade union intervention, however, does not regard only the identification of common interests and objectives but also the mobilisation and the co-ordination of actions at the European level. Cases such as Ford and GME show that EWCs are accepted as negotiating partners not because management is enlightened but because of the capability to mobilise employees and to represent common interests at the EU level which makes it more difficult for management to play off the various plants and national unions against one other.

To sum up, the above-mentioned experiences show that the timely involvement of EWCs in restructuring processes is of course important, but not sufficient to guarantee an effective and positive role for EWCs in the framework of restructuring processes. As regards the rights laid down by the EWC Directive, it would be equally important to accurately define the concept of consultation (a key ETUC campaign issue). Besides the timeliness it is necessary to guarantee the possibility for EWCs to develop alternative proposals to the projects presented by the management. An active interpretation of consultation implies the need for knowledge, competencies and capabilities, which can only be achieved in the context of training programmes. Furthermore, for the successful involvement of EWCs it is imperative that they decide on their role in regard to both the development of an autonomous strategy and the necessary actions to be carried out to achieve the jointly agreed objectives.

The cases of Ford, GME and, to a certain extent, also Electrolux show that it is possible for trade union organisations and EWCs to develop European-wide strategies able to counterbalance management's restructuring plans. Nevertheless, one has to be aware that so far these examples represent only positive exceptions, while in the majority of cases, even in the context of restructuring processes, EWCs do not succeed in going beyond the level of a 'service EWC' (Lecher *et al.* 2002). As it has been shown, in order to conclude agreements it is necessary to guarantee, first of all, close co-operation between EWCs and trade union organisations at the various levels. Furthermore, the co-operation between EWCs and national works councils as well as between European and national trade union organisations is indispensable for the success of a European-wide strategy of co-ordination of mobilisation and negotiation. From the point of view of the EWCs the support of both the trade unions and the national structures of interest representation is also an important source of legitimisation of the EWCs' activities. It is obvious, at least in theory, that the added value of an effective involvement of interest representation bodies at the European level consists in the possibility of overcoming the limits of local responses, which are often characterised by a logic of competition between the different production sites. At the European level, on the contrary, EWCs have the possibility of trying to develop a commonly agreed European-wide response to management strategies.

To date, the most interesting experiences have occurred in the European metalworking industry. This is probably due to the fact that we find the highest unionisation rates here, a prerequisite for mobilising members as well as exerting pressure on management. Another explanation might be that not all European industry federations are convinced of the usefulness of assigning an active role to EWCs in the context of restructuring processes. The policy of European trade union federations is therefore another important prerequisite for a successful European-wide strategy of interest representation. Pulignano's contribution in this book shows that there are in fact substantial differences in the strategies of European trade union federations. Of course, developing a European-wide strategy is a rather complex challenge requiring considerable resources. This is probably another reason for the still very limited number of cases in which this approach has been successfully applied.

Following EU enlargement the development of a European-wide strategy has become even more complex and demanding as the differences between eastern and western European sites in terms of costs, working conditions and industrial relations remain considerable, so much so that it might become difficult to develop a common strategy. Therefore, according to Tholen *et al.* (2005), EWCs are not yet ready to take on an intermediary role in a co-operative network which has to involve eastern European sites. Again in these cases the close co-operation between European industry federations and EWCs will prove important in overcoming the present limitations.

The development of a European collective identity – a twofold challenge

Finally, we will try to draw conclusions from the case studies with regard to the development of a collective identity within EWCs. First of all we have to address the relevance of a European collective identity. In general, identity is considered the central aspect of consciousness. In the case of the EWCs this would mean the appropriation and definition of their specific characteristics as well as the definition of their position in relation to other actors. Identity is therefore the result of a process in which awareness of the specificity of the EWC as a European-level body of interest representation is built. This process includes the definition of the specific interests and values of an EWC as well as concrete objectives arising from its interests and values. Only on the basis of such an awareness can the EWCs become an effective body of interest representation.

EWCs, therefore, need to develop a stable and consistent identity with the function of orientation and organisation in order to be able to face social complexity. The process of identity-building takes place through processes of internal and external interaction. In general, identity-building is a complex and differentiated process as the EWC members are covering different roles. At times it may be difficult to bring them into agreement with each other.

If identity has an important function of orientation and organisation, not addressing the issue of a European collective identity would mean surrendering an important tool at EU level or, at any rate, under-using it. On the other hand, to ensure the identification with the role as *European* employee representative appears particularly difficult as for EWCs the development of a European collective identity represents a twofold challenge. First of all, the identity-building process is linked with the genuine function of *interest representation*. The second challenge regards the development of a specific *European* identity of EWCs. The two challenges are of course closely linked and they are treated here separately only for analytical reasons.

The first challenge for EWCs, therefore, involves becoming a *real actor of interest representation*. So far, the rights of EWCs are limited to information and consultation; they do not have any negotiation or co-determination rights, which might allow them to try to influence management decisions. This means that up to now the EWC cannot be considered an effective body of interest representation. This lack of rights leads in the major part of the cases to practices typical of 'symbolic' or 'service EWCs' (Lecher *et al.* 2002), which in many cases have a negative impact on the motivation of the delegates. If it is right that a collective identity is able to develop on the basis of common activities aimed at achieving jointly defined objectives, it will remain difficult for EWCs to develop such a collective identity as long as the EWC Directive relegates them to a more or less passive and subordinated role *vis-à-vis* management. Therefore, the EWC's lack of rights can be considered a major obstacle with regard to the development of a genuine identity in the form of a collective structure of interest representation at European level.

As a consequence, EWCs have to identify ways to become a real structure promoting interest representation. As was shown earlier, given the existing legal basis there are two possibilities for EWCs to develop strategies of action at a European level and, as a consequence, to contribute to the formation of a European collective identity. The first one consists in identifying common interests and trying to obtain a *voluntary* legitimisation by management. The second one is in general the result of conflicts between EWCs and management arising in the context of restructuring processes. In these cases EWCs develop a European-wide strategy in order to obtain a *forced* legitimisation by management. It is, however, extremely difficult for EWCs to become an evenly matched counterpart as long as there is no clearly defined right to strike. To conclude, it can be argued that in order to develop an effective European-wide strategy, EWCs are required to go beyond the provisions set by the EWC Directive.

Finally, there is of course the institutional approach to be considered, the EWC obtaining real interest representation rights at European level through a modification of the EWC Directive itself. The success of this approach, which is supported by the European Trade Union Confederation (ETUC), also depends to a certain extent on the success of the above-mentioned EWC strategies.

The second challenge, the development of a specific *European* identity, regards factors such as intercultural learning, mutual trust and internal cohesion. That means that the process of developing a European identity is the result of learning processes and experiences: of course, both depend very much on the time factor, the availability of resources and the quality of external support.

If as indicated above the development of European-wide strategies goes hand in hand with the development of a European collective identity, the positive cases presented in this chapter may provide some indications concerning the prerequisites for the development of a European collective identity and the factors that might influence this development process.

On the basis of the above-described experiences, it can be concluded that the development of a European collective identity of EWCs depends on the capability of its members to autonomously identify common interests and values, to agree on following step on common objectives and, finally, to define and carry out a common strategy. The development of a common strategy presupposes that the delegates are faced with a common challenge and agree on the role the EWC should take on *vis-à-vis* this challenge. To assign an active role to the EWC implies that there exists the conviction among the members of the EWC that the European level is the appropriate level of action.

Besides these basic prerequisites it is possible to identify at least eight factors influencing the process of identity-building:

- The first one is the *time factor*, which is of crucial importance as there are a number of necessary conditions to be met in order to make the forming of a European identity possible. The development of a European collective identity is, therefore, the outcome of medium or long-term processes.
- Time is also necessary in order to allow *internal cohesion* to develop as it is the outcome of learning processes and practical experiences that are at the basis of the development of mutual trust.
- The development of the *subjective factor* consisting, among other things, in an improvement of the individual capabilities, is relevant not only to foster intercultural learning but also to create the necessary awareness with regard to the potential role of EWCs. Besides the development of individual capabilities, it is equally important to guarantee the motivation of the single EWC members that may also be influenced by a number of other factors described in this paragraph.
- Another factor influencing the process of identity-building is represented by the *internal functioning* of EWCs. Only an EWC operating efficiently will be able to organise continuous communication processes which can guarantee an adequate involvement of all delegates in EWC activities.
- The fifth factor regards the dimension of external relationships of EWCs, i.e. its capability of *integration, co-operation* and *co-ordination*. In order to be able to define common objectives and a jointly shared strategy, EWCs must develop adequate relationships with both company-level structures of interest representation and trade union organisations in various countries and at various levels.
- Furthermore, the *legitimisation* of EWC activities can have a significant impact on the process of identity-building. In this context it has to be borne in mind that there are different sources of legitimisation. The first one regards the institutionalised rights at the European level. In the case of activities going beyond the EWC Directive, EWCs depend on the legitimisation by management, the national structures of interest representation and in certain cases also the national and European trade union organisations.
- The improvement of individual capabilities and the internal functioning as well as the processes of integration, co-operation and co-ordination depend on the availability of adequate *resources*. It is, therefore, of crucial importance for the functioning of EWCs to verify all the existing possibilities of obtaining the necessary resources in order to guarantee an effective and efficient operation.

- Resources as well as the extension of rights are likewise important in order to guarantee the *autonomy* of EWCs as European-level bodies of interest representation.

The above-mentioned factors regard various dimensions of the identity-building process. First of all, there is the *individual* dimension regarding the development of the subjective factor. Second, we have the *collective* dimension, which relates to the internal dynamics of the EWC. The relevant factors influencing the identity-building process at this level are the internal functioning, the internal cohesion and the autonomy of the EWCs. The factors integration, co-operation and co-ordination as well as legitimisation represent the dimension of *interaction* between EWCs and the other actors at the various levels. Finally, there are the factors of resources and time that represent a *horizontal* dimension affecting all the other already mentioned dimensions.

Referring to the classification of Lecher *et al.* (2002), we can conclude that a European collective identity is likely to develop in *project-oriented* and *participative* EWCs as these EWCs are able to take on an active role in overcoming a passive and subordinated attitude *vis-à-vis* management, which is typical of symbolic and service-oriented EWCs. Project-oriented and participative EWCs are characterised by their capacity to identify common interests and objectives from an autonomous point of view; being able therefore to develop independent agendas and to develop a jointly shared strategy.

Notes

1 The project 'Quality inventories on the operation and results of European Works Councils' has been funded from the budget heading B3–4003 of the Directorate General for Employment and Social Affairs of the European Commission. It was carried out in co-operation with the European Trade Union Confederation. The research group was composed of Heinz Bierbaum (Germany), Peter Kerckhofs (Belgium), Lionel Fulton (United Kingdom), Udo Rehfeldt (France), Olle Hammarström (Sweden) and Volker Telljohann (Italy).
2 We refer to Volkswagen, DaimlerChrysler, Audi and Porsche.
3 It should be to be observed that at the time of writing the Electrolux case has not yet been concluded. Our observations regarding this case therefore have a very preliminary nature.

References

Carley, M. (2001) *Joint Texts Negotiated by European Works Councils,* Luxembourg: Office for Official Publications of the European Communities.
Erne, R. (2004) 'Organized labour – an agent of a more democratic EU?' paper presented at the European conference 'Organised labour – an agent of EU democracy? Trade union strategies and the EU integration process', Dublin, October.

European Metalworkers' Federation (2005a) 'The EMF/GME restructuring and framework agreements. An example of EMF European Company Policy', unpublished report, European Metalworkers' Federation, Brussels.

—— (2005b) '21st October – first European Action Day to protest against Electrolux management', press information, European Metalworkers' Federation: Brussels.

Hall, M., Hoffmann, A., Marginson, P. and Müller, T. (2003) 'National influences on European Works Councils in UK- and US-based companies', *Human Resource Management Journal*, 13 (4): 75–92.

Hammarström, O. (2005) 'EWCs and the trade unions – the case of Sweden', in V. Telljohann (ed.) *Quality Inventories on the Operation and Results of European Works Councils*, Bologna: Fondazione Istituto per il Lavoro, 67–75.

Hancké, B. (2000) 'European Works Councils and industrial restructuring in the European motor industry', *European Journal of Industrial Relations*, 6 (1): 35–59.

Huzzard, T. and Docherty, P. (2005) 'Between global and local: eight European Works Councils in retrospect and prospect', *Economic and Industrial Democracy*, 26: 541–68.

Klebe, T. and Roth, S. (2000) 'Die Gewerkschaften auf dem Weg zu einer internationalen Strategie', *Arbeitsrecht im Betrieb*, 12: 749–59.

Knudsen, H. (2005) 'Scandinavian scepticism: Danish and Swedish trade unionism in the European context', paper presented at the International Workshop 'Europeanisation and organised labour: an unsolved dilemma?' Warwick, November.

Köhler, H.D. and Begega, S.G. (2005) 'Co-ordinating labour policy in European firm level social dialogue. The case of Arcelor's European Works Council', paper presented at the 7th European Sociological Association Congress, 'Rethinking inequalities', Torun, September.

Lecher, W., Platzer, H.-W., Rüb, S. and Weiner, K.P. (2002) *European Works Councils: Negotiated Europeanisation. Between Statutory Framework and Social Dynamics*, Aldershot: Ashgate.

Rehfeldt, U. (2004) 'European Works Councils and international restructuring: a perspective for European collective bargaining?' in E. Charron and P. Steward (eds) *Work and Employment Relations in the Automobile Industry*, London: Palgrave Macmillan, 183–94.

Telljohann, V. (2003) 'Regolazione sociale a livello transnazionale: un nuovo modello di azione sindacale?' *Economia & Lavoro*, 1: 29–46.

—— (2004) 'Globalisation, enterprise restructuring and the role of pacts for employment and competitiveness' in F. Garibaldo and V. Telljohann (eds) *Globalisation, Company Strategies and Quality of Working Life in Europe*, Frankfurt am Main: Peter Lang, 87–106.

—— (2005a) 'The European Works Councils – a role beyond the EC Directive?' *Transfer*, 11 (1): 81–96.

—— (ed.) (2005b) *Quality Inventories on the Operation and Results of European Works Councils*, Bologna: Fondazione Istituto per il Lavoro.

Tholen, J., Cziria, L., Hemmer, E., Kozek, W. and Mansfeldovà, Z. (2005) 'Die Auswirkungen von Direktinvestitionen deutscher Unternehmen auf die Arbeitsbeziehungen in Mittel-/Osteuropa', unpublished research report, University of Bremen and Institut Arbeit und Wirtschaft.

Weiler, A. (2004) *European Works Councils in Practice*, Luxembourg: Office for Official Publications of the European Communities.

10 The European Works Council and the feeling of interdependence[1]

Hermann Kotthoff

The frequently recognised limited ability of European Works Councils (EWCs) to act is explained by the fact that the members of these committees see themselves as delegates of national interests and not as actors of a genuine European (transnational) institution. They lack a European identity. According to this perspective the construction and development of a European identity is viewed as the solution to the problem of a 'limited ability to act'. This perspective is theoretically and practically not imperative. For its opposite is also plausible, namely the thesis that the cause of the EWC's low level of European identity is its limited ability to act, and that therefore an increase of that ability is the solution to the problem. Such chicken-and-egg constellations are not uncommon in the social sciences. Often it appears that both theses prove false, and only the opening up of new perspectives shows a way out of the dilemma. Such an attempt has to begin with a careful examination of the terms. What does European identity mean in this context?

The sociological concept of collective identity, or of collective consciousness, leads to a difficult and slippery terrain. This is particularly the case within the German context. It is often noted that the Germans fail to identify with their country, so that a reduced form of identification, namely with the constitution, is suggested as a line of direction (*Leitlinie*). The discourse on collective identity is particularly difficult because modernisation processes, globalisation and widespread migration result in a dissolving of old identities in all regions of the world. Hence, an essential feature of the identity discourse is the more or less openly formulated complaint and regret over a painful loss. As a reaction to this, in recent years more and more authors have resorted to the opposite position: the dissolving of old collective identities represents a chance, an expansion of the horizon. They claim that previous views about identity have been ontological and backward-looking, too oriented towards stability, firmness and duration (Yildiz 2006). In contrast, a post-modern view is proposed in which identity is something that is flowing and has to be continually reproduced by people (Pries 2001). In particular, authors who consider the issue of identity in connection with the globalisation or migration phenomena speak about 'plural', 'operative', 'dialogical', 'narrative' or 'hybrid' identity concepts, which are distinguished critically from the so-called strong identity concepts of 'home' and 'nation'. The paradigmatic constellation is no longer marked by a secure identity of descent nor by a clear picture of a different, identity-founding future, but rather the 'in-between', the 'life in plural' or even the 'nomadic self'.

The discourse about a European identity has become severely dampened since the vote against the draft European constitution in France and the Netherlands. Europe, at least at this particular stage, is not an image or a concept that gets people's hearts racing and encourages identification. On the other hand, the widespread scepticism concerning Turkey joining the European Union shows that in the emotional household of the population there appears to be something like an emotionally loaded conception of Europe, at least a 'vague' notion of identity.

This current European political background certainly also has parallels to EWC identity. One parallel is that the demand for a European EWC identity raises expectations that possibly may be disappointed. I assume that this is a demand too high, when one understands identity in the full sense as the self, the core and the middle of a person. Presumably the current robust national identities of EWC members will not be simply replaced by a robust European identity. Such a change should not be imagined as a bus trip from A to B. I would like to see whether more modest and therefore also more realistic concepts of identity are available.

To this end I will take a quick look at the history of sociological theory in which collective identity ('we-feeling') is a central concept, representing the mutual penetration of individual and society. For this reason the terms 'identity' and 'identification' are two sides of the same coin. You can approach the phenomenon from both sides. From the perspective of the individual it is about the constitution of the self (self-becoming, self-understanding, self-perception, the core and middle of the personality) through internalisation of the perspective of the Other (society) as well as the creative individual interpretation and modification of this perspective. This process in its classical form is depicted by G.H. Mead's concept of 'me' and 'I' and S. Freud's 'super ego' and 'ego'. The process of interpenetration is interpreted as an affective as well as a cognitive event.

From the perspective of society, interpenetration is constructed through the identification with a collective, as collective consciousness and as solidarity. The specific knowledge interest does not concern the constitution of the self but rather the conditions that make society as such possible, i.e. the cohesion, the integration and the duration of collectives. Each theoretical sociological approach deals with this cardinal theme. However, for fundamental socio-theoretical insights from this perspective we are first and foremost indebted to E. Durkheim and T. Parsons, whose entire works are centred around these questions.

Collective identity in sociological theory

According to Durkheim (1992), collective identity (we-feeling, solidarity) arises from the division of labour, i.e. through the reciprocal dependency of specialists who as such are no longer self-sufficient. The division of labour increases the frequency of contact and this in turn increases the willingness to co-operate, which forges people into a collective. The central term is the feeling of interdependence. Something purely functional, namely the specialisation of the social organisation of work in society, gives birth to something moral, namely solidarity. Concerning this concept by Durkheim, N. Luhmann (1992: 34) critically notes:

> The premises state that contact generates morals. When one accepts this, when one ignores the hostile aspects of morals ... then in fact the expectation of an interactional recovery of society appears as an arguable future perspective.

The demand that EWCs develop a European identity is a form of interactional recovery of society in the spirit of Durkheim. However, Luhmann treats such a position sceptically: identification, collective feelings, solidarity – these do not inevitably lead to something good but just as easily lead to hostility and war, for the we-feeling is often linked with an increased exclusion of others.

T. Parsons (1964), however, who is very close to Durkheimian thinking, explains the origins of feelings of collectivity and solidarity as the result of normative factors rather than interaction, and like Durkheim has been charged with being blind to the social fact of conflict. Parsons bases the co-operation, cohesion and stability of an action system on norms and values. They stem from the 'cultural system', which means an ordered connection between cultural symbols:

> Actually Parsons sees things so: the values from the cultural system have to be anchored in the action systems, and this through two processes: through the process of internalization in the personality system and the process of institutionalization in the social system.
>
> (Joas and Knöbl 2004: 99)

The theoretical programmes of Durkheim and Parsons are primarily concerned with overcoming utilitarian thought which in the nineteenth century, especially in Anglo-Saxon countries, dominated thought about society and social action. Neither doubt that co-operation and cohesion can develop through selfish (utilitarian) behaviour. But this, they claim, is simply by chance and arbitrary, and for this reason too weak and unstable to base a society on. They are looking for something more stable and solid which is not subject to the voluntarism of unreliable and erratic individuals.

A third variant is the modern utilitarian criticism of Durkheim and Parsons by contemporary authors. It questions the connection between an increase of contact and solidarity (and between norms and solidarity) by arguing that close contacts often lead to a functional-rational 'business relationship' but not to a collective feeling and a deep sense of community. The argument claims that Durkheim failed to see the possibility and the usefulness of egoistic-utilitarian co-operation. It continues, that a social bonding exists that does not require deep feelings of belonging as a precondition, but is based on purpose-rational motives and functionality (Müller and Schmidt 1992: 515). This utilitarian-functionalist concept appears to me to be suggesting a variant of identification that is less conditional than Durkheim's. It derives from the theoretical tradition to which A. Smith also belongs, whose 'invisible hand' converts egoistic behaviour, behind the back of actors so to speak, into something co-operative and socially constructive. It does this without recourse to morals and feelings. However, a closer look reveals that A. Smith takes an already existing stable institutional order for granted, so that in his case the chicken-and-egg reference does not come to a halt. Thus, we must continue to put this question to Durkheim and Parsons. But in this short chapter we will not try to solve this theoretical dilemma.

A fourth explanation of collective identity is not argued in an interactionist, normative or utilitarian way, but refers to the sociology of power. In a similar way to Durkheim, M. Weber comprehends collective identity primarily as a quality of feeling, but he anchors this to the sociology of power and authority: it is the common *belief* in the legitimacy of an authority which forms a number of people into a collective (Weber 1972: 122 ff). H. Popitz follows a similar train of thought by seeing the social historical starting point of collective identity in the archetypical role of the patriarch, the general and the judge (Popitz 1986: 122 ff). From all three arises an authority relationship in which authority must be understood in a double sense as commitment to an authority as well as subordination under its superior power/force. This need for commitment to an authority consists of the need for recognition by a superior authority and subordination under its effective protection. Authority takes on the meaning of socially 'refined' constructive power that provides effective protection and as such creates cohesion/identification and strengthens the collective. The military commander, for example, provides effective protection in an emergency or threatening situation and through this gains recognition and authority that welds the collective together. Of course, this approach is able to best explain the strongest forms of collective identity that we know, namely patriotism and national feeling. Historically, national feeling is a relatively new phenomenon – but without doubt it dominates the entire discourse about collective identity. The called-for European identity has to be measured against this, too.

When considering the EWC from the perspective of Popitz, who has an anthropological starting point, then the question of the real need for commitment as well as situations of distress and danger becomes central. The feeling towards a collective arises out of practical needs and necessities in everyday life (and therefore has utilitarian elements). Their satisfaction though – one could say here, too, behind the back of actors – leads to the creation of authority, which becomes the push for institutionalisation, integration and identification. This approach becomes interesting for us when it involves the transfer of authority, the change from one sovereign to another. This is exactly the case in many multinational firms when, through an increase in the internationalisation of structures, factory managers lose power and must pass it over to the firm's central management. This phenomenon of changes in authority is the historical reason for the existence of the EWC Directive. The inability of employee representatives within foreign subsidiaries to get access to the place where the real power resides was *the* original main argument for demanding European representation.

In a short journey through the history of theory we have discovered four different versions of how collective identity is constituted: through close interaction (Durkheim), through normative ties (Parsons), through utilitarian purposeful rational behaviour (Smith) and through the dynamics of power and authority relationships (Popitz, Weber). Which version is meant when the European identity of the EWC is discussed?

Identity in different types of EWCs

In an empirical study of EWCs I asked the question concerning European identity at three levels (Kotthoff 2006):[2] first, at the level of action, the politics and effectiveness of the committee; second, at the level of EWC members' self-reflection regarding the question 'Is there a European solidarity within the EWC?'; third, at the level of repercussions of the EWC on the consciousness of national works council members who are not delegates to the EWC. For this reason, in each firm studied, two national works council members were interviewed. The result is as expected or as feared: a European identity is not very developed. But it takes on a different shape on each of these levels. It decreases with the growing distance from the European stage.

At the level of action and politics it concerns whether and in what form the EWC as a new transnational institution within the firm has gained weight and significance. Indicators for this are the characteristics of its internal organisation (among others the frequency of full and steering committee meetings; the intensity of contacts between meetings) as well as, and first and foremost, the content and intensity of its work (e.g. which subjects are dealt with? are common positions to particular issues developed? how intensive and effective is the communication with central management?). That is: how effective is it as a cross-border employee representation within the firm?

It became clear that one cannot lump together all EWCs, but rather five different types of EWCs exist. Contrary to the Euro-sceptical prognoses, it is possible to discern that three types of EWCs quite clearly have cross-border effects. They have attained a weight and relevance in the firm, even though this might be in very different forms and measures. Half of the firms studied belong to these types. The other half do not develop any comparable effectiveness. For the debate concerning the current theme, a further result is especially relevant: among the three effective types there is only one which can to some extent be classified as having characteristics of European identity. It is the 'EWC as a participating working team'. Only a minority (a quarter) of the case studies belong to this type.

What is meant when I suggest that this type possesses a European identity? In the main, it means that it has a transnational political understanding, that it concentrates on common questions and problems, i.e. not on parochial questions but rather on transnational corporate policies, and that it attempts to influence these. It acts within the framework of a trans-local perspective. A further characteristic is its internal organisation: it is a working team. That means in particular that the steering committee meets often (eight to twelve times a year), that the members of this committee as well as other active EWC delegates communicate between meetings, and that the chair of the EWC uses a much higher percentage of his/her time budget (around 25–30 per cent) for this function compared to chairs of other types of EWCs (5–10 per cent). Beside or together with national and local employee representatives, the EWC has gained a noticeable relevance in the corporation. It has become a reality to be reckoned with.

This EWC type can be found only in firms in which no single European country plays a dominant role, but in which Europe is rather reflected as a unified area, namely through Europeanised management structures and through highly integrated production structures. Such firms no longer differentiate between the individual countries; they treat them all the same. They are in fact the opposite of parochialism. They are 'Euro-companies'. It is not surprising, then, that no German firm belongs to this type – rather, US-American and a British-Dutch firm.

But even these EWCs do not have a strong European identity in the sense of Durkheim's definition, i.e. in the sense of strong affective bonds and collective feelings. On the contrary, it is rather a European identity with a functional and businesslike meaning. Like other Europeans, these EWC members do not feel strongly about Europe. Europe is a sober place of work, a 'building site'. The essential concern is not the 'collective Europe', the new society or the 'European idea', but rather, in a sober and pragmatic way, the members of the committee, and of these only those who are engaged, often only the members of the steering committee who do the work. Europe is reduced to actual contacts in different places with colleagues from different countries with whom questions of common concern are discussed. In accordance with Durkheim's and Parsons's tradition, this identity lacks the mythical, which is inherent to the term 'collective': the feeling that arouses emotions. Admittedly the committee members have on a personal level become closer over time and mutual understanding has improved, but a bonding that makes a solidary European community out of a loose meeting of national delegates is not apparent.

Most of the committee members are definitely European-minded in the sense that they display an international understanding and good neigh-bourliness, and in this respect they are very likely to surpass the average population by a long way. However, the realisation of the European collective, the EU, they perceive as a business contact with standing orders that function amazingly well.

The transnational collective, which for them has a larger relevance, is the inner world of the firm. And as the firm becomes more transnational, the perspective of EWC members' becomes more transnational. Often there is no great difference between a European and global transnationalism. In some firms even the employee representatives have a closer relationship to non-European than European countries because they have more to do with them. The EWC members could equally be world works council members. This would hardly change anything of what I have discussed about identity. The core of the transnational employee representation is access to the relevant decision-making level within the firm, the question of the correct counterpart for consultation and negotiation. If, for example, the group management is based in Germany, and if the German works council via co-determination has a direct or even a personal access to central management, then it is not to be expected that the EWC has a specific European identity. Such an EWC is well advised to appreciate these chances to push things through as an asset, and to take advantage of them, i.e. to connect itself to the practiced employee representation within the firm's headquarters. This does not mean it will gain a German identity; rather, this is a rational-functional arrangement with a strategy for action that reflects chances offered by German co-determination. These characteristics in fact apply to the following EWC type.

This second type, though less effective, I characterise as 'the German works council chair as the advocate for the Diaspora'. This type can only be found in firms with German headquarters in which a strong German co-determination exists and where the national works council chair (or the deputy) is also the EWC chair, with a direct contact to the firm's top management. When employee representatives from a foreign subsidiary have a problem which can only be solved with the firm's central management, then the German chair/EWC colleague addresses this problem and has a word with central management on their behalf. The EWC's identity is a kind of appendix of German co-determination: when necessary, foreign subsidiaries can also benefit from this. The political perspective is not transnational or European, but local and bilateral: problems are considered and dealt with as local and individual, though cross-border. And it is here that I see the effectiveness of this type: the foreign subsidiaries no longer disappear from the surface, but have an advocate in cases of emergency. Not only does this type of EWC lack an affective European identity, but it also lacks a European identity in the sense of practical work and business contacts and a strategy for action. It starts moving, but not in a genuinely European game; rather, it plays a nationally dominated game, but now with some other nation included in the package.

In the main this also applies to the third type, 'the EWC as an information analyst: the fencing foil'. This is the French variation of a nationally dominated game with foreign themes and problems in the rucksack. Because of limited space, this and the two remaining types of EWCs, which I term 'the EWC running in vain – the toothless tiger' and 'the marginalised EWC: a wrong start', will not be treated in this chapter.

The second level in which European identity is addressed is the reflection of questioned EWC members on whether 'European or international solidarity' exists within the committee. The general answer to this was a clear 'no', and this even from respondents who belonged to the 'participating working team' type of EWC. Respondents spontaneously have the same understanding of solidarity as Durkheim's, namely feelings of identity/ identification, i.e. empathy, sympathy and compassion, out of which emerge a corresponding readiness to help. Some respondents refined this with the example of a threat to close a plant: EWC members and employee representatives from other countries would not be willing to strike or demonstrate in this situation. The standard formulation in explaining this was as follows: it is totally normal that charity begins at home. Respondents emphasised that solidarity in its full meaning represents too high a demand. 'When it really comes to the crunch then everyone considers their own plant, their own country,' as one EWC respondent said. Another EWC member talked about a case where German EWC members were pleased when they heard that the Czech plant had to stop production because of flooding. The comment was, 'Love does not stretch that far.' (The eastern enlargement of EWCs is the subject in Kotthoff (2005).)

The third identity-relevant level in the research is the 'everyday Europeanisation', i.e. the effect of the EWC on the home works council. Is Europe becoming an everyday dimension of national plants? The hypothesis was that without such roots the EWC project would be left dangling. In most of the studied cases, the EWC members themselves consider the interest in the EWC among their works council colleagues at home, and even more that among the workforce, to be very limited. The exception is only those companies with a very high percentage of highly qualified employees (with a university education) in the workforce as well as in the works council. Here a large section of the workforce has contact to other countries through their everyday work, and many have at times worked or visited abroad. One respondent reports from a pharmaceutical firm: 'It has to do with our firm structure that one has a feeling of being allied with colleagues from other countries. We work together!' This comparatively large interest in the EWC within highly qualified firms even exists where the EWC has only a limited significance.

Statements from interviewed national works councils about their own interests in the EWC and those of other national works councils are congruent with statements of the questioned EWC members: interest in, as well as knowledge about, the EWC is limited.

> It plays no role here, is hardly discussed. Official information takes place, that they have returned from the meeting, that they are learning English. But in terms of policy, in everyday life it does not play a role up to now.
>
> (Member of a German works council)

Another respondent noted:

> For us here it is far away. It is really far, far away. Such an EWC for me is extremely far away. So far I have not thought about what kind of committee it is, what positions they take up.

Interviews with works council delegates from the home country confirm the observation that only in firms with many highly qualified employees does a degree of interest in the EWC exist. The limited interest also goes for firms in which the EWC corresponds with the EWC-type 'participating working team'. This contradicts my own hypothesis concerning roots (*Bodenhaftung*) being a condition for the possibility of an effective EWC. Obviously the EWC is an arrangement of specialised functionaries. Its development and significance, at least in the current stage, do not depend very strongly on the European identity of the workforce and of the home works council members, but rather on its own identity, which in turn mainly depends on the structural characteristics of the firm.

In contrast to interests, the expectations of home works councils towards the EWC are big and very standardised. They demand that the EWC stops the transfer of production to low-wage countries and that it raises labour costs and social standards in the other countries up to the German standards. Some see the EWC as a European office for the allocation of work, which distributes jobs between all the production sites in a just way. These immense expectations are abstract. They express a wishful thinking that is connected not to an interest in the EWC but rather the opposite, to the small degree of reality that the EWC contains in their eyes.

Types of identity in EWCs

From R. Münch (1988: 152) comes the concise sentence, 'the common identification based on solidarity in an institutional order is steered through affective bonds'. If this alone makes up identification, the EWC has none. The quoted sentence also contains the reason why it cannot have one: European employee representation does not have an 'institutional order'. Yes, it is true that many observers view the EWC as the pioneer that must create this institutional order. For this reason we have to reformulate the question: what kind of identity can a pioneer (or a reformer) have at all? Belonging to a stable order and to a firmly established collective does not apply to the pioneer. For he/she leaves the old and established order and penetrates socially new land. The pioneer is a wanderer between different worlds, in a milieu of transition.

This indicates that the post-modern identification concepts referred to at the beginning, which speak of a hybrid, plural and operative identity, are more applicable to the situation of the EWC than Durkheim and the other old ones. Although the plural and operative aspect is an adequate description of the situation, I do not want to pursue this approach as it touches our topic only from the point of view of the individual and the self. The post-modern authors ask how individuals can assert themselves under insecure, fluid conditions – the 'in-between'. They do not conceptualise the object from the point of view of society and do not question how society and lasting collectives are possible. The conditions for co-operation, cohesion and identification are not their subject. Hence, for the purposes of our problematic we cannot expect much from them.

My suggestion would be to continue to operate with the classical approaches described above. It is clear that in the case of the EWC we should not strain the full variant of identity as solidarity. That would be too high an aim. We have to content ourselves with weaker variants. Therefore the question is: what can give the EWC co-operation and cohesion beyond Durkheim?

I believe the 'participating working team' EWC in my empirical section possesses certain indicators of such variants. I list them once again:

1 Identification in the total meaning of Durkheim as affective relationship, we-feeling, feeling of interdependence, solidarity. (This too-strong variant we have to place in the realm of the ideal.)
2 The EWC possesses a 'European thinking'. This is not primarily an affective relation, but rather a functional and rational one. The problem definition, the 'way of seeing things', the policy and strategy of the EWC has a European framework, it has a European view of things and a transnational agenda. This can definitely be the result of national and local interests; solidarity does not have to be the primary motive. Such thinking demands international interaction and co-operation. This is *institutionalised international co-operation*. The EWC is a team for European co-operation within the company. In this variant the cognitive and strategic aspects are in the foreground.
3 The role of EWC delegates becomes routine, habitual and professional. This happens first and foremost through an effective internal organisation, relatively high time budgets and natural working contact between members that fulfil an organisational role within the committee. In this variant the operative aspect is in the foreground.

4 Intensification and institutionalisation of access to relevant management at group level: private discussions between the EWC chair and the CEO; a meaningful and effective programme on the second day of an EWC meeting ('information provided by management'); open access also to top sector and division management.

5 Networking: regular contact also between members who are not involved in the organisation or work of the committee; getting to know each other; getting closer to each other; exchanging information about everyday life; getting to know the standards of employee representation practices in other countries (cultural diversity). Here, non-functional situations are especially important: the evening social programme that goes with EWC meetings, coffee breaks, visits of foreign colleagues who are on holiday, etc. In this variant the life world aspects are in the foreground.

Even if 'European identification' (variant 1) remains too distant, the intensification of contacts and co-operation in variants 2 to 5 represent a wide area for further institutionalisation and for the creation of EWC identity. These are variants that realistically can be brought into play. In each of these dimensions identification means more investment in transnational co-operation of representative bodies in the company and more contacts with colleagues from other countries who are working on the same projects.

Our views on interest representation are strongly influenced by the national political history of the representation institutions; that is the history of resistance and battles for recognition. However, for the EWC neither the national nor primarily the European frameworks are the playing field, but rather the internal world of the global company. The world of the multinational company is so big, comprehensive and complex that it has a tendency towards self-reference and self-sufficiency. The external world becomes more irrelevant because the company itself becomes a world system. With regard to the EWC this means that it is not Europe's political construction that is the point of reference, but rather the internal world of the multinational company. 'Company group (*Konzern*) works council' would be the more exact term if it were not already taken up by the German works council, for which it is not quite the correct choice, as the term 'group' today implies at the same time the adjective 'global'. This means: what is the state of European identity of a committee which calls itself a *European* Works Council, but which in many cases is about to become a *World* Works Council?

If we look back at the theoretical tradition there are a few clear indicators about what can contribute to the growth of co-operation and cohesion. According to Durkheim, this is mainly the feeling of interdependence. It arises through the division of labour – today we would rather say through production networks (working together). But there also exists a felt interdependence through competition, i.e. through mutual exchangeability when one can be made superfluous by the other.

Through interdependence arises a sense of being affected. What the Other does, and how he or she is doing, concerns me, for it has noticeable effects on me and vice versa. This interactive way to a collective identity is dependent on whether a firm through its production and organisation structure creates pre-conditions and possibilities for tangible   not only abstract – transnational affectedness. At firms with a high percentage of highly qualified employees, we have seen how the structural realities (transnational organisation) intensify the direct interaction ('working together') and bring about a sympathy with foreign colleagues ('feeling connected') that is positive for the interest in the EWC.

Another road is the sociology of authority. When plant management loses power and influence and the decisive matters are determined by group or European management, then we are dealing with another authority. The altered organisational chart is directly followed by altered feelings of protection as well as subordination. What occurs is a drastic change in sovereignty. The authority of the national manager declines. People in the firm hope for what is most important, namely recognition, protection and direction from those who alone can offer such things: from the central, transnational management. The EWC is forced to become European when management becomes so. This isomorphism of the organisation, this reorientation of aerials and new alignment of working practices and communication channels, I consider to be the strongest motor for European identity of the EWC. It occurs faster and more intensively the bigger the need for protection and recognition, i.e. particularly in situations of distress and danger, in which people move closer together. Therefore, it would be an interesting question to study how far the dramatically endangered situation of many General Motors Europe plants in the autumn of 2004 strengthened not only the ability of the EWC to act, but also its European identity in terms of the affective version of collective consciousness. The national institutions for interest representation are the outcomes of suffering, fighting and hoping in historical battles. The EWC stands just at the beginning of such exciting experiences, which form identity.

Notes

1 This chapter was translated from German by Michael Whittall in co-operation with Susanne Wöllecke-Whittall and Herman Knudsen.
2 The project was a comparative case study covering twelve MNCs (seven German, two British-Dutch, two US and one French company). In each company interviews were conducted with two German members of the steering committee of the EWC, one non-German EWC member, two members of the German *Betriebsrat* (who were not members of the EWC), one corporate HR manager and one union representative. The main subjects of the study were the influence and role of the EWC in company politics, the internal communication and integration of EWC members, the repercussions of the EWCs on the national works councils, and the assistance provided by trade unions (Kotthoff 2006).

References

Durkheim, E. (1992) *Über soziale Arbeitsteilung. Studie über die Organisationhöherer Gesellschaften*, Frankfurt: Suhrkamp.

Joas, H. and Knöbl, W. (2004) *Sozialtheorie*, Frankfurt: Suhrkamp.

Kotthoff, H. (2005) *EU-Osterweiterung: die aktuelle Herausforderung für den Europäischen Betriebsrat*, Arbeitspapier 109, Düsseldorf: Hans-Böckler Stiftung.

—— (2006) *Lehrjahre des Europäischen Betriebsrats. Zehn Jahre transnationale Arbeitnehmervertretung*, Berlin: Edition Sigma.

Luhmann, N. (1992) Arbeitsteilung und Moral. Durkheims Theorie, Einleitung, in E. Durkheim (ed.) *Über soziale Arbeitsteilung. Studie über die Organisation höhere Gesellschaften*, Frankfurt: Suhrkamp, 19–40.

Müller, H.-P. and Schmidt, M. (1992) Arbeitsteilung, Solidarität und Moral, Nachwort, in E. Durkheim (ed.) *Über soziale Arbeitsteilung. Studie über die Organisation höhere Gesellschaften*, Frankfurt: Suhrkamp, 481–521.

Münch, R. (1988) *Theorie des Handelns. Zur Rekonstruktion der Beiträge von T. Parsons, E. Durkheim und M. Weber*, Frankfurt: Suhrkamp.

Parsons, T. (1964) *Social Structure and Personality*, New York: Free Press.

Popitz, H. (1986) Macht und Herrschaft. Stufen der Institutionalisierung von Macht, in H. Popitz, *Phänomene der Macht*, Tübingen: Mohr (Siebeck), 37–67.

Pries, L. (ed.) (2001) *The Emergence of Transnational Social Spaces*, London: Routledge.

Weber, M. (1972) *Wirtschaft und Gesellschaft*, 5, Aufl. Tübingen: Mohr (Siebeck).

Yildiz, E. (2006) Identitätsdiskurs zu Beginn des 21. Jahrhunderts, *Soziologische Revue*, 29 (1): 36–50.

11 Preparing the ground for a social Europe?

European Works Councils and European regulatory identity

Miguel Martínez Lucio and Syd Weston

The 1994 European Union directive on the establishment of European Works Councils (EWCs) has stimulated considerable research and debate. For some observers, it is a major contribution to workers' rights in multinational companies (MNCs) and a platform on which to develop more meaningful forms of cross-border co-operation between worker representatives and their trade unions (Weston and Martínez Lucio 1998; Whittall 2000). For others, on the contrary, it matches current trends in the management of MNCs and facilitates the creation of company-centred and management-driven employment relations across Europe (Deppe 1995).[1] It has also been noted that the development of EWCs is consistent with decentralisation in political and industrial relations systems and may well assist MNCs in weakening their ties with national industrial relations systems (Streeck and Schmitter 1991). Furthermore, there is concern surrounding the support mechanisms of EWCs due to the major institutional differences of the trade unions throughout Europe, particularly those regarding their decision-making mechanisms. It is suggested that such differences may significantly undermine the ability of the trade unions to counter the development of a more managerially driven employment relations systems from evolving (Stoop 1994). There is therefore a range of perspectives surrounding the potential development of European Works Councils, with UK contributions tending to be slightly more pessimistic (see Fitzgerald and Stirling 2004).

Our position is that EWCs should not be seen simply as the instruments of management, but that in certain circumstances they do offer trade unions and worker representatives the opportunity to influence corporate decision-making. We suggest that EWCs are one aspect of new complex interactions between supranational regulation and evolving international labour structures. The EWC initiative can be seen as a new form of regulatory strategy to overcome some of the political and economic constraints facing the European Union (EU) in the context of 'globalisation'. Within the new context developments *in and around* EWCs can have spin-off effects on the form and character of worker representation in Europe. These effects can condition management decision-making and organisational outcomes, implying a new form of 'joint regulation' in European industrial relations.

In this chapter we first discuss the shift in the pattern of regulation within the EU, and how and why new forms of regulation have emerged. We follow this with an account of how EWCs can be understood as one aspect of this form of regulation. We go on to analyse the tensions and limitations with this type of regulation and EWCs in particular and how other commentators draw their conclusions. The final section of the chapter will reaffirm our thesis that the *form* of regulation and the *context* within which EWCs function need to be at the centre of future research. In this respect, we suggest that EWCs need to be understood as part of a broader array of actors and players, an element of a broader regulatory logic, which includes communities and networks of organisations and individuals exchanging information and developing actions and policy. We attempt to demonstrate how the move to reinstate a regulatory logic of a social nature within the European Union, through such developments as EWCs, is based on a more flexible view of regulation (Keller and Platzer 2003; Marginson and Sisson 2004). To what extent this is an outcome of design or an awareness of the structural limitations of transnational European regulation and state systems is, however, another matter. Regulation is not about intervention, it is about linkages between different actors (MacKenzie and Martínez Lucio 2005). It is about the position and context of institutions, be they formal or informal. In addition, it is also a question of how these forms of regulation develop an identity, i.e. a purpose and values.

The emergence of new forms of regulation in the European Union

EU economic and social policy emerged in a period of crisis for the Keynesian welfare state and the model of corporatist intermediation associated with it. The principal orientation of EU intervention of recent years has been based on market integration and deregulation, exemplified by the Single European Market and Maastricht Treaty. Integration along market lines was embraced in order to contribute to the restructuring and unification of a 'European' capitalist base, the implicit assumption being that European capital possesses cultural and political characteristics that allow for a more organised and regionally committed capitalist constituency to emerge. There remain, however, major political and economic questions as to how the changing constituency of capital in Europe is to be regulated and supported in a more global and liberalised economic space, and how much it should be wedded to the social character of traditional European regulation. This is more pronounced in light of increasingly overt tensions within the EU between supposed 'Anglo-Saxon' models of regulation and Franco/German ones.

Recent events such as the 2005 referendums in France and the Netherlands have continued to demonstrate that the major constraint for the EU is the political dimension. The nature of decision-making is such that on most issues the tendency is to seek a lowest common denominator, which can be supported by most national actors. EU policy has rarely gravitated towards 'best practice' in the social regulation of the employment relationship. Instead, it seeks a common reference point that inevitably, given the diversity of social regulation and welfare systems, tends to be of a minimum standard (Platzer 1998; Leisink and Hyman 2005: 279). This is also driven by the procedural orientation of the EU and the manner in which decision-making is developed across a longer time frame and with complex forms of policy inputs (Platzer 1998).

Consequently an interest in alternative forms of regulation emerged to address economic and fiscal issues within the EU and problems of its decision-making processes (Cohen and Sabel 1997). Within a complex and at times contradictory policy-making context the outputs have varied from direct forms of intervention (based on strategic alliances between economic and industrial groups) to more indirect support involving facilitating contacts between a range of economic actors and public bodies. For example, the EU scientific and academic exchange programmes are evidence of how networking activity is facilitated and organised within the European political space. The aim is to create a supportive framework within knowledge-based communities that consistently interact with the projects of the EU and the new actors involved in the process. This networking is crucial for understanding the way EU policy is made, implemented and developed. Policy implementation, like the decision-making described earlier, is based on a broader articulation and combination of actors (Jensen *et al.* 1999; Peters 1994).[2] To this extent networking is not solely a feature of labour movement activity within the European Union. It is a central development in the way 'successful organisations' are believed to operate. The notion is that traditional bureaucratic processes of organisational behaviour (in terms of modern hierarchies and decision-making processes) are too rigid and inflexible for the new economic climate. In particular, the new globalisation forces call for new forms of information exchanges across less restrictive and bounded forms of organisations and actors. Castells (1998) sees this as the fundamental organising logic of the informational economy and highlights why there is ongoing interest with networking as an organisational form.

Thus, a new discourse of 'state intervention' has been progressively emerging within the EU that has digested these views. This new form of regulation can be labelled as 'regulation from below' (Moody 1997), 'indirect regulation' (Majone 1997: 265) or what various other commentators have termed 'flexible regulation'. A good example of this type of regulation can be seen in the regional dimension of EU policies where the EU connects with regional administrative systems and social actors. It is our contention that, while being formally different from the EWC initiative, the latter conforms to the same pattern in that they attract a range of interest groups into action.

The logic of this process is that the EU, as an emergent supranational quasi-state, bypasses the nation-states and locks into the activity and new roles established within the local and regional states in the form of regional (e.g. Catalonia) or city-based governance (e.g. Barcelona). It provides the local state with specific resources and economic support in its relations with MNCs and capital more generally. For example, training programmes or aid for assisting with the outcomes of restructuring are used to allow the local state and local actors to intervene in the local labour market. Transnational *networks* between the key agents of local state systems are elaborated and supported by the EU, so that local economies may continue to prove attractive to international and European capital. New strategic alliances and loose neo-corporatist arrangements that involve local economic interests at the micro level emerge to sustain this new role and 'symbio-tic' relationship between state and capital (Hirst and Thompson, 1996: 147–51). Information is therefore exchanged on 'good practice' in terms of governance.

This has been seen as a new logic of state intervention and support which has been characteristic of EU interaction with regional levels of regulation. It rests on the fact that global capital is still organisationally and envir-onmentally dependent on local political, economic and social contexts (Hirst and Thompson 1996; Panitch 1995; Peck 1996). The aim is to con-struct what Hancher and Moran (1989) call a regulatory space with estab-lished relations and processes capable of sustaining regulatory functions (for a discussion of such concepts see MacKenzie and Martínez Lucio 2005).

> Accordingly, what is clearly evolving is a shift to forms of regulation based upon information and persuasion, rather than on command and control mechanisms; and ... this needs to be acknowledged as part of the general reappraisal of the role of public policy in an increasingly complex and interdependent world.
>
> (Majone 1997: 69)

A whole new range of institutions is being constructed, capable of mon-itoring and regulating the economy. What therefore seems to be emerging throughout various arenas of regulatory activity within the EU is a new logic of governance that underpins the attempts of the EU to locate itself in the new economic order. EU agencies enter the political arena as organisers and transmitters of information. Within such a set of relations, information becomes a political resource (Castells 1998). Thus, a new form of govern-ance is entertained and propagated that is based on an interaction between different societal and political actors and their growing interdependence (Kooiman 2003). Consequently, the process of intervention becomes dependent on the role of the recipients and the diverse users of policy as much as on its instigators (Kooiman 2003).

There is therefore an attempt within the EU to create new legal and political contexts through which other actors can participate in the regula-tion of capital:

Use of regulatory policy measures allows the European Commission to 'call the tune without paying the piper' in the field of social policy. Thus by making use of regulatory policies in the area of social policy, rather than those involving direct Union expenditure, EU social policy, in a number of specific areas, sets the standards to be adhered to in member states while incurring minimal Union costs.

(Cram 1994: 210).

In our opinion, EWCs fit into the logic of this regulation process because they attempt to undertake the function of regulation in terms of conducing or coercing employers towards 'high-road' forms of economic strategy and social policies. They provide a framework of discussion for the corporate and employment issues to be acted on within the context of a view of social regulation that (may) fit the more social aspects of the EU's strategy but without the EU directly interfering in the policies of the firm (Sisson 1999). The EWC Directive is therefore a form of intervention into the corporate governance of MNCs and fits the logic of regulation outlined above. Within the internal and external constraints of the EU political process, the directive creates new structures of regulation, in this case through worker representation in decision-making. It ties together distinct socio-economic constituencies, political elites and projects through an alternative mode of regulation (Jensen *et al.* 1999). This is its strength but may also be its weakness.

EWCs as a new form of regulation

If European Works Councils are to be a new form of regulation – or a pivotal feature of the new tapestry of regulation – then we need to evaluate what role they may play and, in particular, try to capture whether their identity tends towards any specific actor's agendas or projects. There is a tension as to whether they will be subsumed within specific management orientations and projects, and therefore internalised within the boundaries and identity of the corporation; or, on the other hand, whether they will feature as part of the identity of a broader form of labour co-ordination and social agendas. To do this we need to assess EWCs in terms of their links to actors, the internal organisational developments of the forums themselves, the extent of co-ordination within labour and capital, and the way early initiatives define their progress.

It has already been noted that indirect, flexible regulation has limitations and problems. Majone (1994: 79), for example, suggests how these new types of economic regulation contain weaknesses as well as strengths. The first main problem is that they can be 'captured' by the actors they are intended to control; becoming an extension of the very interests they were meant to regulate. Second, as with all organisational bodies they may be open to bureaucratic inertia and fail to connect with their original purpose;

or their objectives may become vague and dysfunctional. Another problem is the potential lack of co-ordination among the different regulatory actors and bodies, and their projects. Finally, the very way such new forms of regulation have been developed may undermine their accountability and democratic status. Hence the new mechanisms may be transformed to function in ways unintended and unanticipated.

Such risks clearly exist in the case of EWCs (see Martínez Lucio and Weston 2004 for a discussion of distinct perspectives on EWCs). A key concern of many commentators is that employers can use, and capture, EWCs as a vehicle for communicating business as opposed to any social issues, and for constructing special relations within these arenas with certain labour representatives at the expense of others (Tuckman and Whittall 2002; Weston and Martínez Lucio 1997). Also, Hyman (1994, 2001) has noted the ongoing lure of the market as the basis of union identity and the tensions this may create for traditional forms of class and social identity. EWCs may therefore facilitate the development of 'enterprise-plant egoism' within the European labour movement and within privileged, elite firms. Consequently, EWCs can, in certain cases, reinforce a corporate identity within its union constituency, creating new cleavages within the labour movement (Deppe 1995; Royle 1999; Wills 2000).

It is understandable that the economic context of different countries (along with the home base of those multinationals effected by the directive and trade unions within them) will influence the internal politics of EWCs. It is also clear that labour's international structures are still relatively limited when compared with those of transnational capital (Lecher 1998; Platzer 1998; Schulten 2003) and not difficult to conclude that such factors will undermine the strategic linkages that labour would require to regulate international capital. As a consequence of the project of 'new regulation', governance structures may become institutionally 'stretched', constructed in a more precarious and complex manner, and articulated in broader spatial and organisational terrains: hence making regulatory processes and outcomes more complex and potentially no more than symbolic. In internal terms, questions have already been raised concerning the accountability of EWC representatives, their gender and ethnic profile and their political complexion (Meissner 1994). The agendas of such structures will be the subject of competing interests and interventions. In addition national interests will continue to be mobilised by employers, managers and worker representatives within these forums (Weston and Martínez Lucio 1997, 1998).

Another concern is that EWCs do not build on any strong state tradition or organised and regulated system of industrial relations at European level (Streeck and Schmitter 1991: 157). If anything, the tendency is towards greater decentralisation in political and industrial relations terms (Keller 1998). Any articulation of industrial relations at the transnational level will occur within a context of privileged firms and be apolitical and voluntaristic in nature (Streeck and Schmitter 1991: 158). Thus EWCs are likely to undermine traditional, solidaristic forms of industrial relations as regulation becomes internalised within the firm and in effect *captured* by employers, as mentioned earlier. Institutions such as EWCs can only become effective and autonomous actors with the support of a strong state tradition and 'public power', which at the EU level does not exist (Streeck and Schmitter 1991: 142). As Hyman puts it:

> The underlying flaw in the pursuit of European-level regulation by supranational equivalents of collective bargaining or legal enactment is that such processes and the resulting instruments lack the support of the more diffuse shared perspectives and normative commitments which give them much of their effectiveness at national level.
>
> (Hyman 2001: 176)

The question is therefore not solely of regulatory congruence or political influence. It is also one of identity. By identity, we refer to the manner in which EWCs are visualised by other actors and how they present themselves *vis-à-vis* their internal and external organisational environments. We also include the values and purpose underpinning the EWC as a system of regulation.

European Works Councils in a new context

Management and EWCs

The above issues do raise real concerns with the prospect of EWCs becoming primarily extensions of corporate decision-making and agendas. They may become part of the internal coalition of interests that firms and trade unions build in the face of the market. To this extent their regulatory identity could be linked more closely to the neo-liberal or market dimensions of European Union politics. However, this is not inevitable. EWCs are emerging in the context of new managerial developments: benchmarking, exhaustive (although not always consistent) performance measurement techniques, and an obsession with 'communication' (Knudsen 1995; Garrahan and Stewart 1992; Sewell and Wilkinson 1992; Ferner and Edwards 1995). In this context, information is becoming a major vehicle of transnational management control but at the same time it provides a new arena of engagement and a potential resource for transnational employee representatives. This provides 'windows of opportunities' into which labour can make effective interventions (Martínez Lucio and Weston 2004). For example, internal benchmarking may well be a powerful mechanism for diffusing best practices by senior management, but it can be met by various forms of resistance from local management as well as from labour (Weston and Martínez Lucio 1997).

To argue that EWCs have no effect on management and that they will inevitably be incorporated into managerial agendas is to ignore the complex organisational processes within MNCs. Many commentators exaggerate the power resources and consistency of management strategy (Hyman 1994). Internal power systems within organisations are invariably incomplete and precarious (Ferner and Edwards 1995). As Storey (1985) points out, there are numerous axes of internal tensions: departmental or hierarchical divisions (Lowe 1993), professional identities (Armstrong 1989), national and local interests (Doz *et al.* 1981). Along these fault lines within organisations, information flows and controls inevitably become the focus of disagreement, especially when the structures of companies are changing as a result of mergers, takeovers and organisational volatility.

At local level, gaps in management information systems are exposed by alternative information flows and informal circuits (Paauwe and Dewe 1995: 71). One EWC case study indicated how corporate performance measurement systems varied between plants, with local managers being set different targets in different areas, forcing complex internal negotiations and responses from local managers and trade unionists in some cases (Weston and Martínez Lucio 1997). These types of issues have begun to emerge within discussions among EWC union members and, in turn, conditioned local pressures for change. Given the ongoing nature of organisational politics it seems highly unlikely that a central management communication system will overcome these ongoing contradictions.

The new managerial structures and practices can therefore become problematic as a strategy in the face of new institutions that bridge the distinct sites of employment that are benchmarked against each other. Within this context, EWCs are a forum and a point of reference for exchanges of information across different plants, with the new managerial regime attempting to generate competitive pressures between them. What is more, EWCs are being constructed when such management strategies have intentionally increased employee representatives' interests in the new management performance and productivity measurements techniques (Weston and Martínez Lucio 1997). Much, of course, will depend on the structure of production and the links between sites within transnational corporations. Cross-referencing is probably most developed in manufacturing, but the development of detailed performance measurement systems in other sectors such as financial services and telecommunications (especially call centres) has made this the subject of transnational union exchanges here also. The EWC Directive, allowing the use of 'experts' by employee representatives, in some cases enables organised labour to exploit the new informational resources. Furthermore, the identified training needs for EWC representatives can go some way in making better use of such information flows.[3]

Alternative linkages and identities: regulation and the co-ordination of EWCs

As well as the formal institutional vehicles for the development of transnational labour relations, there are informal ones involving a whole range of informational and political circuits relating to the activities and management practices of MNCs. A good example is the development of a range of networks among trade unionists in GM Europe, who organised meetings throughout the 1990s formulating and sharing counter-strategies on issues such as teamworking. This was mainly related to qualitative issues within the context of the 1990s (the development of new forms of work organisation and patterns of automation). In the past few years the concerns have shifted to questions of restructuring and change (Pulignano 2005). In this particular case, the EWC has become a conduit for discussions that link a range of networks and trade union activists. EWCs are therefore influenced by broader structures of employee representation. For example, there has been growing evidence both of wage comparison across the EU (Marginson 2000; Walsh *et al.* 1995) and that EWC agreements have stimulated international comparisons in local collective bargaining within the enterprises (Fulton 1995: 237; LRD 1994), although evidence is not always easy to find.[4]

Even at this early stage of their development there is emerging evidence, albeit anecdotal, that EWCs are generating and making linkages to alternative networks and the more traditional institutional mechanisms of trade union relationships. There is evidence that such supports can be effective even in Royle's (1999) sober assessment of the McDonald's EWC, where the absence of a union infrastructure limited the effectiveness of the forum. In the case of Renault, the EWC helped unions co-ordinate a short international stoppage in 1997 in reaction to the closure of the Vilvoorde plant in Belgium, even though opposition was not ultimately successful. Moreover, the EWC became a forum for the development of an alternative viability plan for the plant and broader discussions and relations. The episode led to widespread recognition within the EU of the need for a stronger underpinning of EWCs through improved consultation and information rights (Rehfeldt 1999). EWCs are also part of an increasingly organised system of supranational interest intermediation, involving for example the ETUC and the European industry federations. At regional level the embryo of a more structured industrial relations system has also been steadily developing (Gollbach and Schulten 2000).[5]

The concern that there must be some co-ordination within and between European Works Councils, and related trade union constituencies, has been formally acknowledged and responded to by the European Trade Unions Congress. The 2003–6 TRACE project (Trade Unions Anticipating Change in Europe) is very much concerned with developing the industrial relations capacity of trade unions and their activists within these forums, among others. Ensuring trade unions are in themselves connected and working across boundaries in novel ways is a vital precondition for the co-ordination of such institutions as EWCs. Increasingly, questions of co-ordination require the development of a variety of networks, knowledge systems and information processes. These are vital for networks to be active, as is having access to information, strategy formulation and a common sense of identity (Wills 2001: 194–8).

Supporting EWCs

The picture we have at this time is that EWCs as networks and the networks that underpin EWCs vary such that they do not form a cohesive whole with a given purpose. Jensen (2004: 76) argues that networks vary between those based on 'similarity and boundedness' ('clubs'), those based on 'difference and functional relations' ('chains') and those based on much looser and undefined relations ('acquaintances'). The need in European industrial relations is to recognise the needs of such distinct networks (authority structures, information-sharing, and knowledge needs respectively) and to provide regulatory and organisational supports for them. Moreover, the aim is to try and ensure they move from the category of 'acquaintances' to that of 'clubs', or at least systematic 'chains'.

The above points fit into the concept of epistemic communities. While it is normally used to describe professional communities, Haas (1992) argues that this is a useful term for understanding international policy co-ordination. Epistemic communities are networks of experts that share knowledge about an area but also share normative principles and beliefs (Haas 1992). These can influence the policy framework and debates of international communities as seen in various topics or international matters: circulating ideas and influencing policies. For the kind of regulatory process of an indirect nature as outlined above to function and operate, it will need such communities framing debates and developing policy. These communities would form links that sustain an ongoing dialogue on developments such as European Works Councils that will allow for an awareness of their development and the prospect of recalling activities and communicating them. A history and 'glossary' of developments can be sustained by such communities and, therefore, allow for more informed choices regarding their role, i.e. whether they evolve as a focus for worker solidarity and not corporate internal marketing.

Socially oriented figures and bodies in the European Union, through some of its funding programmes, have begun to realise that the relations inside European Works Councils will depend on the relations established within and between them: that is to say, the link between the European Works Councils in particular sectors, the link they have with trade union constituencies, and the input of autonomous and non-corporate epistemic communities (including academic, quasi-academic, political activists and other interests). Although the politics and internal differences are not an issue to ignore, in general terms the aim is to have such communities raise and push for alternative forms of restructuring, social support and progressive economic development within the confines of corporate Europe. That is why more focused approaches to trade union training and industrial relations capacity-building programmes are necessary. One could even argue that the social capital of trade unionists through the development of mutually beneficial reciprocation and organisation across trade union communities would further strengthen the community in question and its regulatory potential. Much hinges on the extent to which the social capital of trade unionists inside and around European Works Councils develops. By social capital Bourdieu (1986) refers to the resources that are linked to membership of a durable network of relationships of mutual acquaintance, and the mutual recognition that is institutionalised to varying degrees. In this instance, it would mean the linkages a trade union representative would have, the types of information they could access through formal and informal channels, and the relations across boundaries they could count on.

Within the EU institutions, the Commission's approach to the drafting and development of new regulations in the area of worker rights and involvement has been based on a process of negotiation and interaction which becomes consolidated over time (Jensen *et al.* 1999: 127). This 'elite-based' interaction may provide a source of tension in terms of the politics of the labour movement, but it provides a series of support structures and decision-making processes. There is regularity in regulation, or such is the objective. Hence, the development of new forms of transnational worker representation interlocks with major developments in the behaviour and structures of labour and capital at the political level of the EU. This can generate more 'windows of opportunity' for labour. For example, Knutsen (1997) saw prospects for the consolidation of 'Euro-corporatism', while Falkner (1996: 202) interprets the Maastricht Social Agreement as a demonstration of such a process, and suggests that through such initiatives as the Working Time Directive 'Euro-corporatism' may 'cascade' down to company and workplace level. Whether this is likely to happen or not depends on how the 'links' between levels of industrial relations and within circuits of power develop and require further investigation and analysis along the lines we suggest above. Indeed, industrial relations as a discipline needs to engage with the realities of regulation and the manner in which it is shared and moulded in broad and multiple ways (Martínez Lucio and Weston 2004; MacKenzie and Martínez Lucio 2005; Visser 2005).

Conclusion

Increasingly the EU has developed, and come to rely on, external forms of regulation for its own regulatory structures to operate. In this respect there is not so much a 'hollowing out of the state' but more of a complex process of interaction and external dependency – an outward search for allies. This means that new modes of regulation will depend on developments beyond 'public power'. Much may depend on how other types of softer regulation (for example at the regional level) and the constituent actors (such as supranational trade union organisations) are articulated with EWCs if 'capture' by capital is to be avoided. Consequently, the development of further support in terms of legislation, transnational networks and political links needs to address the question as to how EWCs can be supported from the 'centre' to perform the function of influencing management priorities and decision-making.

Methodologically, the study of EWCs should also go beyond the content of agreements, their structures or their pattern of bargaining – no matter how important these issues are. The reality is that EWCs are shaped by the environing political and social context. The interconnections between different types of regulation, state support, political action and ideological projects will be crucial for the development of this new form of regulation. A broader remit in EWC research is not solely an academic issue but also a political one. If we are to understand the twin problems of EWC capture and isolation, we need to comprehend the strategic preconditions for effective counter-measures.

This chapter has suggested that there is a new dynamic of transnational worker representation emerging with repercussions for the regulation of the international division of labour and capitalist organisational structures. It may be embryonic, and based on loose articulations between different sites of regulation, but it is emerging nevertheless. Given the complex nature of their construction, how will these new models of regulation develop and sustain themselves? Will they be subsumed within distinct and pre-existing systems of worker involvement or will they stimulate a new era of international labour politics? Either way, the strategy of indirect and flexible regulation leads to a new set of issues between capital and labour within the EU. They illustrate the evolution of new forms of transnational employment and industrial regulation that must be studied in terms of their complex political development, structure and context.

On a final note, there is the ideological make-up of EWCs. Forms of regulation require political values and visions of their purpose in order to function and sustain legitimacy. This is especially the case when they rest on such new forms as discussed above that are premised on loose and varied networks, diverse communities of knowledge, and the manner in which they intersect with others. The risk (or reality) is that such communities or networks connect in contradictory ways and become subsumed or allowed to drift (Jensen 2004). Regulatory identity is currently being contested as market-oriented approaches line up against more state-led and socially oriented traditions. The events in the EU during 2005 in terms of the national challenges to the EU project are a testament to that. The direction of the different elements of this new system of regulation and the way it provides linkages may well depend on whether there are common views of the way work should be regulated. In this respect it will be in the realm of the political and in broader forms of affiliation that a new transnational worker identity and co-ordination may evolve by acting as 'glue' for a renewed project of social inclusion and representation (Martínez Lucio and Weston 1995).

The identity of any regulatory process will ultimately stabilise in the longer term, when the links between its different features, institutional contours and the realisable and transparent nature of outcomes become clearer. To judge such systems without a longer time frame might be ill-judged, even if the time frames of regulation are not as extensive as they used to be. To expect a mode of representation, which is what EWCs are, to develop alternative, social and political identities in themselves and as objects of study is naïve. They will only do so as part of an extension and set of linkages that are, in turn, underpinned by alternative discourses and values.

Notes

1 An earlier version of this chapter was originally published in the *European Journal of Industrial Relations*, Vol. 6, No. 2, pp. 203–16 with the title 'European Works Councils and flexible regulation: the politics of intervention'. This version has been developed to include themes related to social capital, epistemic communities and discussions of regulatory identity in general.
2 For example, one of the criticisms of EWCs is that they would be no more than a 'weekend in Paris' for the trade unionists involved.
3 We use the term 'articulation' in a different way from Crouch, who writes of an articulated organisation as 'one in which strong relations of interdependence bind different vertical levels, such that the actions of the centre are frequently predicated on securing the consent of lower levels and the autonomous action of lower levels is bounded by rules of delegation and scope for discretion ultimately controlled by successively higher levels' (Crouch 1993: 54–5). Crouch points to this dimension within trade unions as being a key factor in countries with 'stable bargained corporatism'. We use this concept in a different way, drawing on the work of Stuart Hall (1988) as well as Laclau and Mouffe (1984). According to Hall, 'articulation is thus the form of connection that *can* make a unity of two different elements, under certain conditions. It is a linkage which is not necessary, determined, absolute and essential for all time' (Grossberg 1996: 141).
4 For a fuller discussion of the forces pushing and pulling EWCs *vis-à-vis* capital see Martínez Lucio and Weston (2004).
5 Such transnational exchanges of information between constituencies of employee representatives will not necessarily be 'solidaristic' and evenly organised between distinct groups. While groups of employee representatives from different countries may collaborate through information networks (formal and informal), the lack of consistency in such structures means that most of the time the employee representatives are isolated from each other, which has been the case in previous attempts noted by researchers in this field. Thus employee representatives may 'free-ride' by utilising information gathered from networking as a means to consolidate and strengthen their own local position.

References

Armstrong, P. (1989) 'Limits and possibilities for HRM in an age of management accountancy', in J. Storey (ed.) *New Perspectives on Human Resource Management*, London: Routledge, 154–66.
Bourdieu, P. (1986) 'The forms of capital', in J.G. Richardson (ed.) *Handbook for Theory and Research for the Sociology of Education*, New York: Greenwood, 241–58.
Castells, M. (1998) *The Rise of the Network Society*, Oxford: Blackwell.

Cohen, J. and Sabel, C. (1997) 'Directly-deliberative polyarchy', *European Law Journal*, 3 (4): 313–58.

Cram, L. (1994) 'The European Commission as a multi-organisation: social policy and IT policy in the EU', *Journal of European Public Policy*, 1 (2): 195–217.

Crouch, C. (1993) *Industrial Relations and European State Traditions*, Oxford: Clarendon.

Deppe, F. (1995) 'Trade unions and industrial relations in the European Union', paper presented at an international symposium 'Europe 1992/3', Delphi, May.

Doz, Y.L., Bartlett, C.A. and Prahale, C.K. (1981) 'Global competitive pressures and host country demands: managing tensions in MNCs', *California Management Review*, 23 (3): 63–74.

Falkner, G. (1996) 'European Works Councils and the Maastricht Agreement: towards a new policy style', *Journal of European Public Policy*, 3 (2): 192–208.

Ferner, A. and Edwards, P. (1995) 'Power and the diffusion of organisational change within multinational enterprises', *European Journal of Industrial Relations*, 1 (2): 229–57.

Fitzgerald, I. and Stirling, J. (2004) *European Works Councils: Pessimism of the Intellect, Optimism of the Will?* London: Routledge.

Fulton, L. (1995) 'Meetings on European multinationals: the experience so far', *Transfer*, 1 (2): 229–44.

Garrahan, P. and Stewart, P. (1992) *The Nissan Enigma*, London: Cassell.

Gollbach, J. and Schulten, T. (2000) 'Cross-border collective bargaining networks in Europe', *European Journal of Industrial Relations*, 6 (2): 161–79.

Grossberg, L. (1996) 'On postmodernism and articulation: an interview with Stuart Hall', in D. Morley and Kuan Hsing-Chen (eds) *Stuart Hall: A Critical Reader*, London: Routledge, 131–50.

Haas, P. (1992) 'Introduction: epistemic communities and international policy co-ordination', *International Organisation*, 46 (1): 1–35.

Hall, S. (1988) *The Hard Road to Renewal*, London: Verso.

Hancher, L. and Moran, M. (1989) 'Organizing regulatory space', in R. Baldwin, C. Scott and C. Hood (eds) *A Reader on Regulation*, Oxford: University Press.

Hirst, P. and Thompson, G. (1996) *Globalisation in Question*, Cambridge: Polity.

Hyman, R. (1994) 'Industrial relations in Western Europe: an era of ambiguity', *Industrial Relations*, 33 (1): 1–24.

—— (2001) 'European integration and industrial relations: a case of variable geometry', in P. Waterman and J. Wills (eds) *Place, Space, and the New Labour Internationalism*, Oxford: Blackwell.

Jensen, C.S., Madsen, J.S. and Due, J. (1999) 'Phases and dynamics in the development of EU industrial relations regulation', *Industrial Relations Journal*, 30 (2): 118–34.

Jensen, T.E. (2004) 'The networking arena', in T.E. Jensen and A. Westenholz (eds) *Identity in the Age of the New Economy: Life in Temporary and Scattered Work Practices*, Cheltenham, UK, and Northampton, MA: Edward Elgar.

Keller, B. (1998) 'National industrial relations and the prospects for European collective bargaining: the view from a German standpoint', in W.E. Lecher and H.-W. Platzer (eds) *European Union: European Industrial Relations*, London: Routledge, 47–64.

Keller, B. and Platzer, H.-W. (2003) 'Conclusions and perspectives', in B. Keller and H.-W. Platzer (eds) *Industrial Relations and European Integration*, Aldershot: Ashgate, 161–78.

Knudsen, H. (1995) *Employee Participation in Europe*, London: Sage.

Knutsen, P. (1997) 'Corporatist tendencies in the Euro-Polity: the EU Directive of 22 September 1994 on European Works Councils', *Economic and Industrial Democracy*, 18 (2): 289–323.

Kooiman, J. (2003) *Governing as Governance*, London: Sage.

Laclau, E. and Mouffe, C. (1984) *Hegemony and Socialist Strategy*, London: Verso.

Lecher, W.E. (1998) 'European Works Councils: experiences and perspectives', in W.E. Lecher and H.-W. Platzer (eds) *European Union: European Industrial Relations*, London: Routledge, 234–51.

Leisink, P. and Hyman, R. (2005) 'The dual evolution of Europeanization and varieties of governance', *European Journal of Industrial Relations*, 11 (3): 277–86.

Lowe, J. (1993) 'Manufacturing reform and the changing role of the production supervisor', *Journal of Management Studies*, 30 (6): 739–58.

LRD (1994) 'Meetings on European multinationals: the experience so far', *Labour Research*, September.

MacKenzie, R. and Martínez Lucio, M. (2005) 'The realities of regulatory change: beyond the fetish of deregulation', *Sociology*, 39: 499–517.

Majone, G. (1994) 'The rise of the regulatory state in Europe', *West European Politics*, 17 (3): 77–101.

—— (1997) 'The new European agencies: regulation by information', *Journal of European Public Policy*, 43 (3): 262–75.

Marginson, P. (2000) 'The Eurocompany and Euro industrial relations', *European Journal of Industrial Relations*, 6 (1): 9–34.

Marginson, P. and Sisson, K. (2004) *European Integration and Industrial Relations: Multi-level Governance in the Making*, Houndmills: Palgrave Macmillan.

Marin, B. (1990) 'Generalised political exchange: preliminary considerations', in B. Marin (ed.) *Generalised Political Exchange*, Frankfurt: Campus, 37–66.

Martínez Lucio, M. and Weston, S. (1995) 'Trade unions and networking in the context of change: evaluating the outcomes of decentralisation in industrial relations', *Economic and Industrial Democracy*, 16 (2): 233–51.

—— (2004) 'European Works Council: structures and strategies in a new Europe', in I. Fitzgerald and J. Stirling (eds) *European Works Councils: Pessimism of the Intellect, Optimism of the Will?* London: Routledge.

Meissner, D. (1994) *The Role of European Works Councils in the Future*, Brussels: European Federation of Chemical and General Workers Unions.

Moody, K. (1997) 'Towards an international social movement unionism', *New Left Review*, 225: 52–72.

Paauwe, J. and Dewe, P. (1995) 'Organisational structure of multinational corporations: theories and models', in A. Harzing and J. Van Ruysseveldt (eds) *International Human Resource Management*, London: Sage, 75–98.

Panitch, L. (1994) 'Globalisation and the state', *Socialist Register 30*: 60–93.

Peck, J. (1996) *Workplace: The Social Regulation of Labour Markets*, New York: Guilford.

Peters, B.G. (1994) 'Agenda-setting in the European Community', *Journal of European Public Policy*, 1 (1): 9–26.

Platzer, H.-W. (1998) 'Industrial relations and European integration: patterns, dynamics, and limits of transnationalisation', in W.E. Lecher and H.-W. Platzer (eds) *European Union – European Industrial Relations*, London: Routledge, 81–117.

Pulignano, V. (2005) 'Going national or European? Trade union politics within multinational business contexts', paper presented to 'Europeanisation and organised labour: an unsolved dilemma?' international workshop at Warwick Business School, University of Warwick, United Kingdom, 18–19 November.

Rehfeldt, U. (1999) 'European works councils and international bargaining', *La Lettre du GERPISA*, 8–11 November.

Royle, T. (1999) 'Where's the beef? McDonald's and its European Works Council', *European Journal of Industrial Relations*, 5 (3): 327–47.

Schulten, T. (2003) 'Europeanisation of collective bargaining: trade union initiatives for the transnational coordination of collective bargaining', B. Keller and H.-W. Platzer (eds) *Industrial Relations and European Integration*, Aldershot: Ashgate, 112–37.

Sewell, G. and Wilkinson, B. (1992) 'Empowerment or emasculation? Shopfloor surveillance in a total quality organisation', in P. Blyton and P. Turnbull (eds) *Reassessing Human Resource Management*, London: Sage, 97–115.

Sisson, K. (1999) 'The "new" European social model: the end of the search for an orthodoxy or another false dawn?', *Employee Relations*, 21 (5): 445–62.

Stoop, S. (1994) *The European Works Councils: One Step Forward*, Amsterdam: FNV Centrum Ondernemingsraden.

Storey, J. (1985) 'The means of management control', *Sociology*, 19 (2): 193–211.

Streeck, W. (1997) 'Neither European nor works councils: a reply to Paul Knutsen', *Economic and Industrial Democracy*, 18 (2): 325–37.

Streeck, W. and Schmitter, P. (1991) 'From national corporatism to transnational pluralism: organised interests in the single European market', *Politics and Society*, 19: 133–64.

Tuckman, A. and Whittall, M. (2002) 'Affirmation, games and insecurity: cultivating consent within a new workplace regime', *Capital and Class*, 76 (Spring): 65–94.

Visser, J. (2005) 'Beneath the surface of stability: new and old modes of governance in European industrial relations', *European Journal of Industrial Relations*, 11 (3): 287–306.

Walsh, J., Zappala, G. and Brown, W. (1995) 'European industrial relations and the pay policies of British multinationals', *Industrial Relations Journal*, 26 (2): 84–96.

Weston, S. and Martínez Lucio, M. (1997) 'Trade unions, management and European Works Councils: opening Pandora's box', *International Journal of Human Resource Management*, 8 (6): 764–79.

—— (1998) 'In and beyond European Works Councils: the limits and possibilities of trade union influence', *Employee Relations*, 20 (6): 551–64.

Whittall, M. (2000) 'The BMW European Works Council experience: a cause for European industrial relations optimism?' *European Journal of Industrial Relations*, 6 (1): 61–83.

Wills, J. (2000) 'Great expectations: three years in the life of a European Works Council', *European Journal of Industrial Relations*, 6 (1): 85–107.

—— (2001) 'Uneven geographies of capital and labour: the lessons of European Works Councils', in P. Waterman and J. Wills (eds) *Place, Space and the New Labour Internationalism*, Oxford: Blackwell.

12 Coming of age

The development of a collective identity in European Works Councils

Torsten Müller and Stefan Rüb

In the light of the growing transnationalisation of companies, the adoption of the EWC Directive in September 1994 represented an important step to redress the imbalance between the strategic options of transnational companies (TNCs), which transcend national borders, and labour's limited capacity to act, which had until then been closely circumscribed by national boundaries. Since the EWC Directive provides the statutory basis for the first genuinely European institution of employee interest representation which aims to 'bridge the gap between increasingly transnational corporate decision-making and employees' nationally defined information and consultation rights' (Hall 1992: 547), the establishment of EWCs was heralded by the European labour movement as a useful tool to counter the intensified competition both between and within companies resulting from the TNCs' growing flexibility and capacity to shift production from one country to another.

However, if an EWC is to fulfil this function, it must develop its own capacity to act. Numerous case studies of EWC practice have demonstrated a close link between an EWC's capacity to act and its ability to develop a collective identity on which cross-border co-operation rests. It has yet to be specified, however, what the term 'collective EWC identity' actually means, nor have the social processes which give rise to such a collective identity been explored in any detail – at least not prior to the research presented in this book. Instead, much empirical research on EWCs confines itself to the identification of structural, cultural and political barriers which inhibit the development of a collective EWC identity, and many contributions go on to suggest concrete measures designed to overcome these barriers. While these empirical contributions have considerably extended our knowledge about the EWCs' potential capacity to act, what we still lack is a more conceptual reflection on the meaning of the term 'collective EWC identity' and the factors and processes involved in its generation.

In an effort to conceptualise the development of a collective EWC identity we propose a model in which the collective EWC identity is made up of three components: European identity, works council identity and trade union identity. This composite identity is shaped by the EWC delegates' individual socialisation which shapes their more general understanding of their role as employee representative, the constellation of actors surrounding the EWC, and structural framework conditions such as the broader context of EU regulation, company structure and national IR arrangements. Figure 12.1 provides a graphic illustration of this model.

As can be seen in Figure 12.1, the impact of these factors is mediated by the social interaction processes which take place within the EWC itself; it is these interaction processes among EWC delegates which ultimately determine form and content of the EWC's collective identity.

In this contribution, we attempt to model the development of a collective EWC identity. We begin by exploring its three components – European identity, works council identity and trade union identity. We then go on to explore the ways in which the emergence of a collective EWC identity is shaped by various factors. We conclude with an assessment of the risks and opportunities involved in the process of creating such a multi-dimensional collective EWC identity.

What do we mean by collective EWC identity?

Following Hyman's conception of trade union identity, the collective identity of EWCs can be defined as the collectively shared perceptions and views

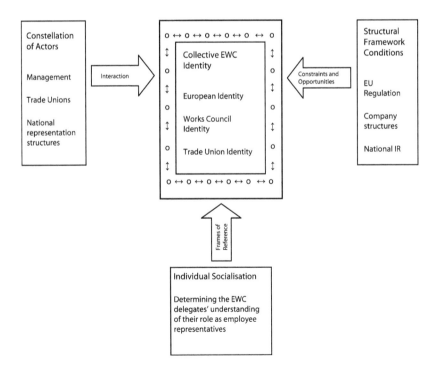

Figure 12.1 Model of the development of a collective EWC identity.

of the EWC's underlying purpose, its priority objectives, the appropriate forms of action, and the desirable pattern of industrial relations (Hyman 1994, 1996a, 1996b, 2001). This definition points to two fundamental functions of the collective identity of EWCs. The first aspect highlighted by this definition is the notion of sameness of the EWC delegates' views of the general purpose and function of an EWC. The collective identity of an EWC therefore fulfils an integrative function by creating and fostering among its members a sense of belonging together. Thus in the words of Crouch, 'identity demarcates shared membership of a group' (Crouch 1996: 93). In doing so, the collective identity also comprises an exclusive component to the extent that it demarcates EWCs as autonomous entities *vis-à-vis* other IR actors such as management, national employee representation bodies and trade unions.

In addition to this inwardly oriented integrative function, the collective EWC identity also specifies the purpose and objectives of EWCs as collective actors in the context of interaction processes with other IR actors. The second fundamental function of the collective identity of EWCs is therefore to guide the behaviour of the EWC members by setting out the primary objectives and the manner in which these objectives can best be achieved. In doing so, the collective EWC identity provides the basis for a specific strategic and programmatic orientation. The collective identity of an EWC can therefore be viewed as a guide to action, which assists the members of an EWC in interpreting external developments and challenges, and in choosing an appropriate course of action.

Having established the main functions of an EWC's collective identity we now turn to its operationalisation. In order to do so, we suggest distinguishing between three interconnected processes which constitute the EWCs' collective identity: first, the development of a European identity; second, the development of a works council identity; and third, the development of a trade union identity.

The development of a European identity

With respect to the development of a European identity, EWCs are 'caught between a national, international and supranational identity' (Lecher 1999: 280), which manifests itself in the EWC members' specific notion of the function and purpose of the EWC and their internal mode of interaction. It is useful to explore each of these identities in turn. If an EWC works exclusively within national frames of reference, then the EWC is considered by its members to be a mere extension of the national systems of interest representation. There is no ongoing contact among the EWC delegates and the information obtained through the EWC at European level from central management is used exclusively for the pursuit of national interests. If an EWC has an international identity, then the European body may go beyond the pursuit of purely national interests, but the internal relations among the delegates are marked by the dominant position of the representatives of the company's home country who tend to monopolise the link with group management. As a consequence, the capacity to act of an EWC with an international identity heavily depends on the home country delegates' willingness to use their national power resources for the pursuit of the interests of the EWC as a whole. By contrast, an EWC with a supranational identity is characterised by its capacity to develop a new overarching set of transnational values and practices which transcends national traditions and interests (Miller 1999). This means that the structure and activities of an EWC with a supranational identity are no longer primarily shaped by EWC delegates' national frames of reference. In such a supranational EWC, the members are well aware of the structural and cultural differences between the various national systems of interest representation. They do not attempt to suppress these differences. On the contrary, they accept them and view them as an opportunity to make the EWC more than the sum of its parts. The activities of supranational EWCs are therefore based on the EWC delegates' inclusive understanding of their role as employee representatives, a role which comprises the interests of all employees of the company – rather than the pursuit of selective national interests – and which is geared towards the solidary balancing of the interests across different countries. The geographical scope of the EWC delegates' inclusive understanding of their role as employee representatives does not necessarily stop at the European level. It can also extend to the global level, as illustrated by the international framework agreements on social minimum standards which have been concluded by EWCs most recently (EWCB 2004; Miller 2004). As Hoffmann (2005) illustrated in her analysis of the lessons to be learned from the construction of solidarity within German Central Works Councils, the internal relations among the delegates of an EWC with a supranational identity ideally follow the principles of equality and transparency, which enable all EWC members to participate in the internal processes of decision-making and interest aggregation. However, the emergence of such a supranational-European frame of reference is only one dimension of the development of a collective EWC identity. Another important factor is the development of an autonomous works council identity.

The development of a works council's identity

Depending on the national IR background, the term 'works council' means something very different and is usually associated with different functions of an employee representation body in different countries (Rogers and Streeck 1995). In particular from a German perspective, the term 'works council' is linked with legally guaranteed employee participation rights which go beyond the information and consultation rights foreseen in the EWC Directive. This discrepancy between the understanding of consultation as dialogue and exchange of views inherent in the EWC Directive and the conventional German understanding of consultation as more far-reaching employee participation in the sense of co-determination led Streeck (1996) to contend that EWCs are not actually works councils at all. The perceived functional determinism and ideological underpinnings of the term 'works council' also led several managements to insist that it be avoided in the name of their company's European employee representation structure. Accordingly, the range of different names found in practice, such as 'European Forum', 'European Dialogue', or 'European Committee', reflect such attempts to signify the qualitative difference between the European employee representation body and a national works council endowed with far-reaching legally guaranteed employee participation rights.

Following our definition of collective EWC identity as the collectively shared perceptions and views of the EWC's underlying purpose, the development of a works council identity is based on the generation of an autonomous transnational conception of the functions and activities of an employee representation body, rather than on merely transferring one particular national model to the European level. The normative guideline for such an autonomous cross-border conception of works council identity could be to develop the EWC into an employee representation body which is able to effectively mobilise, aggregate and defend the interests of the (European) workforce as a whole.

On the basis of Lecher *et al.*'s (2001) ideal types of EWCs, it is possible to distinguish three different developmental stages of a works council identity which manifest themselves in varying degrees of the EWCs' capacity to act. In the case of a 'symbolic' EWC, the EWC members are unwilling or unable to develop a common works council identity, since for the most part they remain passive and show little interest in developing the EWC's capacity to act. The members of a 'service-oriented' EWC view the EWC primarily as a forum for the exchange of information and provision of mutual support. Although the 'service-oriented' EWC's capacity to act as a collective representation body *vis-à-vis* management is only limited, it fulfils an important role as an information hub among the EWC members and as a source of information from management which would not have been available at national level. In other words, the primary function of a 'service-oriented' EWC is to improve the co-operation among the EWC members. The third stage of the development of an autonomous works council is exemplified by Lecher *et al.*'s 'project-oriented' and 'participative' EWCs, whose explicit objective is to represent and defend the employees' interests *vis-à-vis* management. The difference between a 'project-oriented' and a 'participative' EWC is that the activities of the former are more strongly geared towards the development of its internal capacities and structures because of management's refusal to recognise the EWC as a negotiation partner. However, in order to strengthen their internal cohesion and capacity to act, both 'project-oriented' and 'participative' EWCs systematically establish internal working structures, such as a select committee and/or issue-specific project and working groups which aim at the egalitarian inclusion of the representatives of peripheral sites. The establishment of their own autonomous working structures not only strengthens the EWC's internal capacity to aggregate the potentially conflicting interests of its members and to develop common positions which transcend the confines of national constituencies, but also represents an important power resource in the pursuit of these common positions *vis-à-vis* management.

The development of a trade union identity

The development of a trade union identity is the third fundamental component of a collective EWC identity. As Martínez Lucio and Weston (2004: 37) point out, EWCs are caught between distinct pressures in terms of push and pull factors between labour and capital both inside and outside the firm: there are dual pressures within these environments that both push unions towards managerial agendas and pull them towards autonomous labour ones.

This means that in developing a collective identity, EWCs are caught up in the field of tension between corporate identity and trade union identity. Against this backdrop, the central objective of developing a trade union identity is to avoid company egoistic tendencies and the potential co-optation of the EWC by management by ensuring that the EWC's activities are not one-sidedly geared towards the pursuit of company-specific interests.

A crucial prerequisite to prevent the corporate identity becoming paramount and overriding social and solidaristic considerations (Martínez Lucio and Weston 2004: 36) is the creation of an awareness among the EWC members of the necessity to take into consideration and represent the broader, cross-company, sectoral interests of trade unions. An important means to create such an awareness is the establishment of close links between EWCs and trade unions. In the light of the fact that the EWC Directive currently makes no explicit mention of trade unions and *de facto* limits their role to that of external experts, the establishment of close links with EWCs often represents a major challenge to trade unions. In particular, since in many cases the main obstacle to the establishment of close links between EWCs and trade unions is not so much the EWC members' unwillingness, but the lack of efficient support and co-ordinating structures within trade unions. Thus, if trade unions are to make a contribution to the development of the EWCs' trade union identity, they have to develop their own internal capacity to provide ongoing strategic support to EWCs which goes beyond the provision of legal advice during the phase of negotiating an EWC agreement. They furthermore have to develop a clear conception of the political functions of EWCs within an emerging European multi-level system of IR. In the light of the empirically observable change in many EWCs' function, which manifests itself in the increasing negotiating activities of EWCs, a key issue for trade unions is the development of a strategic position towards EWCs as negotiating bodies at European company level. This question has thus far not figured prominently on the trade unions' agenda.

So far, this chapter has explored the meaning and function of collective EWC identity. However, the novelty of EWCs as collective institutions of employee interest representation at European company level raises questions. What are the origins of this multi-dimensional collective EWC identity? And what are the sources of the collectively shared views of the EWC's underlying purpose and its aims and activities which constitute its collective identity?

The development of a collective EWC identity

As the studies by Lecher *et al.* (1999), Miller (1999) and Stirling and Tully (2004) demonstrate, the development of a collective EWC identity is the result of social interaction processes on which the EWC delegates bring to bear their own individual perceptions and views of the EWC's purpose. However, these social interaction processes do not take place in an institutional or political vacuum. On the contrary, the development of the EWC's collective identity is influenced by a range of factors which can be broadly grouped into three categories: the EWC delegates' individual socialisation, the specific constellation and strategies of other IR actors with which the EWC interact, and structural framework conditions. There is no deterministic relationship between these three sets of factors and the specific nature of the EWC's collective identity; rather their impact is mediated and filtered by the social interaction processes among the EWC members and their individual perceptions of the role and function of the EWC.

Individual socialisation processes

In addition to their role as employee representative at European company level, most EWC delegates fulfil a range of other representative functions in the national context, for example as members of company-level representation structures at the local or national level, or as lay or full-time union officials. As a consequence of these multiple representative functions, each EWC delegate 'wears different hats' and is exposed to a variety of different and often contradicting expectations and interests of different constituencies. Thus, the EWC members' individual perception of the role and function of EWCs and the interests they pursue at European level heavily depends on how they negotiate the various demands placed on them and on their socialisation within their specific own national IR context. Depending on the EWC delegates' role and position within the national IR context, they may have a feeling of accountability and loyalty to specific constituencies which shapes their prioritisation of interests and their understanding of their role as EWC representatives. Accordingly, EWC delegates may view themselves primarily as representatives of their union, of the employees of a specific business division of the company or of a particular occupational grouping. These potentially different and conflicting loyalties not only shape the EWC delegates' frames of reference, but, as Stirling and Tully (2004: 78) point out, they potentially also provide the basis for the emergence of strategic alliances among like-minded EWC delegates which cluster around perceived commonalities of interest. The emergence of strategic alliances could lead to hegemonial relations within the EWC which shape the definition of the primary objectives and functions of the EWC. The situation is further complicated by the potential cultural and language barriers, which are further factors that could lead to the formation of sub-groupings within EWCs and inhibit informal contacts and the development of mutual trust.

Against this backdrop, the development of internal cohesion is hampered not only by the varying role perceptions and interests among the EWC delegates, but also by the different – conflictual or co-operative – styles of politics with which they pursue these interests. The insufficient knowledge of different national IR backgrounds and national frames of reference can itself lead to misunderstandings, conflicts and factionalism within the EWC (Miller and Stirling 1998; Lecher *et al.* 1999; Stirling and Tully 2004).

However, EWC delegates are not only employee representatives. As human beings they are also part of the wider civil society. This means that their individual frame of reference through which they interpret and make sense of reality is also informed by their loyalty to different social collectivities as they are defined by religion, ethnicity, gender or political (and ideological) orientation, for example. It is the complex interplay of all these potential influences within the context of the individual socialisation process which constitutes the EWC delegates' individual perception of their role as employee representative and their notion of the primary aims and function of EWCs as collective structures of employee representation at European company level. Furthermore, as Hyman points out, 'the priorities of one over the other can shift according to time and circumstance' (Hyman 1996a: 64). As a consequence, any EWC will be marked by different and often conflicting views of its underlying purpose and its appropriate strategic orientation. Ultimately, the collective identity of an EWC is the outcome of a continuous internal struggle among the different conceptions of the purpose of the institution which are held by its individual members.

Constellation of actors

As collective employee representation bodies, EWCs interact with other collective IR actors, such as management, trade unions and national employee representation structures, whose activities influence the development of the EWCs' collective identity. One such framework condition is the transnationalisation strategy pursued by management. In the EWC literature, there are strongly divergent assessments of the impact of transnational restructuring initiatives on the development of internal cohesion within EWCs. Pessimistic observers, such as Hancké (2000) and Tuckman and Whittall (2002), argue that restructuring initiatives and the frequently concomitant intensification of competitive relations between different sites undermine the EWC's capacity to develop a collective identity, since in such a competitive situation the EWC delegates use the EWC to pursue their national or even plant-centred interests in order to achieve the most for their national constituency (see also Chapter 3 in this book). Based on the analysis of restructuring processes at General Motors and Renault, Hancké (2000) concludes that instead of becoming a pan-European vehicle for employee and trade union co-operation in order to combat competition, EWCs themselves become one of the major carriers of a new competition regime. A similar argument is put forward by Streeck (1996, 1997a, 1997b), one of the main proponents of this pessimistic line of argument, by contending that EWCs are likely to reinforce regime competition and the emergence of micro-corporatist arrangements at European company level. He even sees the danger that in an increasingly competitive environment, EWCs could contribute to the formation of new coalitions between management and domestic workforces which are no longer based on common class interests of labour to seek protection against the competitive forces of free markets, but on national interests of labour to out-compete labour in other countries.

However, as Martínez Lucio and Weston (2004: 39) point out, the use of benchmarking techniques and coercive comparisons in the context of restructuring initiatives is a 'contradictory process' which can also have the opposite effect by creating among the EWC delegates an increased interest in autonomous cross-border networking and co-operation. Empirical support for this more optimistic assessment is provided by Klebe and Roth (2000) and Zimmer (2003) whose contributions show how the EWCs at General Motors and Ford, when faced with transnational restructuring initiatives, developed an autonomous capacity to act which in turn served as the basis for the conclusion of an agreement with central management on how to implement the process of restructuring. As Klebe and Roth (2000: 753) emphasise with respect to the EWC at Ford, the mere process leading to the conclusion of the agreement with central management changed the internal relations within the EWC dramatically by fostering mutual trust and a heightened awareness among the EWC members of the necessity to co-operate transnationally and to take joint action *vis-à-vis* management.

These divergent empirically based assessments demonstrate that the companies' transnationalisation strategy is an important framework condition for the development of a collective EWC identity, but they also highlight that its actual impact depends on the EWC delegates' perception of the problem at hand and the development of an appropriate strategic response in the context of EWC-internal interaction processes.

The same applies to the potential impact of management's more general approach towards the EWC on the development of a collective EWC identity. A supportive approach by management increases the likelihood that it will provide the EWC with the necessary resources in terms of time, money, information and power. This in turn creates favourable framework conditions for the development of a collective identity, since as Lecher points out, 'the better the EWC can equip itself in terms of these four "claims", the greater its chance of developing a European identity and to act effectively' (Lecher 1999: 281). However, it is as plausible to argue that an antagonistic approach by management strengthens the EWC delegates' sense of belonging together and of the need to take joint action *vis-à-vis* management. Thus, management's approach towards the EWC is an important framework condition, but its influence on the development of a collective EWC identity is mediated by the EWC delegates' collective response.

Besides the interaction between EWCs and management, the relationship between EWCs and trade unions plays a crucial role in the development of a collective EWC identity. We have already mentioned the importance of close ties between EWCs and trade unions for the development of the EWCs' trade union identity if company egoistic tendencies are to be avoided. In addition, through the provision of training and education programmes, trade unions also play an important role in developing the other two components of an EWC's collective identity: the European identity and works council identity. Since many EWC delegates are not accustomed to performing their role as employee representatives in a multi-cultural and multi-lingual setting, trade union training programmes are often an essential prerequisite to equip the EWC delegates with the skills needed to develop internal cohesion and a collective identity (Gohde 1995; Miller 1999; Miller and Stirling 1998). According to Harazim (1998), two sets of qualifications can be distinguished: on the one hand, issue-related training which includes basic knowledge about the different national IR systems and collective bargaining arrangements, the legal background of the EWC Directive and the national transposition laws, and the broader economic context in which the EWC operates; on the other hand, individual qualifications which comprise communication, language and conflict resolution skills. By providing these two sets of qualifications, trade unions not only raise the EWC delegates' awareness and understanding of the differing national interests and modes of action, but they also facilitate EWC-internal processes of communication and interest aggregation and, in doing so, the development of an autonomous transnational conception of the role and function of EWCs.

However, the transfer of language and social skills needed by EWC delegates to perform their role successfully in the multi-cultural context of an EWC poses manifold challenges to trade unions. First of all, the development of a more coherent approach to EWC training represents a methodological challenge, because as Miller and Stirling (1998) highlight, the traditional approach taken by European trade unions towards EWC training was ad hoc and pragmatic. Miller (1999: 356) therefore calls for a new 'pedagogy of transnationality' which takes into account the specific cross-national training needs of EWCs in terms of the content, method and the organisation of delivery of training. However, the development of a new transnational approach to EWC training which facilitates the development of internal cohesion is above all a political challenge for trade unions, because it presupposes a more general shift in their political priorities. As Lecher *et al.* (2001) emphasise, past trade union policy predominantly focused on negotiating additional EWCs rather than on providing ongoing substantial and strategic support for existing EWCs. Particularly in the more advanced developmental stages of an EWC, trade union support needs to assume a more explicitly political role in helping to shape EWC policies *vis-à-vis* management. Some sectoral European industry federations have responded to the new demands placed upon trade unions by mature EWCs by setting up company-specific EWC task forces which aim to establish effective European-wide support structures and improve strategic co-ordination among their national affiliates (see Chapter 5 in this book). While such developments will continue to represent an important platform for co-ordinating EWCs and in developing a shared conception of the potential role of EWCs within the larger arena of European IR, this process needs to be complemented at the national level. Trade unions themselves need not only to clarify the status and role of EWCs within their overall strategies, but also to reassess the ways in which their national-level strategies in other policy areas may need to become Europeanised as well.

The relationship between EWCs and national representation structures is the third field of interaction which influences the development of a collective EWC identity. The crucial issue with respect to this field of interaction is the significance and legitimacy attributed to EWCs by national employee representation structures. As Lecher *et al.* (1999) emphasise on the basis of their comparative studies, the development of the EWCs' capacity to act depends heavily on whether the EWC members manage to anchor EWCs within national representation systems by convincing national representation structures and workforces of the significance of EWCs as an employee representation structure at European company level. The successful anchoring of EWCs within national representation structures provides the EWC delegates with the necessary legitimacy to develop the EWC into a body which is capable of efficiently defending the interests of the workforce at European company level.

So far, we have looked at the potential impact of the EWC delegates' individual socialisation processes and of the constellation of actors on the development of a collective EWC identity. The following section will deal with the potential impact of the main structural framework conditions – EU regulation, company structure and national IR arrangements – on the emergence of a collectively shared conception of the role and purpose of EWCs.

Structural framework conditions

An important structural framework condition which influences the EWC delegates' individual perception of the role and function of EWCs is the broader context defined by the existing body of EU regulation more generally and, most obviously, the provisions of the EWC Directive in particular. Research has demonstrated that EWCs tend to closely mirror the subsidiary requirements laid out in the EWC Directive – in particular, most if not all EWC agreements have adopted the EWC Directive's limitation of the competence of EWCs to information and consultation.

More recent EU legislation on worker participation – in particular the Framework Directive on information and consultation and the provisions contained in the legislation for the European Company (SE) – contains more stringent definitions of information and consultation for example. It is possible that EWCs will attempt to orient themselves more closely towards these higher standards. At the same time, EWCs are likely to be influenced by the ideological bias of the EWC Directive which manifests itself in the strong emphasis placed on the development of consensual dialogue between the two sides of industry and the explicit stipulation in Article 9 of the directive that 'central management and the European Works Council shall work in a spirit of co-operation with due regard to their reciprocal rights and obligations'.

Moreover, further EU Directives, which define certain minimum standards across the EU, for instance in the fields of health and safety, data protection, anti-discrimination and equal opportunities, create a new arena for EWCs because these soft issues offer a common reference point for the development of joint projects, activities and strategies within EWCs. That EWCs are increasingly discovering these soft issues as an interesting area of activity can be seen in several more recently concluded EWC agreements on such qualitative issues (Carley 2001). At a more general level, the paradigm shift in EU social policy regulation has fostered the 'corporatist tendencies in the Euro-polity' (Knutsen 1997) so that, as Martínez Lucio and Weston point out, 'EWCs will be part of a web of institutions and bodies which can provide them with alternative reference points, resources, trajectories and narratives' (Martínez Lucio and Weston 2004: 42), which potentially influence the EWC delegates' notion of the purpose of EWCs.

Further structural framework conditions which shape the development of the EWCs' collective identity are company structure and national IR arrangements. The empirical investigation by Marginson *et al.* (2004) of the impact of EWCs on management decision-making in Anglo-Saxon companies highlights that interaction, and co-ordination among EWC members tends to be more intensive in companies with a single business structure whose operations are spread across several countries, coupled with the existence of a European management structure which acts as a direct counterpart to the EWC. The influence of national IR structures and practices on the practical operation of EWCs more generally and the EWC delegates' understanding of their role as employee representatives in particular is well documented in the EWC literature (Hall *et al.* 2003; Lecher *et al.* 1999; Müller and Hoffmann 2001; Wills 2000). In the specific context of structural framework conditions, one aspect deserves particular emphasis: the nationally varying IR structures and practices define different constraints and opportunities for employee representatives to handle transnational developments at national level. These different constraints and opportunities, however, shape the EWC delegates' perception of both the increasing transnationalisation of economic activity and the necessity to deal with the consequences of these developments at European level through the EWC.

Against this background, all the structural framework conditions described above – EU regulation, company structure and national IR structures and practices – represent important factors which influence the development of the EWCs' collective identity by defining points of reference and the range of strategic options. Whether and how these are taken up by the EWC delegates in their internal interaction processes depends on their individual perception of the pressure to act and the opportunities to do so.

Conclusion

The foregoing analysis of the function and meaning of a collective EWC identity and the factors that potentially shape its form and content underscores the complexity and openness of the EWC-internal social interaction processes. The analysis furthermore demonstrates the importance of the EWC members' awareness of the need to focus on the balanced development of all three partial identities which constitute the EWCs' collective identity. At the same time, however, the process of developing such a balanced multi-dimensional collective EWC identity is complicated by the fact that the three partial identities can potentially contradict each other.

EWCs therefore face the difficult task of finding a solution to the dilemma that on the one hand their capacity to act depends on the development of a balanced collective EWC identity while on the other hand the potential tensions between the three partial identities increase simultaneously with the EWCs' capacity to act. A case in point is the development of the EWC at General Motors, which played a crucial role in the implementation of the company's transnational restructuring initiatives by negotiating European framework agreements. As Pulignano (2006) illustrated in her succinct analysis of transnational union co-operation at General Motors, the EWC's capacity to act is essentially based on the EWC members' awareness of the need to develop the EWC's European and works council identity in order to counter management's strategy of concession bargaining.

At the same time, however, the negotiating role assumed by the EWC put pressure on the trade unions to stay involved in the activities of the EWC and to ensure that the EWC also develops its trade union identity in order to avoid the development of company-egoism. If the members of an EWC focus primarily on the development of the EWC's European and works council identity and, in doing so, disregard the broader sectoral interests of trade unions in negotiations with management, the EWC might reinforce trends towards more decentralised and company-specific forms of regulation. Particularly in dualistic systems of IR, this could undermine the trade unions' core business of negotiating collective agreements (Keller 1995; Schulten 1996).

At General Motors, the European Metalworkers' Federation responded to this risk by setting up a European trade union co-ordination group consisting of EMF officials, representatives of the national trade unions concerned by the transnational restructuring initiative and EWC members. The aim of this co-ordination group was to support the EWC in its negotiations with management by developing a jointly agreed strategy and to agree on common rules of how to respond to management attempts to pit workforces from different European production sites against each other.

This example demonstrates the need to develop all three partial identities simultaneously, because it is their smooth and effective interaction on which the EWCs' capacity to act is based. Any one-sided focus on a single dimension of the collective EWC identity will lead to insufficient results. If, for example, the EWC members primarily focus on the development of a European identity at the expense of the EWC's works council and trade union identities, the EWC will largely remain at the stage of a symbolic employee representation structure. In other words, while delegates may get along well and develop a mutual understanding of each other's problems, they will essentially fail to develop effective means to defend the interests of the European workforce *vis-à-vis* management. In the worst case, such an EWC amounts to little more than cultural Euro-tourism.

By the same token, the practical implications of an EWC with a strong trade union identity coupled with a weak European and works councils identity might be that trade unions instrumentalise the EWC as an arena for their ideological confrontations at the expense of the pursuit of concrete company-specific interests. Since in this case the EWC members would primarily view themselves as representatives of their union's interests, such an EWC would exclude the interests of non-unionised employees and, because of its remoteness from company-level developments, might also lack the legitimacy to speak on behalf of the European workforce as a whole *vis-à-vis* management.

If, however, EWCs manage to avoid the fallacies of a one-sided focus on only one of the three partial identities and manage to develop a balanced multi-dimensional collective identity, they can be expected to play a pivotal role in the development of a European multi-level system of IR.

References

Carley, M. (2001) *Bargaining at European Level? Joint Texts Negotiated by European Works Councils*, Luxembourg: Office for Official Publications of the European Community.

Crouch, C. (1996) 'Trade unions and ideology: unions and industrial relations systems', in P. Pasture, J. Verberckmoes and H. De Witte (eds) *The Lost Perspective? Volume 2: Significance of Ideology in European Trade Unionism*, Aldershot: Avebury, 90–106.

EWCB (2004) 'Global agreements – state of play, part one', *European Works Councils Bulletin*, 52: 5–10.

Gohde, H. (1995) 'Training European Works Councils', *Transfer*, 1 (2): 258–72.

Hall, M. (1992) 'Behind the European Works Councils Directive: the European Commission's legislative strategy', *British Journal of Industrial Relations*, 30 (4): 547–66.

Hall, M., Hoffmann, A., Marginson, P. and Müller, T. (2003) 'National influences on European Works Councils in UK- and US-based companies', *Human Resource Management Journal*, 13 (4): 75–92.

Hancké, B. (2000) 'European Works Councils and industrial restructuring in the European motor industry', *European Journal of Industrial Relations*, 6 (1): 35–59.

Harazim, H. (1998) 'Qualifizierungsbedarf der mitglieder von europäischen betriebsräten', *Arbeitsrecht im Betrieb*, 19 (9): 500–505.

Hoffmann, A. (2005) 'The construction of solidarity in a German central works council: implications for European Works Councils', PhD thesis, University of Warwick.

Hyman, R. (1994) 'Changing trade union identities and strategies', in R. Hyman and A. Ferner (eds) *New Frontiers in European Industrial Relations*, Oxford: Blackwell, 108–39.

—— (1996a) 'Union identities and ideologies in Europe', in P. Pasture, J. Verberckmoes and H. De Witte (eds) *The Lost Perspective? Volume 2: Significance of Ideology in European Trade Unionism*, Aldershot: Avebury, 60–89.

—— (1996b) 'Changing union identities in Europe', in P. Leisink, J. Van Leemput and J. Vilrokx (eds) *Challenges to Trade Unions in Europe: Innovation or Adaptation*, Cheltenham: Edward Elgar, 53–73.

—— (2001) *Understanding European Trade Unionism – Between Market, Class and Society*, London: Sage.

Keller, B. (1995) 'Perspektiven europäischer kollektivverhandlungen – vor und nach Maastricht', *Zeitschrift für Soziologie*, 24 (8): 243–62.

Klebe, T. and Roth, S. (2000) 'Die gewerkschaften auf dem weg zu einer internationalen strategie?', *Arbeitsrecht im Betrieb*, 21 (12): 749–59.

Knutsen, P. (1997) 'Corporatist tendencies in the Euro-Polity: the EU directive of 22 September 1994 on European Works Councils', *Economic and Industrial Democracy*, 18 (2): 289–323.

Lecher, W. (1999) 'Resources of the European Works Council – empirical knowledge and prospects', *Transfer*, 5 (3): 278–301.

Lecher, W., Nagel, B., Platzer, H.-W., Jaich, R., Rüb, S., Weiner, K.-P., Fulton, L., Rehfeldt, U. and Telljohann, V. (1999) *The Establishment of European Works Councils – From Information Committee to Social Actor*, Aldershot: Ashgate.

Lecher, W., Platzer, H.-W., Rüb, S. and Weiner, K.-P. (2001) *European Works Councils – Developments, Types and Networking*, Aldershot: Gower.

Marginson, P., Hall, M., Hoffmann, A. and Müller, T. (2004) 'The impact of European Works Councils on management decision-making in UK and US-based multinationals: a case study comparison', *British Journal of Industrial Relations*, 42 (2): 209–33.

Martínez Lucio, M. and Weston, S. (2004) 'European Works Councils – structures and strategies in the new Europe', in I. Fitzgerald and J. Stirling (eds) *European Works Councils: Pessimism of the Intellect, Optimism of the Will*, London: Routledge, 34–47.

Miller, D. (1999) 'Towards a European Works Council', *Transfer*, 5 (3): 344–65.

—— (2004) 'The limits and possibilities of European Works Councils in the context of globalisation: experience in the textile, clothing and footwear sector', in I. Fitzgerald and J. Stirling (eds) *European Works Councils: Pessimism of the Intellect, Optimism of the Will*, London: Routledge, 198–210.

Miller, D. and Stirling, J. (1998) 'European Works Councils training: an opportunity missed?' *European Journal of Industrial Relations*, 4 (1): 35–56.

Müller, T. and Hoffmann, A. (2001) *EWC Research: A Review of the Literature*, Warwick Papers in Industrial Relations 65, Coventry: IRRU, University of Warwick. Online. Available HTTP: http://users.wbs.warwick.ac.uk /irru/publications/ papers.html (accessed 15 December 2005).

Pulignano, V. (2006) 'Going national or European? Local trade union politics within multinational business contexts', paper presented at international conference 'Global unions – global research – global companies – global campaigns', organised by Cornell University, New York, 9–11 February.

Rogers, J. and Streeck, W. (1995) *Works Councils – Consultation, Representation and Cooperation in Industrial Relations*, Chicago: University of Chicago Press.

Schulten, T. (1996) 'European Works Councils: prospects for a new system of European industrial relations', *European Journal of Industrial Relations*, 2 (3): 303–24.

Stirling, J. and Tully, B. (2004) 'Power, process and practice: communication in European Works Councils', *European Journal of Industrial Relations*, 10 (1): 73–89.

Streeck, W. (1996) 'Neo-Voluntarism: a new European social policy regime?', in G. Marks, F.W. Scharpf, P.C. Schmitter and W. Streeck (eds) *Governance in the European Union*, London: Sage, 64–94.

—— (1997a) 'Industrial citizenship under regime competition: the case of the European Works Councils', *Journal of European Public Policy*, 4 (4): 643–64.

—— (1997b) 'Neither European nor works councils: a reply to Paul Knutsen', *Economic and Industrial Democracy*, 18 (2): 325–37.

Tuckman, A. and Whittall, M. (2002) 'Affirmation, games and insecurity: cultivating consent within a new Workplace Regime', *Capital and Class*, 65: 65–94.

Wills, J. (2000) 'Great experiences: three years in the life of a European Works Council', *European Journal of Industrial Relations*, 6 (1): 85–107.

Zimmer, R. (2003) 'Europäische Solidarität – Beispiele positiver Arbeit europäischer Betriebsräte', *Arbeitsrecht im Betrieb*, 24 (10): 620–5.

13 Tackling the identity dilemma

Fred Huijgen, Michael Whittall and Herman Knudsen

Each and every one of the contributors to this book is linked by a common assertion, a recognition that our individual and collective ability to command some degree of sovereignty over our lives, in this case working lives, is diminishing with the advance of global economic and political forces. We take heart in the fact that we are not alone in our concerns, as witnessed by a vast number of NGOs and social movements addressing the negative consequences of globalisation. In the case of employment the emergence of what Manuel Castells (1996) terms the 'network society' provides the technological know-how not only to increase the mobility of production and investment, but equally to develop a degree of transparency in relations between capital and labour never known before. In the case of the latter, this has led to a rise in the control over the labour process, an attack on employment terms and conditions, derecognition of labour representation and an increase in the level of job insecurity.

In the context of internationalisation the European project is first and foremost a concern with economic power, at its centre guided by neo-liberal policies. This concern is potentially at odds with European social policy, with the realisation of the European social model and with the interests of labour. Moreover, it might endanger the development of a sense of belonging of the European citizens and the development of a common European identity.

However, the task facing us involves not only documenting the harsh realities of employment in a world where capital is no longer confined within national borders. The real challenge concerns what Ross Poole (1999) defines in his work on Cosmopolities, the development of institutional communities that stretch beyond the traditional parameters defined and implemented by the nation-state. Based on our current research, we believe evidence exists, as presented throughout this book, to suggest that the EWC represents a preliminary platform which allows European workers, employed in highly international sectors, the chance to regain some influence over decisions taken in relation to their working life. Though the EWC to all intents and purposes remains a Eurocentric institution, and one which continues to cover a relatively small percentage of employees within the

European Union, it possesses certain qualities which make it an interesting cosmopolitical institutional role model. To justify our claim it is necessary to again consult Poole's (1999: 157) work on cosmopolitanism, particularly the issue of human association via interaction within an institutional setting: as we enter into relationships and institutions, or find ourselves involved in them, we discover that we are implicated in complex networks of moral commitment and obligation to others in those relationships and institutions.

Seen from this perspective we believe that the EWC is symbolic of a cosmopolitical institution, a body which potentially possesses the ability to raise and link traditionally parochial communities into a meaningful supranational network. In the area of employment this would amount to EWCs helping to complement, not replace, the diminishing influence of nationally oriented systems of industrial relations. However, as preceding chapters testify, such a huge leap is not an inevitable result of the so-called economic 'spill-over' effect. The development of 'moral commitment and obligation' within EWCs is not preordained by God; rather, what can often be nothing more than a temporary experience has to be conceived through the actions of actors.

In summary, then, we contend that evidence presented in the previous chapters documents that there are 'windows of opportunity' to counteract some of the negative consequences of globalisation. This book has investigated the windows opened by the 1994 European Works Council Directive.

The EWCD is an attempt to go some way in redressing the imbalance between economic and social policies by granting employee representatives the right to meet at a supranational level as well as to be informed and consulted by top management at least once a year. The EWCD has created a genuine space at EU level for worker participation. However, the key question raised in this volume is if, how and under which circumstances EWCs are able to participate successfully. Can EWC representatives make sense of their new European role? Earlier evidence suggested that the development of a common, collective identity within the EWC is a decisive step in ensuring that this forum becomes a key player within a European civil society and a European corporate system. But will EWC delegates be able to develop common perspectives, mutual understandings and a common identity? Will EWCs remain merely symbolic institutions or will they develop into strong integrated groups or even institutions with common identities? Can EWCs play a role in overcoming international factionalism, regime competition and social dumping? Moreover, may EWCs play a role in developing supranational industrial relations? As we shall now demonstrate, the contributors to this volume have gone some way in trying to answer these questions. The basic aim of the book has been a concern with analysing developments within EWCs from the perspective of European identity-building. Focusing on the issue of identity, the book represents a new departure in the study of EWCs. Involving researchers from eight countries who were asked to focus closely on the main theme, identity, the foregoing chapters represent a unique and extensive consideration of the processes and problems related to developing European identities within EWCs.

In Chapter 1 Knudsen, Whittall and Huijgen offered a conceptual understanding of the multiple identities of employee representatives seated on EWCs and identity-building processes at the European level, as well as a general discussion of this issue not only within the general economic context but also against the background of European social policy. The next chapter, by Gold, traced the development of proposals for employee participation at EU level over the last forty years or so. In Chapters 3–9 empirical findings from a variety of case studies were presented concerning factors and conditions influencing the identity-building process. In Chapter 10 Kotthoff interpreted his findings in the light of a critical examination of the concepts of identity and European identity. In Chapter 11 Martínez Lucio and Weston argued that the EWC initiative can be seen as a new form of regulative strategy to overcome some of the political and economic constraints facing the EU. And finally, in Chapter 12 Müller and Rüb presented a conceptual reflection of what the term 'collective EWC identity' means, as well as discussing the factors and processes involved in its generation.

In this final chapter, after a summary of the foregoing contributions, we address lessons that can be learned from the research presented in this volume, focusing in particular on identity-shaping in EWCs.

The European Works Councils Directive

In Chapter 2 Michael Gold tracks the emergence of worker participation as an area for EU regulation, along with the changing rationales for its development.

Worker participation is the most controversial of all areas regulated by social and employment policy of the EU. Problems surrounding the introduction of worker participation have been compounded by a variety of factors. The complications are related to the diversity of legal and institutional frameworks, varying roles played by trade unions and the fact that attitudes towards worker participation have undergone phases of interest, support and hostility.

The EU eventually adopted the EWCD in 1994, a breakthrough later followed by the European Company Statute (2001) and the 'general framework' Directive (2002). Gold sketches four sets of rationale that underpin the Commission's interest in employee participation, namely company law harmonisation, participation as a productive factor, prevention of social dumping, and political factors such as union and political pressures for workers' rights. The main reasons for the Commission to adopt the EWC Directive were:

- Support of progressive parties and the ETUC to the extension of workers' rights to information and consultation in exchange for support for trade liberalisation: the ETUC was eager to promote collective bargaining across multinationals located in the EU. In their opinion EWCs would help establish a firm foundation for EU-level industrial relations within multinationals.
- Several multinationals had set up their own information and consultation committees on a voluntary basis. These emerging practices proved very influential with the Commission.
- The Commission drew heavily on the existing proposals for the European Company Statute. The ECS required the introduction of a European Works Council. This proved a helpful precedent. The Commission adapted the concept for the purpose of the EWCD.
- The EWCD can be considered a major juncture in the creation of worker participation at EU level. This unique EU institution means that the structure is there, 'but the issue now is: will EWCs rise to meet the challenges?'

Our original concept of EWC identity

As a premise and point of departure for this book it was stated in Chapter 1 that we believed it to be an open question whether EWCs would remain 'series' in character or would develop into strongly integrated groups or even institutions with common identities – with a European identity. The question of European identity-building was our main focus.

In the following two sections we summarise the main findings presented in the foregoing chapters concerning factors and conditions which impede or promote the development of this European identity. After that we present our conclusions regarding the role and identity of EWCs. The structure of the following is reflected in Figure 13.1.

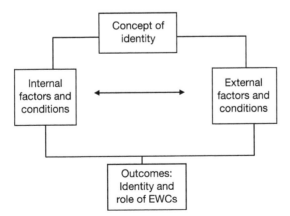

Figure 13.1 Identity and role of EWCs.

EWC-internal factors and circumstances influencing the identity-building process

An EWC brings together delegates from different parts of a MNC, from different countries, i.e. actors with diverging interests, ideas and ideologies, different attitudes towards and expectations regarding the role and function of the EWC. Moreover, the delegates often are confronted with restricted resources, lack training and have difficulties communicating with each other because of different cultural backgrounds and different languages. In addition, time restrictions and frequent changes in the composition of the EWC (frequent changes in membership; short tenure) only help to compound the problems of EWC delegates. In other words, there are many factors and conditions which may impede an EWC's capacity to act, to overcome national self-interest, namely to develop into a countervailing institution with a transnational perspective – in short, obstacles which hamper the EWC's ability to form into a transnational collective identity on which cross-border co-operation rests. These findings are demonstrated in several of the contributions and are in line with and partly supplement earlier research.

The social interaction processes within the EWC itself ultimately determine the form and content of the EWC's collective identity (Müller and Rüb, Chapter 12). The development of a specific collective or European identity regards aspects such as intercultural learning, mutual trust and internal cohesion. It is the result of learning processes and experiences that depend very much on the time factor, availability of resources and quality and patterns of formal and informal communication.

Possibilities for interaction are related to the frequency of and time for meetings. The statutory minimum is one meeting per year. This may be a minimum basis for 'industrial relations tourism': short trips to foreign countries, with all expenses paid (Scott 1999). It is obviously not enough for developing the necessary capacity to act. For example, more advanced EWCs do meet more often (Bicknell, Chapter 7). Time in between meetings is also important. In the first place, time and again it is demonstrated that informal activities and encounters outside the formal meeting, i.e. during coffee breaks, in the bar or at dinner, are important for making personal contacts, building relationships as well as learning more of the 'basics' from other countries (Andersson and Thörnqvist, Chapter 6). Next, regular contacts between meetings are highly important. Telljohann (Chapter 9), for example, points to the important role played by select committees in facilitating communication, above all in the period elapsing between the regular meetings. Thus they ensure certain continuity in the EWCs' activities.

Most authors in this volume stipulate that language is a major factor. Language is the basic tool for human communication. Communication across language barriers is a minimum requirement for the functioning of EWCs. Translation and interpretation facilities do help, but are not sufficient. Andersson and Thörnqvist (Chapter 6) demonstrate that language barriers may develop from being only obstacles for communication to the separation of people, especially in the context of informal contacts. They point to the risk that rather than genuine internationalisation, the EWCs may experience a 'regionalisation of identity', namely a situation whereby most contacts take place within different (language) regions.

EWC delegates come from different countries, characterised by different cultures. Cultural hindrances, including differing national political interests, are covered by several chapters in this book. Cultural differences are serious obstacles to effective transnational co-operation and trust, forming the foundations of parochialism and the continued predominance of national identities. Culture-based or nation-based identity constructs may be prioritised over and above a possible common EWC identity. They turned out to be, for example, normative obstacles, leading to conflict and mutual suspicion in the context of the Corus EWC (Timming and Veersma, Chapter 3). Cultural differences must be recognised and understood. Regular communication, informal contacts and an open mind for cultural differences and communalities and intercultural learning may, over time, help EWC members to overcome cultural obstacles.

Telljohann (Chapter 9) points to the relevance of the development of the subjective factor consisting, among other things, in an improvement of the individual capabilities. This is relevant not only in order to foster intercultural learning but also in order to create the necessary awareness with regard to the potential role of EWCs. Formal training and informal learning by doing (which takes time and requires active membership) are helpful in reaching these aims.

EWC delegates come not only from different countries and cultures, but also from different industrial relations backgrounds. Their expectations and interest definitions often are directly related to that. These different interests turn out to be difficult to overcome and are often a major obstacle in the process of finding common interests and developing a transnational collective identity. 'Near is my shirt, but nearer is my skin' is the proverb which typifies the practice within most EWCs. Only under certain conditions (see, for example, Whittall, Chapter 4; Bicknell, Chapter 7) were delegates able to transcend their different interests to concentrate on common European issues and to define a common course of action. Whittall demonstrated that in his Rover case the EWC delegates were committed to moving forward, developing new appropriate modes of representation in a world of increased global competition, but nevertheless were forced to acknowledge the continued importance of their respective industrial relations systems, their main source of power. The concern here is what he refers to as the catch-22 syndrome of EWCs: delegates trying to straddle the past and the present.

The composition of the EWC, the distribution of seats, its internal structure, is another relevant phenomenon when it comes to explaining the functioning of the EWC. This structure is directly related to the overall structure of the multinational. As Bicknell (Chapter 7) makes clear, the numerical relationship between delegates belonging to the parent company and delegates from subsidiaries in the other EU countries, and especially the dominant industrial relations system(s) of the office holders, are very relevant factors for explaining how EWCs function.

Whittall (Chapter 4) points to another phenomenon, namely what he calls the 'corporate identity' of the delegates. Corporate identity in this context refers to the part of the organisation with which the delegates identify. In his BMW-Rover case the EWC delegates demonstrate a close association with their respective part of the overall company.

Telljohann (Chapter 9) concludes that the development of a European identity of EWCs 'depends on the capability of its members to autonomously identify common interests and values, to agree on a following step on common objectives and, finally, to define and carry out a shared strategy'. What we learned from the contributions is that only a minor share of the EWCs were able to reach this advanced state of development. Next to the internal dynamics summarised above, external support and conditions are imperative to the development of a common identity. The external relations and conditions are the subject of the following section. Here we want to conclude that learning processes are key to the development of EWCs as collective actors. Several cases presented in this volume demonstrate that EWCs are not a static institution but a dynamic reality that may move from one phase of development to another. The process of developing a collective identity is the result of learning processes and common experiences; thus it depends very much on what Telljohann calls the 'time factor'.

EWC-external factors and circumstances influencing the identity-building process

'As collective employee representation bodies, EWCs interact with other collective IR actors, such as management, trade unions and national employee representation structures, whose activities influence the development of the EWCs' collective identity' (Müller and Rüb, Chapter 12). These external relations are the focus of this section.

Relations with national employee representation structures at company level and with national and local trade unions

EWC delegates are very often members of employee representative bodies, such as works councils, in their home country. Most EWC delegates are also active trade union members. As such their expectations and ideas about the possible role and functions of the EWC are influenced by their experiences with national systems of industrial relations. Within Europe, these systems are very diverse. As Timming and Veersma (Chapter 3) argue, the system of industrial relations within a given nation-state sets the norm for common cognitions, or a common way of 'thinking' about the employment relation.

A major obstacle to the development of a common approach towards management in the Corus case was the difference in the frames of reference of the UK and Dutch representatives, which generated different attitudes: low versus high trust *vis-à-vis* management, mutual antagonism versus an expectation of partnership. These different cognitions turned out to be difficult to overcome since they hampered co-operation and trust among non-compatriotic workers.

Telljohann (Chapter 9) and Müller and Rüb (Chapter 12) stress the importance of anchoring EWCs within national representation structures, which provide the EWC delegates with the necessary legitimacy to develop the EWC into a body which is capable of efficiently defending the interests of the workforce at European company level. As is obvious from several case studies presented in this volume, national representation structures vary as to the significance and legitimacy attributed to EWCs. The Spanish experience, reported by Köhler and Gonzáles Begega in Chapter 8, is a case in point. It may be that the Spanish minority delegations sometimes feel like 'guests in somebody else's house'. But, as the authors argue, 'the EWC process has a pedagogical component for the actors of industrial relations in Spain'. The Spanish case demonstrates that it is possible to join and learn from participating in EWCs. However, the development of a genuine Spanish contribution to EWC identity will take time.

Relations with EU-level unions

Evidence on EWCs' practice suggests that these bodies of interest representation may develop over time, from a largely 'symbolic' existence to bodies with a genuine collective identity distinct from that of the structures of representation in the national countries. Pulignano (Chapter 5) demonstrates that the development into active and even 'participatory' bodies is conditioned, among other things, by the operation of trade unions at EU level. In particular, European industry federations may and sometimes do play a crucial role in promoting a collective identity by offering advisors' support, through the provision of training and education programmes and through horizontal and vertical co-ordination among and between diverse levels of employee and union representation. Müller and Rüb (Chapter 12) underline the (possible) important role of trade unions, too. They point to the relevance of close ties between EWCs and trade unions for the development of what they call EWCs' 'trade union identity' and of the provision of training programmes for the other two components of an EWC's collective identity which they distinguish: the 'European identity' and the 'works council identity'.

Structure of the MNC and relations with central management

The capacity of EWCs to act varies considerably, not only with the support of trade unions and sector (Pulignano, Chapter 5), but also with the international nature of the company concerned (Marginson and Sisson 2004; Kotthoff, Bicknell, Whittall, Pulignano, Müller and Rüb in this volume). First, the extent to which business operations are spread across several countries, or concentrated in one, influences the composition of EWCs. In the last case the EWC is usually numerically dominated by delegates from the home country of the corporation, which may be an obstacle for defining common interests (Bicknell, Chapter 7; Whittall, Chapter 4). The same holds true where there are multiple business activities, which may be differently spread across countries (Marginson and Sisson 2004). In the third place, integration of production and other activities across borders, especially where there is a single business focus, foster similar and directly interdependent employee interests, as argued in the work of Marginson (2000). As pointed out by Telljohann (Chapter 9) as well as Kotthoff (Chapter 10), it seems easier for a common identity to evolve in MNCs whose headquarters are located outside Europe. This is probably because employee representatives here experience themselves and each other as being on a more equal footing with their EWC colleagues; there are no home country representatives with possible close links to top management. The practice of EWCs is further influenced by management's approach to the EWC and, related to this, the quantity, quality and timeliness of the information processes. Telljohann (Chapter 9) points to the fact that in most cases management is determined to maintain its prerogatives and consequently tries to limit the EWC's scope for action. Another management strategy is characterised by the attempt to manipulate and control the EWC for management's strategic objectives, which may lead to internal divisions and the subordination of the EWC. However, as Telljohann notes, in a minority of companies, especially in cases of international restructuring processes, management demonstrates a more constructive role, demonstrating that it is available to grant some entitlements that go beyond the contents of the directive. Thus, attitudes of management towards the EWC, and its legitimisation as a body of interest representation, are an important framework condition for the development of a collective EWC identity.

Above, the internal and external factors and conditions which influence the practices of EWCs and the development of the collective identity of these bodies of employee representation have been summarised. However, we have to keep in mind that the EWC is a structure of discourse, interaction and interpretation. For this reason outcomes will be informed by the interaction of internal and external factors, as demonstrated above.

The identity and role of EWCs

Collective transnational identity rather than European identity

How far have EWCs come in developing a collective European identity? That has been the central question for this book. The answer has been sought by studying the behaviour and attitudes of employee representatives in European Works Councils and the factors and conditions which are related to this. What can we learn from this study concerning the relevance of the concept of European identity?

In the foregoing contributions, the terms 'European identity' and 'collective identity' have sometimes been used alternately, in other cases as concepts with a different meaning. Müller and Rüb (Chapter 12), for example, define collective identity as a more encompassing concept, consisting of the dimensions European identity, works council identity and trade union identity. According to their view, a European identity refers to the EWC delegates' inclusive understanding of their role as employee representatives, a role which comprises the interests of all employees of the company – rather than the pursuit of selective national interests – and which is geared towards solidaristic balancing of the interests of labour across different countries. However, according to these authors the geographical scope of the EWC delegates' inclusive understanding of their role as employee representatives does not necessarily stop at the European level. It can also extend to the global level. In this case the frame of reference is not the European workforce of the company, but the workforce of the whole company, organised at a supra-European level. Using the term 'European identity' in this context might be misleading.

In Chapter 10 Kotthoff presents a critical review of the discourse about collective identity. Based on fundamental theoretical sociological approaches which deal with collective identity and on his own empirical research, he concludes that identification in the total meaning of Durkheim, as affective relationships, we-feeling, feeling of interdependence, is too strong a variant which has to be placed in the realm of the ideal. 'Europe' as a political construction is not the playing field. On the contrary, at best it is the internal world of the corporation. The point of reference for the members of an EWC is not 'Europe', but the common interests of the workforce within the multinational, be it a 'Eurocompany' (Marginson, 2000) or a global company.

Both contributions, that of Müller and Rüb (Chapter 12) and the one by Kotthoff (Chapter 10), are critical about the concept 'European identity'. What they have in common is the question: with whom do the EWC delegates collectively identify? But Kotthoff's contribution is more fundamental, in the sense that he questions the notion of European identity as such. The EWC representatives do not identify with 'Europe', but at best with the common interests of labour at an international level.

As Kotthoff argues, in studying the solidarity issue it is fruitful to complement the Marxian position with Durkheimian insights. According to Durkheim the 'feeling of interdependence' can contribute to the growth of co-operation and cohesion. The feeling of interdependence arises through the division of labour, through working together. Therefore, the corporate structure 'through its production and organisation structure creates preconditions and possibilities for tangible – not only abstract – transnational affectedness'.

Thus, a common identity may develop within EWCs, but at the same time an identity which is not particularly European. The national identities of employee representatives are not being complemented by, and certainly not replaced by, a type of European identity which is comparable to the national ones. What we see is rather the development of a collective, transnational identity among the representatives. This identity is first and foremost linked to the challenges and problems posed by the transnational corporation in which they work and earn their income. Only secondarily, so to speak, may this identity also be European.

Thus, the fact that European legislation with the EWC Directive defines a space for transnational representation of employee interests across European borders is apparently not a sufficient condition for the creation of a European identity within EWCs. On this purely formal basis national identities may prevail, or they may be extended and modified with elements of transnational or global identity. A European identity seems to develop only if and when other institutions and structures pull in that direction.

One such structure may be that of the company. If the MNC is genuinely European – with a European perspective and with activities and workforces spread more or less evenly over many European countries, or, as for instance in the case of GM Europe, with a distinct organisation for Europe, then 'Europe' becomes a more meaningful entity for employee representatives to relate to. As already mentioned, and paradoxically, such European identity-building seems to be strongest in EWCs belonging to MNCs based outside Europe. General Motors and Ford are the notorious examples. Identity theory, however, helps us to dissolve the paradox: in such cases, 'the Other' is located outside Europe.

Other structures of significance are those of European trade union organisations, notably the industry federations. Some of the most active and cohesive EWCs operate in close contact with the sector's European industry federation which again bases its support on European trade union policies. As shown by, in particular, Pulignano (Chapter 5) and Telljohann (Chapter 9) this strengthens 'Europe' as a relevant reference point for EWCs.

On the whole, the contributions in this book demonstrate that, although national identities are strong and often dominate the scene, there is clear evidence that EWCs have the potential to host a development of collective, transnational identities. Compared with this, the European component of EWC identities is much more fragile. A stronger European identity must await a broader development of European organisations and institutions. In the meantime, we may perceive EWCs as stepping stones towards more global forms of identities and solidarities in the labour movement – some EWCs expanding into world works councils (da Costa and Rehfeldt 2006). That role may be just as important, or even more so, than their role in constructing an integrated Europe.

The growth of the capacity of EWCs to act

The research findings presented in this volume clearly demonstrate that quite a few EWCs are in a process of change, are following development paths (Lecher *et al.* 2001) from mere symbolic to more influential institutions. The most advanced EWCs have been typified as 'project-oriented' and 'participatory'. They are able to play a pro-active role *vis-à-vis* central management, and some of them have even surpassed the legally set restriction to information and consultation rights by entering the realm of co-determination (for example, Ford and GM).

A very important – maybe the most important – factor conducive to this, alongside the support by EU-level unions and the significance of company structure (see above), is external pressure and risks. Pressure and risks are certainly evident in the case of central management trying to implement transnational restructuring of the corporation. This typically leads to uncertainty, work intensification and possibly redundancies, thus endangering the employment and working conditions of the workforce. As stressed by Telljohann (Chapter 9), restructuring may strengthen the ability of the EWC to act, and Kotthoff (Chapter 10) argues that such situations of change and danger are likely to promote more institutionalised, and perhaps also more affective, forms of co-operation. In combination with the support of especially the European industry federations, this may not only lead to greater transnational interdependence of the EWC delegates as the basis for development of a collective identity, but it may also empower the EWCs to force central management in the direction of co-determination.

We expect that the more EWCs move in this direction, the more pressure will be built up to revise the existing EWC Directive. The further regulation of worker participation at EU level will thus be a process reflecting the real processes in the context of Europeanising industrial relations. The emergence of the EWCD 1994 is a case in point, well explained by Gold in Chapter 2: legislation follows action.

The transnational renegotiation of capital–labour relations

During the last two decades capital–labour relations have changed dramatically, mainly to the disadvantage of labour. With the further transnationalisation of capital and the strong neo-liberal wind whipping across Europe, the prospects of redressing this imbalance seem to be quite weak. However, there are positives next to the negative signs.

To start with the negative trends, the progress of Europe as a political and social entity seems to have been halted since the rejection of the Constitution in France and the Netherlands. In addition, the Europeanisation of industrial relations, which received strong impetus during the last decade of the twentieth century, appears to have slowed down in recent years. Next, the output of the social dialogue increased quite remarkably during the

1990s thanks to strong support from the Commission, but has slowed down recently. And the advancement of collective bargaining at EU level has proven quite slow. Pessimists would claim that redressing the imbalance is virtually impossible as long as a new system of regulation at EU level has not yet been fully developed. According to our evaluation of recent trends, however, there are a number of signs warranting a more positive estimation. At the same time as regulatory approaches have become softer, organised labour has been granted a much more promising role in EU social regulation. Maybe, as the pessimists underline, the output is still meagre. But on the other hand these kinds of developments take time. Moreover, the processes are still moving in the right direction. Furthermore, it may be that collective bargaining at EU level is still in its infancy, but more and more European industry federations have started a certain co-ordination across borders and are proving in the meantime to be able to act as an influential collective actor.

In Chapter 1 we introduced the EWCD as 'a window of opportunity'. Having seen the empirical data concerning the functioning of EWCs, we may conclude that since 1996, when the directive came into force, at least a minor share of EWCs have begun to play a relevant role in and against the new model of production and management characterised by Castells (1996: 238) as the 'simultaneous integration of the work process and disintegration of the workforce'. According to Martínez Lucio and Weston (Chapter 11) EWCs in certain circumstances do offer trade unions and worker representatives the opportunity to influence corporate decision-making. They see EWCs as one aspect of new complex interactions between supranational regulation and involving international labour structures. They sketch the emergence of new forms of regulation in the EU of which EWCs are a part and suggest that 'there is a new dynamic of transnational worker representation emerging with repercussions for the regulation of the international division of labour and capitalist organisational structures'.

Although Müller and Rüb (Chapter 12) called their chapter 'Coming of age', and thus correctly pointed at the time factor and learning processes as central for the development of EWC identity, we must remember that measured by history's yardstick the European Works Council is still in its infancy. However, in our view the research collected in this book clearly demonstrates the potential of the EWC. It may turn out to be a stepping stone to a renegotiation of capital–labour relations and the playing field for the development of modern forms of solidarity. Moreover, the EWC is a platform for the development of EU-level bargaining and EU-level industrial relations. At least a relevant share of EWCs have risen to meet the challenges posed by global capital.

References

Castells, M. (1996) *The Rise of the Network Society. The Information Age, Economy, Society and Culture*, vol. I, Oxford: Blackwell.

Da Costa, I. and Rehfeldt, U. (2006) 'European unions and American automobile firms: from European Works Councils to world councils?', paper presented at the 58th Annual Meeting of Labour and Employment Relations Association, Boston, 5–8 January.

Lecher, W., Platzer, H-W., Rüb, S. and Wiener, K.-P. (2001) *Verhandelte Europäisierung: Die Einrichtung Europäischer Betriebsräte – Zwischen gesetzlichem Rahmen und sozialer Dynamik*, Baden-Baden: Nomos Verlagsgesellschaft.

Marginson, P. (2000) 'The Eurocompany and Euro industrial relations', *European Journal of Industrial Relations*, 6 (1): 10–34.

Marginson, P. and Sisson, K. (2004) *European Integration and Industrial Relations: Multi-level Governance in the Making*, Basingstoke: Palgrave Macmillan.

Poole, R. (1999) *Nation and Identity*, London: Routledge.

Scott, R. (1999) *Europäische Betriebsräte: Entwicklung und Strategie*, Bremen: Universitätsarbeitskammer, Dezember.

Index